The Threshold Is High

日本

Kanji for Japan (Nippon)

The Threshold Is High

The Brethren in Christ in Japan

Doyle C. Book

Evangel Press
301 N. Elm St.
Nappanee, Indiana 46550

The Threshold Is High © 1986 by Doyle C. Book. All rights reserved. No part of this book may be used or reproduced without written permission, except in the case of brief quotations in articles and reviews. For information, address Evangel Press, 301 N. Elm St., Nappanee, Indiana 46550.

Cover design: Weston Phipps

ISBN: 0-916035-15-8

Printed in the United States of America

*To Thelma, my wife,
a true missionary
and my spiritual support during
seventeen years of blessing and struggle in Japan,
and to Charity Kay and Stephanie Dawn,
whose achievements,
partly the result of
growing up in the Japanese culture,
have made me
proud of them and grateful to God.*

Contents

Maps		viii
Introduction		ix
Prologue		xi
1.	A New Adventure	1
2.	The Land of the Rising Sun	12
3.	Early Evangelistic Efforts	28
4.	A New Home	53
5.	The Family Grows	68
6.	Methods in Mission	82
7.	The Emerging Church	100
8.	The Challenge of Growth	123
9.	The Future Mission	144
10.	Into the 1980s	156
11.	Fellowship in the Gospel	171
	Epilogue	184
	Photographs	45, 138
	Japan Missionary Personnel	186
	Mission Chronology—The First Ten Years	188
	Notes	190
	Index	206
	The Author	209

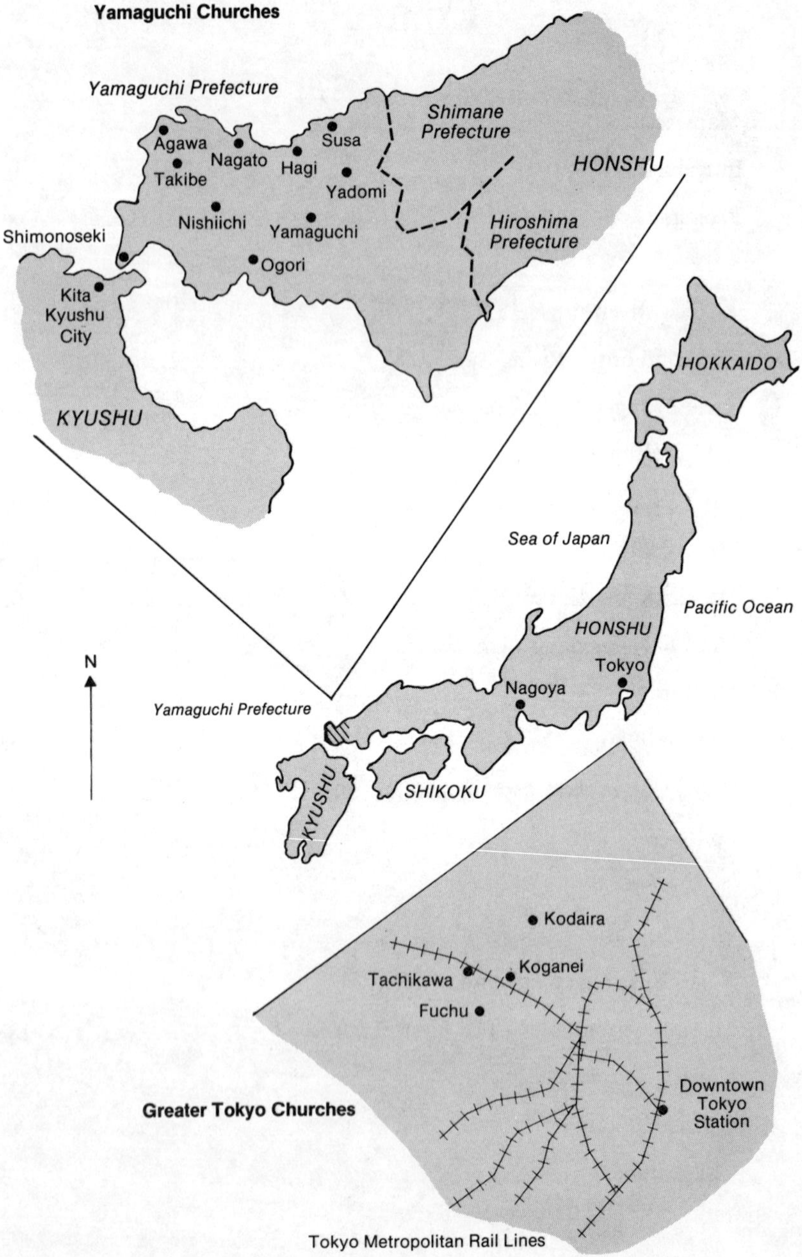
Yamaguchi Churches
Yamaguchi Prefecture
Agawa
Takibe
Nagato
Susa
Hagi
Yadomi
Nishiichi
Yamaguchi
Shimonoseki
Ogori
Kita Kyushu City
KYUSHU
Shimane Prefecture
HONSHU
Hiroshima Prefecture
HOKKAIDO
Sea of Japan
Pacific Ocean
HONSHU
N
Tokyo
Nagoya
Yamaguchi Prefecture
KYUSHU
SHIKOKU
Kodaira
Koganei
Tachikawa
Fuchu
Downtown Tokyo Station
Greater Tokyo Churches
Tokyo Metropolitan Rail Lines

Introduction

In telling the story of the Brethren in Christ in Japan, I have tried to do three things. First, I have attempted to record the main incidents and some details involved in the beginning of the mission, the development of its work and the growth of the church from 1953 to 1985. In this sense, the book is a historical narrative, with details gathered from published articles, correspondence, mission and church files, interviews and the personal experiences of the author.

Second, I have endeavored to give insights into the dynamics involved in communicating the gospel across cultural barriers. Through glimpses into different ways of thinking, different customs, and the personal struggles and adjustments of the missionaries, I hope to create an awareness in the reader of factors that must be considered in sharing Jesus with people of a different culture.

Third, I have sought to evaluate the reasons for the growth of the church, or its lack of growth, and to assess the policies used by the mission in its approach to evangelism. I have also offered suggestions for the future church and mission in view of the fact that even today only one-half of one percent of the Japanese people is Christian.

The book is thus intended to be a history of the Brethren in Christ in Japan, accompanied by insights into cross-cultural evangelism and principles relating to the growth of the church. I have tried, however, to relate the history in a style and in terms that will interest the person in the pew. I hope that the book will read like a story. It is a story—a story of people committed to carrying the good news of Jesus Christ to those who have never heard of him. It is a story of struggles and failures; no attempt is made to hide the fact that missionaries are human. But it is also a story of adventure and of lives transformed by the gospel.

For those expecting a traditional history, it should be understood that the main incidents of the development of the mission and the church in Japan have been dealt with, although briefly, according to the author's research and experience. The facts are there, along with sources cited. However, I have tried to weave the facts into a narrative, to evoke in the reader the sense of excitement and wonder that I myself felt during seventeen years in Japan. Truly, there is never a dull moment in mission work!

Because the book is designed to be a story, the reader is asked at times to use his imagination. At other times the book takes the liberty of inserting into the experiences of others some of the feelings I myself experienced. This is particularly true in the opening scenes involving the Willmses arriving at the inn in Hagi and their early adjustments in the new culture. Other parts of the narrative throughout the book which are not documented may be assumed to be the impressions of the author.

The narrative is designed to be both topical and chronological. Because of this, some incidents are mentioned more than once. The reader is asked to be patient with what may seem to be repetition; since topics are being dealt with as well as a time sequence, the same matters may appear at various places.

To the recent visitor to Japan, some aspects of the culture may seem to be slightly different from those described in the book. Such an observer is asked to remember two things. First, the story relates, for the most part, impressions gained in the early years of the mission. Second, some practices differ greatly from the country to the city in Japan. The matter of physical contact between persons is one example. Younger people in Japanese cities may be seen today linking arms or otherwise touching or expressing affection. But this is not typical of the small town or rural setting, nor was it true in the experiences of the missionaries for most of the years covered by the narrative.

Arigato Gozaimashita!

Heart-felt thanks are due many loving and helpful people, without whom this manuscript could never have been produced. To missionary colleagues and board members for sharing long hours in interviews and for putting up with pushy questions; to church leaders in Japan who shared from their hearts about struggles of the past and hopes for the future; to members of the Japan churches who provided the author and his family with one of the most exciting months of their lives during a visit to their adopted land in the summer of 1980; to Dr. E. Morris Sider for providing hundreds of pages of material from church archives and offering many suggestions for the manuscript; to Paul E. Engle for assistance in research in the Upland archives; to readers Miriam Bowers, Michael Mates, Elizabeth Mates, John Graybill, Lucille Graybill, and Thelma Book who corrected many errors and offered helpful suggestions; to the Upland church staff, Bob Hempy, Bob Keck, John Jordan, and Joy Stump for supplying a room where hundreds of pieces of paper could be spread out day and night; to custodians Hershey Gramm and Ernest Gramm for keeping the room clean; to Aaron Stern and Lester Saltzman for frequent words of encouragement, sometimes late at night; to Deanna Keck for emergency typing when the pressure was on; to Charity Book and Stephanie Book for assistance in typing; to manuscript typist Eleanor Lehman for long hours of work; and to mentor Dr. C. Peter Wagner and faculty committee Dr. Arthur F. Glasser and Dr. Paul G. Hiebert for much patience, encouragement and helpful corrections . . . God bless you!

Prologue[1]

"I am deeply impressed by verse thirty-five. I am glad to see that 'Jesus wept.' " The words came from one of the class members in a matter-of-fact, quiet way. The surprise the missionary felt, however, was not so matter-of-fact.

The students were deep in their study of John 11. They had seen the thrilling story of Lazarus unfold. They had studied Jesus' words, "I am the resurrection and the life." The missionary asked for further questions or comments. And the class member had responded. He then continued quietly: "I have seen how Jesus did miracles and spoke wonderful words. I was feeling that he must be somebody too great to understand—somebody we couldn't identify with. But I feel much better to see that 'Jesus wept.' Now I see that he is human as well as God."

The missionary had learned to be prepared for anything in the class. The questions which came sometimes jarred him with their frankness. But now he could hardly contain his feelings. He wanted to shout for joy. ". . . human as well as God!" The man who spoke had come to a turning point. He could never be the same again. He had begun to see Jesus for who he really is.

The class had begun almost two years earlier. The missionary had moved to the city wondering how to reach men more effectively in Japan. As his presence was discovered, he was asked to judge English contests and participate in other English activities. Thus he became acquainted with a number of Japanese English teachers in the city. He decided to invite the men he knew best to join an English Bible club. Ten of them quickly responded, and the class was formed.

At times the missionary felt he had never stated, clearly and boldly, the claims of God on the individual life. Most of his statements came in response to questions which were direct and unavoidable. Often he thought as he responded, "Will this frighten them away?" or "Will they turn back when they see the price of following Jesus?"

One night as the class was discussing the betrayal of Jesus and the evil in Judas' heart, a teacher asked, "Couldn't God have kept Judas from sinning? If God is all powerful, why doesn't he prevent men from doing evil in the world?" Once again, the missionary began to explain how God put within each person a free will. He pointed out that each individual could determine the direction of his life by the choices he made. Then the words of Deuteronomy 30:19 came to him: "I call heaven and earth to witness against you today, that I have set before you life and death, the blessing and the curse. So choose life in order that you may live, you and your descendants."

"Choose life! It's up to us!" The words flowed freely as God touched his heart with the message. The men were very quiet. The teacher who had raised the question was nodding his head. God's presence in the room was very real. The missionary looked around the room at the fine men. His heart seemed to burst with love and concern for them. In that moment, he knew by God's Holy Spirit that each man felt Jesus knocking at the door of his heart.

The missionary drove home that night with joy. At the same time he sensed the awesome responsibility involved in sharing God's good news.

The men enjoyed singing together. They learned many songs in English from a little paper-back hymnal. One day while preparing for the class, the missionary noticed a familiar title in the song book. He felt that the song was meant for the class. That night, he could hardly contain his emotions as the men sang together:

> Sweetly Lord, have we heard Thee calling, "Come, follow me!"
> And we see where Thy footprints falling lead us to Thee.
> Footprints of Jesus, that make the pathway glow,
> We will follow the steps of Jesus, where'er they go.

One day the group hiked up a small, nearby mountain. At the summit they sat down in the wind-swept grass. Before them spread the panorama of the Sea of Japan on the right and the Pacific Ocean on the left. Below them lay the city of Shimonoseki, crowded onto the diminishing tip of Honshu. They ate together and chatted. Then one of the hikers suggested that they sing. To the missionary's surprise, each of them pulled a hymnal and New Testament from his small pack. The missionary was the only one who had not come prepared!

"Sweetly, Lord, have we heard Thee calling . . ." The missionary looked at the men. They represented the finest of the Japanese people. Some of them had become his close friends. Suddenly it was very hard for him to think of leaving on furlough. It seemed as though his work had just begun. That day, he claimed them for God—each one. Often after that it seemed that he could hear them singing:

> Footprints of Jesus, that make the pathway glow,
> We will follow . . . we will follow . . .

Chapter One

A New Adventure

It was one of the narrowest streets they had ever seen. It would hardly even be called an alley back home. A few tiny shops with doors wide open were scattered among the grey walls and brown, unpainted buildings which pressed close to the narrow roadway and crowded against one another.

The young American couple stepped quickly through a wide opening in a wall as one of those funny three-wheeled trucks with a front end like a motorcycle clattered around the corner and began honking its way among the bicycles and dodging pedestrians.

The wall through which the pair had stepped enclosed a small concrete courtyard dotted with scrubby bushes and a small pine tree which slanted toward the visitors. Just across the courtyard an old wooden building rose two stories above them. Four sliding doors made of glass enclosed by thick wood frames marked the entrance to the building.

The sliding doors were already open, as if in welcome. The young woman hesitated, glancing up at the long, narrow sign attached vertically to the weathered side of the building. But the crossed and slanted lines of the strange writing there gave her no clue as to the name of the place.

The young man had already stepped through the open doorway and was motioning for her to come in. She joined him in a wide room whose cement floor was damp, as if it had been sprinkled with water not long before. They stood together in the entryway of a typical Japanese inn.

Before them was an unusually high step. It was formed by a thick, polished board with natural grains gleaming through its unvarnished surface. Under the entire length of the board ran a series of tiny sliding doors which suggested a storage space.

The step was a kind of broad threshold into a room which lay next to the lower entryway. The side of the room which faced them resembled a partition with four separate sections made of narrow wooden cross strips within a light wood frame and covered by thin, white paper. The two center sections were slid open, like doors. The other walls of the room consisted also of the white partitions. Beyond them a hallway led deeper into the building.

The couple did not know then that the threshold is called *shikii* and that in Japan there is a saying, *Shikii ga takai*—the threshold is high.

The young man looked toward the open partition and ventured, "*Gomen kudasai!*" He had learned that those words meant "Excuse me" or "I beg your pardon" and were the proper expression to use when one stepped into

1

someone's *genkan*. From somewhere inside the building came a quick reply, "*Hai!*" (Yes!).

Moments later a kimono-clad lady appeared at the opening. She dropped to her knees, pressed her hands against the floor with fingers pointed toward the couple and, bowing until her forehead almost touched her hands, murmured, "*Iraashaimase!*"

Recognizing the word for welcome and encouraged by this success in communication, the young couple proceeded to try more of the phrases they had recently memorized. With an emphatic "*Hai, dozo!*" (Of course, please!), the lady motioned for them to step up. Leaving their shoes in the entryway, they followed the figure which moved with quick, short steps along the hallway.

Near the end of the hall, the lady paused, kneeled, and slid open one of the paper-covered partitions. She motioned for the couple to enter. Then, closing the partition and stepping ahead of them once again, she placed some thick cushions at a low table in the center of the room and motioned them to be seated. Uttering something they didn't understand, she bowed low to them, stepped to the partition, kneeled and opened it, and disappeared into the hallway.

The weary young husband and wife glanced at each other, as if to find assurance in each other's presence, and then began to survey their surroundings.

The floor of the room was covered with large, rectangular mats; soft yet firm, fitted closely and neatly together. The surface of each mat was woven of fine, reed-like strands, giving the room a slight odor somewhat like freshly cut straw.

The walls on three sides consisted of the paper-covered sliding partitions called *shoji*. The partitions along the hallway had been closed by the maid; those on the other two sides were open, revealing a narrow strip of wooden floor bordering the room. At each corner of the room was a sturdy post extending all the way to the ceiling. These posts supported the solid sections of the walls which filled the space above the white partitions. The remaining wall was built solid.

An alcove, the floor of which was slightly higher than the mats, took up half the length of the wall. On the floor sat a pottery bowl which held several long-stemmed flowers. A long, narrow picture resembling an open scroll hung on the recessed wall. The alcove was bordered by a magnificent natural wood post which extended from floor to ceiling. Next to the post several sliding panels covered with colorful floral design paper suggested a storage place. A row of large, glass sliding doors formed the outside wall of the building.

This room was located on the back corner of the building, far away from the noisy street. Its sliding doors opened onto a garden of sculptured bushes, neatly trimmed trees and carefully placed stones.

It was all so different, and yet very lovely. The surroundings were strange, and the couple felt tense and uneasy about how they might communicate in this new land. But the quietness of the room and the beauty of the garden

quickly soothed the couple's weary spirits. There was a pleasing fascination about the different sights, sounds and mannerisms they had encountered.
The couple could not help but wonder if this was really happening to them. Was their life now to consist of *tatami* mats, low tables and cushions instead of carpets, couches and chairs? Had they really removed themselves from the comfort of an impulsive telephone call to a close friend or a family member? Was this land actually to be their home for much or all of their remaining lives?
Many thoughts came flooding in upon them. The ways of God that had brought them to this place seemed strange indeed.

The Young Missionaries

Peter A. Willms and Mary Guengerich began their adventure together with their first date in the fall of 1947. Mary lived in Upland, California, with her parents, Erlis L. and Lois Guengerich, a brother and two sisters. Her parents had moved to Upland from an Iowa Mennonite community in 1937. She opened her life to Jesus Christ at the age of nine through the witness of her Sunday school teacher, Salina Armstrong. It was natural for her to attend Upland College, the Brethren in Christ school located in Upland.[1]

Leamington, Ontario, a small Canadian town near Detroit, became Pete's home when he was nine. His parents, Peter and Elizabeth Willms, both had fled Russia to live their life together on a small Saskatchewan farm. The growing family struggled constantly for their livelihood. The only time the children knew the luxury of a piece of fruit was when they received an apple at the Christmas program of their Mennonite Brethren church.

The Willms were strict in their demands upon their six children in matters of honesty, helpfulness, church life and family worship. The children sometimes rebelled inwardly at the discipline. Nevertheless, the entire family took great pride in each other and expressed mutual respect and support.

At the age of twelve Pete attended an "evangelistic meeting" and was "saved." Both of these concepts were completely new in the Mennonite Brethren community at that time. When Pete later expressed stirrings toward the ministry, he heard for the first time that he had been dedicated as a child to the Lord for that purpose.

Pete enrolled in Ontario Bible School, a Brethren in Christ institution at Fort Erie, later to be named Niagara Christian College. He went there thinking he would get a two-year Bible diploma. However, Dorothy Sherk sensed his potential and urged him not to stop short of high school graduation. She worked with him until he was able to catch up in his class.

One day his history teacher, Pauline Herr, read General Douglas MacArthur's call for missionaries to post-war Japan.[2] Pete was so moved inwardly that he almost "fell off his chair." From that moment his heart was set on mission work in Japan. While wondering about further preparation, he heard about work and study opportunities in California from Alvin C. Burkholder, former pastor of the Upland church, who was preaching in the chapel services at Ontario Bible School. Pete enrolled at Upland College in the fall of 1947. Although attracted to Pete, Mary was concerned because she felt no special call to Japan. Pete settled the matter for her one day when he suggested, "Maybe I'm your call!" They were married on July 18, 1950.[3]

Search and Decision

Two things had perplexed young Willms about the call he felt at Ontario Bible School. The first was that his own church, the Mennonite Brethren, had no work in Japan at that time. The second was that at nineteen, he was sure he was too young for mission work. The first problem was answered by Phyllis Pye, on furlough in Canada from India in 1947 with her missionary husband, Arthur. In response to Pete's concern she said simply, "Maybe you should start a new work." The second problem was answered by a poem discovered in the school library. Each stanza of the poem ended with the line, "But surely it is time to strike!" Pete felt that God had cleared away his objections through these two incidents, and he made his call known to his Canadian friends.

Rev. Marshall Winger had taken a special liking to this serious young man. While holding meetings in Upland in the spring of 1949, the Canadian evangelist talked to the California church about Pete's call to Japan. He urged the Brethren in Christ to consider opening the way for Pete's vision to be realized.[4]

Shortly after this, Youth for Christ made plans for a special evangelistic thrust in Japan for the summer of 1951. The plan was to send teams all over the country to preach and call people to decision. The teams were organized by Dave Morken at the urging of Samuel F. Wolgemuth who, as pastor and bishop with the Brethren in Christ, was also working closely with Youth for Christ. Wolgemuth had visited Japan the year before as part of a world tour for that organization.

Three young men expressed an interest in the gospel teams. They were Pete Willms and Gordon Johnson, students at Upland College, and Royce Saltzman, a student at Messiah College in Grantham, Pennsylvania. The Men's Fellowship of the Upland church decided to sponsor the three in their evangelistic venture. At a meeting in the Upland College dining hall, Bishop Jesse F. Lady rose for the final challenge to the men: "It's time that we made some sacrifices. Let's get into our savings if necessary. This is a great opportunity for God's work!"[5]

Hundreds of team members from all over North America gathered in Tokyo in July. The teams, including interpreters and musicians, fanned out over the nation. Some of them campaigned on into the fall. Willms, Johnson and Saltzman held meetings in Tokyo and Osaka, the prefectures of Yamagata and Akita, and on the island of Shikoku.

After the assigned schedule had been fulfilled, Saltzman returned to Messiah College and Johnson tarried in Shikoku for further preaching opportunities. At the request of the Brethren in Christ Foreign Mission Board, Willms set out to visit other areas of Japan. The purpose was to try to discover suitable places for opening a mission work.

Hearing that the north had little Christian witness, Willms journeyed to the top of Honshu, northwest of Aomori. Since no passenger trains were available in that area, he secured rides on lumber trains that wound their way among the scattered towns to the coast. He returned to the States to report that the area along the northern coast of the Sea of Japan had fewer missionaries per capita than the southern part of Japan. He suggested that the Brethren in Christ focus on the north.[6]

But his report to the home church did not conclude so matter-of-factly. If Willms felt stirrings before, he was now overwhelmed with a sense of the spiritual needs of Japan. He called the church to action. He noted that authorities on Japan believed that the best time for reaping a harvest of souls might be rapidly passing. People were no longer as willing to hear the gospel presentation as they had been immediately after World War II. He declared, "Our own church has all but missed even a share in the harvest."[7]

Pete appeared before the California Bible Conference convening in Upland in the fall of 1951 to challenge the church to its opportunities. In the spring of 1952 he and Mary spoke to various churches across the denomination.

Just at this time Bishop Samuel Wolgemuth announced his appointment as director of Youth for Christ in Japan and invited Pete to replace him in the pastorate at Waynesboro, Pennsylvania. Pete thought that perhaps God was telling him that his call to Japan had been fulfilled through the gospel team thrust. He could not accept the invitation, however, because he had previously agreed to pastor the Pasadena, California, church at the request of Bishop Jesse F. Lady. The Willmses moved to Pasadena in July of 1952, and Samuel and Grace Wolgemuth moved to Tokyo with their family in preparation for another great outreach planned for the following year.

The ministry in Pasadena was fulfilling to the Willmses. Invitations to join the staff also came to them from both Upland College and Jabbok Bible School in Oklahoma. These two things again made Pete wonder if his call to Japan had already been fulfilled. But there still remained the deep concern he had felt for that land and a strange drawing toward it.[8]

Events that would eventually press the Brethren in Christ into missions in Japan continued to build up. By this time the Foreign Mission Board was seriously considering opening a work there. In its report to the General Conference of 1952, the board noted the significance of the participation of the three young men in the gospel team project and presented a resolution to Conference that it give "consideration to entering mission work in Japan by approving further study of this field." In the resolution the door was left open for the board to act should the study show the advisability of opening a work there.[9]

Carl J. Ulery was to play a significant role in the study and decision. He had joined the Foreign Mission Board in 1943 and in 1952 was planning a trip to the mission fields in Africa and India. The board asked him to survey Japan on his way home and report to them about possible places for mission work.

With no knowledge of Japan and no contacts there beside Samuel Wolgemuth, he felt very uneasy about the assignment as he arrived in Tokyo on December 1, 1952. But three events occurred that were to prove extremely significant. Two of these took place while he was waiting for Wolgemuth to finish conferences with missionaries and the visiting Billy Graham evangelistic team.

The first event was an unexpected encounter with Edwin L. Kilbourne of the Oriental Missionary Society. Ulery asked Kilbourne for suggestions on places to open mission work. Kilbourne told him that he should consider the western tip of Honshu on the coast behind Shimonoseki. He said there was hardly any Christian work in the area, and added that it was a very conservative area with entrenched traditional religions and many fishermen.

The second event also was an unexpected meeting. Accompanying Wolgemuth to a luncheon with the Billy Graham team in Yokosuka, Ulery sat next to Kenny Joseph, a recent convert who had become an evangelist. Ulery asked him also for suggestions. Joseph said he had been impressed with a place called Hagi while traveling in the western part of Honshu. He urged Ulery to consider that area.

The third event followed shortly. Ulery determined that he must see the western end of Honshu that had been twice recommended. He and Samuel Wolgemuth flew to Osaka, then took an overnight train to Shimonoseki. With only a copy of the *Japan Christian Yearbook* in hand, they sought out Southern Baptist missionary Stanley Howard. Howard's reply to their request for advice was, "I have been working out from Shimonoseki only a few miles. But up the back coast is a place called Hagi. I would seriously consider that area."

Ulery became excited. Three times he had been urged to consider the same area. He and Wolgemuth set out for Hagi. The three-hour ride up the Japan Sea coast from Shimonoseki was not the most pleasant. The train was jammed with people. Ulery and Wolgemuth placed their suitcases in the boarding area between two coaches and sat on them. Choking smoke swirled around them as the train passed through tunnel after tunnel. The train made frequent stops at small towns. Passengers stumbled past Ulery and Wolgemuth, glancing in surprise at the unusual pair. Finally the travelers were able to move inside one of the coaches and find a place on the plain wooden seats.

The adventurers got off the train where the platform sign said "Hagi" and found themselves on a lonely platform. They gazed out over the drab black roofs and unpainted houses. Ulery recalls, "A very strange feeling came over me. I had been praying earnestly for the right place. The Spirit seemed to say, 'No further, this is the place.' " He turned to Wolgemuth and said, "Let's go back to Tokyo. We've found the place."[10]

They investigated the city as best they could in order to prepare a report to the Foreign Mission Board. The report was presented to the board on January 6, 1953, as it met at Messiah Home in Harrisburg, Pennsylvania.

The board acted: "It was decided that we take active steps to open a missionary program in Japan. . . . Decided to approach Bro. and Sr. Pete

Willms and inform them of our desire to have them represent us in Japan."[11] When Pete and Mary were approached, they accepted the invitation on the spot.

Preparation and Journey

The Willmses received the decision of the board in January. Samuel Wolgemuth, anticipating the decision of the board, had already urged them to send Pete and Mary in time for the World Congress on Evangelism which was to meet in August 1953. Only a few months were left for the couple to get ready, and many things had to be done. A transition for the Pasadena church needed to be arranged. Supplies had to be purchased. Language study was urgently needed.

But it was not certain that General Conference, convening in June, would approve their going to Japan. In the first place, conservatives might raise a voice in opposition to the $8,000 budget or the possibility of "spreading ourselves too thin." Second, people might hear of the plans initiated before conference and feel that the Willmses and the board were pulling strings behind the scenes, especially in the unauthorized expenditure of money.[12] Third, some questions had been raised concerning Pete's views on certain doctrines and practices within the church.

In addition, Board Secretary Henry N. Hostetter was concerned about a possible misunderstanding about sending a vehicle along with the Willmses. How was this vehicle to be secured prior to official approval of the Willmses? And what if they were not approved? Hostetter expressed his concern to the candidates about the uncertainty of their appointment and the purchase of a van: "Under these circumstances, a full announcement can hardly be made at present and the news will likely get well spread via the 'grapevine' before it can be officially announced."[13]

But Hostetter was also convinced that preparation had to be started immediately. The decision was made to go ahead and prepare. The board purchased and the Willmses packed as if approval had been given. Pete and Mary plunged into a brief time of language study at Pasadena City College, and Pete entered Fuller Seminary for courses in History of Missions and Biblical Theology.[14]

Happily, the Willmses were approved by General Conference which met, significantly, at Niagara Christian College, where Pete had received his call six years earlier.[15] Conference members also enthusiastically gathered at an outdoor rally to dedicate the new van and pray upon the Willmses the blessing of the Lord. The rally took place at noon on Sunday just before the annual missions program.[16] It was a high point in missions enthusiasm for the Brethren in Christ.

Pete and Mary left immediately for California in the van and quickly gathered and crated their belongings. These were delivered with the van to San Pedro Harbor on Tuesday and the couple boarded ship for Japan Wednesday. It was July 1, 1953.

The voyage was not without discomfort. As if to test the commitment of the youthful pair, a massive storm struck the freighter. The ship rolled dangerously—very close to capsizing, according to later reports from the crew. Much of the lumber which had been piled ten feet high on the deck was lost. The crash of galley dishes and the roar of the wind and waves were the couple's only companions as they tossed from side to side in their bunks.[17]

At last the boat docked in Tokyo harbor on July 16, and the Wolgemuth home provided comfort and respite for the young travelers. Pete assisted Wolgemuth in some of the preparations for the World Congress on Evangelism. Fifteen hundred leaders concerned for world evangelism gathered for sessions of prayer and challenge from August 9-16. Preaching teams were then organized for campaigns in each of the forty-seven prefectures in Japan.[18]

Prior to the convening of the Congress, Pete embarked on a scouting trip to the place where he and Mary were to begin their new ministry. The main purpose for the trip was to find a suitable residence. Boarding a train for the day and night trip, he headed for Hagi, five hundred miles to the southwest. Changing trains in Shimonoseki, he proceeded along the coast to the north and east. As he viewed the fishing villages and small farming towns, he was overwhelmed by the thought that none of them had yet been visited by the message of Jesus Christ. Other thoughts pressed in: "Every one of those villages is my responsibility; the mission begins here!" But how could it happen, he wondered? What experiences lay ahead?

Pete peered from the platform of Hagi station at the same drab scene that Ulery and Wolgemuth had witnessed seven months earlier. "Is this the place?" he thought. "Why here?" He had seen many places throughout Japan that looked more promising than this. He began walking up the street that stretched north between two rows of tightly packed houses and occasional shops. "Is there nothing more to the town than this?" he complained inwardly.

After repeatedly asking directions, he found his way to the city hall. A clerk there arranged for Pete to be taken to the police station. There he met an interpreter who was stationed with the Hagi police to aid in contacts with U.S. occupation forces. To the young missionary's relief, the man spoke good English and offered him a cordial welcome. The interpreter also led him to a large Japanese inn on a very narrow street just behind the main thoroughfare of downtown Hagi.[19] It was the Tomoe Inn, to which we have already been introduced. It was this inn which, one month later, welcomed Pete and his wife, as we have seen earlier, and a traveling companion not yet mentioned, Henry A. Ginder.

Pete stayed at the Tomoe Inn three days. The time was filled with searching for a house to rent, gathering information about the city, and calling on people who were in positions of influence. Pete found that Hagi's population was fifty thousand. He discovered that there was a small Protestant church near the center of town and a larger Catholic church in another section of the city. Although limited in vocabulary, he boldly called on both churches. To his frustration he found the Catholic church staffed by missionaries from Spain. He also found that the one person who might understand English and relay the purpose of his visit, a nun, had just begun her annual discipline of silence and would be unavailable for a week.[20]

There were other frustrations. Pete was having supper his first night in the inn. He was looking forward to a quiet evening for recording his notes on the day's activities when a young man appeared and asked Pete to teach him English. His opening statement was, "Please give me a piece of your knowledge." Pete found that the boy's mother had seen the foreigner in town and had told her son about him. The boy correctly assumed that Pete was staying at the Tomoe Inn. Not wanting to risk offending someone in this new place of ministry, Pete proceeded to give him some of his knowledge—about Jesus! He also was able to glean some helpful information about Hagi from the young man. The "English lesson" lasted three hours, and Pete had to give up recording his notes for that night.[21]

Efforts to rent a house in Hagi at this time proved fruitless. Pete was introduced to a broker who was a member of the small Presbyterian church in town. Mr. Takeshita was warm and helpful, but an extensive search revealed that there were no houses for rent. There was one place for sale, however, and Pete returned to Tokyo to write a detailed letter to the board explaining the situation in Hagi and requesting an immediate decision about the possibility of purchasing the property.[22]

To Hagi

After the World Congress ended, the Willmses set about completing the necessary preparations for the trip to Hagi. It had been decided that Henry Ginder would accompany the Willmses and that they together would form the nucleus of one of the World Congress teams. Other members of the team were to join them in Hagi.

The first task was to get the Chevy "Carryall" van through Japanese customs. This proved to be a more formidable task than anyone could have imagined. Pete was sent from one desk to another with no results. At last, the chief customs officer opened his drawer and handed the keys to Pete. It had taken fourteen separate signatures to release the van—not to mention several days of frustration for the foreigners.[23]

The van was an awful sight. It had been coated with heavy oil to protect it from the salt spray on the ocean journey. Whitish salt crystals clung to the dirty oil. Henry Ginder wondered, "Will this thing ever start?" Pete tried the key and the engine started. "Of course," said Ginder, "it's a Chevy!"

On the way to Hagi, Pete and Mary's companion learned more about Japanese culture. After the first day of driving over narrow, dusty roads, they stopped for the night at a Japanese inn. The Japanese style bathroom with its huge tub of steaming water was a welcome sight. There were a half dozen low wooden stools and some tiny wooden tubs scattered about on the sloping concrete floor. Ginder grabbed the soap and prepared to step into the small pool. He was brought up short by Pete who explained that one must first wash off thoroughly outside the tub. "The little wooden tubs are for dipping and rinsing clean," he explained, and added, "The big tub is just for soaking." That was fine with Ginder, but then he began to think about what he had just heard. "How many people took their baths in this tub before us?" he demanded. The reply sounded like a chuckle, "That's what we don't know!"

Pete's patience, though taxed by the problems with the van, was in better supply than his language ability. Late one evening the party was very much in need of more gasoline. But they could find no place open. They finally found a passer-by and tried without success to ask directions to a gas station. Finally Pete led the man around the car, pointed to the gas cap and blurted, "I need something to put in that place!" The man led them around several corners and they soon had their gasoline.[24]

After three days of bumpy roads and sudden stops to allow other vehicles to squeeze through frequent narrow places, the travelers turned the van inland from Ogori for the final two-hour drive across the mountains to the Japan Sea coast. The roads here were no better, but the mountains were lush with green pines and thick undergrowth. The terraced rice fields, with stalks beginning to bend from the weight of newly forming heads, provided a picture of rare beauty. Finally, the van began to descend along a wide river. Then in the distance they saw Hagi, filling the delta between the two branches of the Abu River which divided at the point where the mountains gave way. On the far edge of the city where the coastline met the sea was the famous little bump of land proudly called "mountain" by the residents. This was the landmark of a former castle that had housed a ruling *daimyo*—a district feudal lord.

Bathed in the evening sun, the scene was magnificent. But Mary's feelings soon changed as they came to the huge shrine on the outskirts of the city. A sense of darkness came over her like an awful weight. She was filled with dread and then loneliness.[25] She saw that here there was no warmth of Christian fellowship. There was none of the brightness that grows out of the knowledge of Christ's love.

She began to realize that the shrine represented the lost condition of the people of Hagi. She did not realize how often she would have to feel the struggle with darkness as the burden for the people without Christ grew within her.

The Tomoe Inn

The paper-covered *shoji* slid quietly open once again as the maid reappeared bearing ice-cold towels for the three travelers' sweaty faces and hands. She then placed cool tea and a tiny, sweet cake in front of each of them. While they savored their treat, she left the room and then reappeared with three thin, kimono-like *yukata*, which were to serve as their robes for going to the bath and their gowns for sleeping.

They returned from a leisurely bath perspiring but refreshed. Supper was being prepared on the low table in their room. Each person's portion was carefully arranged at his place on eight or more colored dishes, some square, some round, each one containing a different item. There was fried fish, white steamed rice, raw fish slices with a hot, mustard-like sauce, deep-fried vegetables, pungent pickles, and some other things they could not identify. Mary couldn't help thinking about the person who would have to wash all the dishes for an inn full of guests!

Shortly after supper, the floral paper-covered doors next to the alcove were opened. Inside was a huge stack of thick bedding resembling over-stuffed comforters. They were brightly colored and looked most inviting to the weary travelers. The narrower, firmer pieces were laid out like mattresses on the woven mats which had served as their sitting space and dining room. The wider, softer pieces were spread like covers on top of these. The pillows looked like overgrown bean bags. Unfortunately they *felt* like bean bags too!

The missionaries would learn to enjoy sleeping on *futon* almost as much as western style beds. But their sleep that night was somewhat fitful. No doubt it was partly because the beds were still strange to them. The pillows were hard, and the *futon* given them as covers were much too thick for a summer night. Perhaps it was also because of the sounds that came through the open sliding doors and into the tent-like nets which protected them from the mosquitoes. The crickets chirped in grand chorus and the cicadas vied for notice with their harsh buzzing. But perhaps their restlessness was also because of a growing awareness that they were no longer visitors in this place. They were here to stay—there was no turning back. It was here they would spend the best years of their lives.

Pete fell asleep before Mary. He had been here before. He had been excited all day about showing Mary and Henry the place that had already become familiar to him. And now he was relaxed.

The missionaries were very young. They couldn't have known what lay ahead. But they knew the Lord. And they knew he had called.

They had taken their first step over a strange new threshold. It was a step of faith. The step was to take them into an adventure of life-changing dimensions. For the threshold was much higher than they realized then.

Chapter Two

The Land of the Rising Sun

It was a shattered people who began to pick up the pieces after Japan's surrender on August 14, 1945.[1] They were shattered both materially and emotionally. The atom bombs dropped on Hiroshima and Nagasaki were the decisive blow in bringing Japan to her knees. But she had already been pressed to the breaking point by the hundreds of fire-bomb raids that gutted most of her major cities. Eighty percent of Tokyo lay in charred ruins. Eight million repatriated soldiers and civilians required food that was not available. Millions were homeless. Many lay burned and disabled without adequate medical care.[2]

Japan's spiritual underpinnings also had been swept away. On January 1, 1946, the emperor acknowledged that he was not divine and that there was no special superiority in the Japanese people.

The dazed survivors of the war were relieved to be able to lay down their bamboo spears prepared for a last ditch stand against anticipated landing forces. But they had to subsist on meager portions of unpalatable wheat kernels and brown bread. Their favorite polished rice had long since become unavailable. Many were amazed to find that the foreign soldiers passed out candy and cigarettes instead of molesting or shooting them or herding them into concentration camps.[3]

The scars of war remained for many years. Rubble was still visible in some of the cities visited by the Youth for Christ team in 1951. Occupation forces came in increasing numbers following the surrender. Prostitutes and beggars proliferated along with them. Homeless shoe-shine boys scrambled for coins or stole when they could.[4] The land that possessed few natural resources had now been hopelessly drained economically. Japan would be a long time rebuilding.

Yet rebuild she did, with a rapidity and tenacity that caused the world to marvel. In the mid-1950s, of course, many conveniences common in the western world were not yet available. The missionaries missed hot, running water most of all. Their custom required that clothes be washed in hot water, but the only source of hot water was the huge, iron, kettle-like *ofuro* used for bathing. In the absence of Japanese washing machines, a large American model had been transported across the ocean. Each washday a fire was built under the iron tub. The hot water was then carried in buckets to the machine. In the 1960s, however, modern conveniences began to appear rapidly. Small washing machines and other appliances became quite common even in the country areas. Soon it seemed that the only houses which did not have television sets were those of the missionaries.

The Japanese auto industry, so impressive today, was almost non-existent after the war. Some large trucks and other vehicles had been reclaimed from the war effort. Gradually, however, a truck-like vehicle began to appear in increasing numbers and various sizes. Its shape fascinated foreigners. Its front resembled an overgrown motorcycle, with a similar driver's seat, handle-bar steering, and a single front wheel. The rear part was like a pick-up truck, with a bed supported by two wheels.

Rail transportation at first consisted of pre-war steam engines pulling soot-blackened coaches. Inside the coaches, square sections seated four people facing each other on wooden seats. The missionaries were long to remember all-night trips to Kobe and Tokyo when an infrequent luxury was to be able to stretch out on the hard bench usually needed for two. More often, their heads bobbed during weary night hours as they sat on suitcases in aisles jammed with sleepy passengers and littered with lunch wrappings.

In spite of such spartan accommodations, one's watch could almost be set by the arrival of the trains.[5] Very soon, gleaming diesel and electric expresses made the discomfort of early travel seem remote.

Early Missions

Japan had not been without Christian witness during the years preceding the new mission. In 1549 Catholic missionaries landed at Kagoshima near the southern end of Kyushu. They were well received as they moved northward toward Kyoto during the first few years. Response to Christianity gained momentum rapidly in some areas as many *daimyo*—district lords—and the noble *samurai* under them gave assent to the new faith.

Yamaguchi Prefecture, part of the vast holdings of the Lord Mori, was strongly influenced by Christianity. Frances Xavier, leading figure among the missionaries, chose Yamaguchi City as a center for worship and outreach. A large church stands there today as testimony to his success. Christian witness was also strong in Shimonoseki, gateway to Honshu from the South.

The earnestness of the missionaries and the strength of the converts resulted in rapid church growth. Xavier set as his goal the entire land of Japan. To him Kagoshima was only a gateway and Yamaguchi a stepping stone.[6] During 1598 and 1599, the increasing missionary force recorded a total of seventy thousand baptisms.[7]

Soon, however, a great persecution of the Christians began. The reasons for the persecution are extremely complex and will not be dealt with here.[8] A group of twenty-six believers and missionaries were crucified in Nagasaki in 1597. In 1614 an official edict of persecution was issued by Ieyasu Tokugawa. Waves of torture and execution decimated the young church over a period of one hundred years. Most church buildings were destroyed. The persecution featured demands for the Christians to recant by stepping on a picture of Christ.

The tenacity and brutality of the persecution testify to the quality of the church. Many believers expressed the depth of their convictions by giving their lives. Their dying words reveal a genuine love for Christ.[9] Because of governmental hostility toward Christianity, Japan was closed to new missionaries for one hundred fifty years. The doors opened once again in 1853 when American gunboats demanded safe harbor and commercial ties.

Protestant missions are acknowledged to have begun in 1859.[10] Growth of the church was exceedingly slow for many years. The most encouraging period of Protestant Christianity until recent times was the decade of 1873-1883. Many church buildings were constructed at this time. The number of believers grew sixty percent in 1879 alone. Japanese leaders of high caliber began to emerge. Mutual respect and support characterized relations of Japanese pastors and missionaries.[11]

An interesting feature of the growth of the church in this decade was the formation of Christian "bands." These were groups of earnest young men who gathered under the intimate instruction of missionary teachers in Yokohama, Kumamoto, Sapporo and other places. Vibrant in their faith and earnest in their commitment, these bands stimulated growth in the church in ensuing years.

A Call for Missionaries

Hopeful signs for Christianity were all but erased by the pressure for military expansion prior to World War II and the Religious Bodies Law in 1939. This law allowed the existence of only large Christian groups which were properly registered with the military-controlled government and which conformed to certain regulations. It forced independent churches and smaller denominations to give up their separate activities and organize together. In this way the *Kyodan*, the United Church of Christ in Japan, was created. Many churches resisted the pressure to submit, seeing the potential dangers of control which could lead to compromise. As a result of their resistance, some of their leaders were put in prison. Most groups, however, acquiesced and thus succumbed to the compromising tendencies demanded by the war effort.[12]

Japan's defeat and the emperor's denial of his right to be worshipped as deity shattered the Japanese image of themselves and their nation. Shintoism, based on emperor-worship, was disestablished as the national religion. The result was a tremendous emotional and spiritual vacuum. General Douglas MacArthur, realizing the implications of this void, called for one thousand missionaries to come to Japan. He also asked for ten million Scripture portions to be distributed.[13] It was this call that had moved Peter Willms so deeply as he sat in the history class at Ontario Bible School in 1947.

Some missionaries responded. Most of them were of evangelical or fundamentalist orientation and came from America. The Southern Baptist Convention and The Evangelical Alliance Mission (TEAM) led the stream of new workers, soon placing one hundred and two hundred missionaries, respectively. By 1954, there were 2,017 Protestant foreign missionaries in Japan; approximately eighty-one percent were American.[14]

The years immediately following Japan's surrender have been termed by some as the "Christian Boom." Richard Drummond indicates that "in the physical devastation and spiritual confusion of those years, large numbers of people who had lost their spiritual moorings visited the churches, not only for services of worship but often at any time of day or night. . . . Many of those who came were earnest seekers after faith."[15]

This condition was to change all too soon. By the time the Willmses arrived in Japan, it was no longer easy to attract a crowd to a gospel presentation. As has been mentioned, Willms saw the trend and warned the church of waning opportunities.[16] Buddhist conventions were held. Shrines were rebuilt, and the number of Shinto worshippers began to increase, indicating a return to pre-war enthusiasm.[17] All Christians combined numbered only 450,000, or approximately one-half of the one percent of the population.[18]

Many observers feared that communism might gain control of Japanese society, now dispirited and with no firm ideological moorings. Wolgemuth warned of a rapidly unfolding communist timetable.[19] Willms cited serious political unrest.[20] However, communism was not to succeed in influencing Japanese society as a whole. It realized some success in cities, but it was largely unable to reach the rural populations.[21] It did, however, make serious inroads in another direction.

The Japanese Church

The wartime Religious Bodies Law was repealed in 1945 under MacArthur's direction. This opened the way once again for religious freedom. By this time, however, members of the smaller Christian groups had been scattered by the pressure of war. The *Kyodan*, though boasting many members and a central organization, had been rendered largely ineffective through theological compromise and capitulation to the government. It is true that it was formed because of extreme pressure from the government—the very existence of the church had seemed threatened. But the *Kyodan* lacked a distinctly Christian, biblical tone. In addition it had offered direct support to the government in its war effort.[22]

Communism had been unable to influence the general populace, but now the *Kyodan* began to embrace its concerns and methodology. The concern of *Kyodan* leaders for social justice (*ningen sogai*) was not misplaced. But they also adopted Marxist policies. Many young people in the *Kyodan* joined the New Left in protests, often violent. Evangelical churches refused the *Kyodan's* ecumenical overtures, and many churches that had earlier joined it withdrew. Its liberal tendencies and its avowal of Marxist methods gradually widened the gap with more conservative churches.[23]

The independent churches and small denominations that had resisted the merger survived the war, their integrity preserved. They regrouped and began to grow. They were joined by the new evangelical personnel and mission organizations. One of these was the Brethren in Christ.

The Brethren in Christ

The Brethren in Christ denomination began about 1780 when a small group of believers began meeting in a farmhouse along Pennsylvania's Susquehanna River. The believers' hearts had been warmed by the winds of revival which swept through the German-speaking community surrounding the town of Bainbridge. They affirmed the historical Christian doctrines of the Trinity, the deity and the humanity of Christ, the atonement of Christ through his death and bodily resurrection, and the rewards and punishments of an afterlife. They insisted, with the reformers, that salvation was through grace by faith alone. But they disagreed with those who promoted the doctrine of predestination. The Brethren (as members came to be known) maintained that Christ died for all mankind and left each individual free to accept or reject his salvation. They also maintained that the Church was a new society composed of regenerated persons gathered in a free covenant relationship.[24]

Historian Carlton Wittlinger shows that three theological streams merged to form the Brethren in Christ. The first was Anabaptism, with its desire to restore the New Testament believer's church and separate the functions of church and state, and with its insistence that baptism required responsible adult confession of faith. The second was Pietism, with its emphasis on a personal experience with Christ, willing service, and intimacy with the Scriptures. The third stream was Wesleyanism. It taught the experience of the Holy Spirit in the believer, resulting in sanctification and power for witness.[25]

Within one hundred years a vibrant missionary consciousness had developed in the church. As members migrated across North America, they took as their responsibility the preaching of the gospel and the beginning of new churches.[26] The denomination was also urged toward foreign missions. This urging came first from concerned members of the Kansas church. Their appeals were backed by their money offerings, and a mission to Africa was inaugurated in 1897. Work was opened in India in 1905. Willing workers increased on both fields until the denomination claimed more than one missionary for every one hundred members at home.[27] The resources of the church were poured into these two fields. It was to be almost fifty years until a new mission field would be opened.

One characteristic of the Brethren in Christ was its concept of churches shepherded by self-supported elders. These elders were, in a sense, lay leaders. This concept was to exert a profound influence on the missionaries who would open this church's third major mission field—Japan—in 1953.

Thoughts Toward Japan

Interest in Japan began long before Peter and Mary Willms found their way to its shores. As had been noted, pressure was mounting in the early 1890's upon the Brethren in Christ to open missions abroad. In the absence of a denominational mission board, the only alternative left for those who felt called to foreign missions was to go out under other societies. One of the earliest Brethren who did so was David W. Zook of Kansas. He went with his wife to India in 1896, under the auspices of Hepzibah Faith Missionary Association of Tabor, Iowa.[28]

On their way to India, Zook worked briefly with F. L. Smelser, a Hepzibah member, in Yokohama, Japan. Smelser had gone to Yokohama in 1895 with L. B. Worcester, also of Hepzibah, who then returned to the States. Zook assisted Smelser until Worcester once again arrived in Japan, this time accompanied by Jeremiah I. Long, also of Kansas.[29] Jeremiah had declined an invitation to join the first group of Brethren in Christ missionaries leaving for Africa in 1897.[30] He felt clearly called to Japan and arrived there in September of that same year.[31] Mary E. Long, Jeremiah's sister, joined him there, but it is not clear when she arrived.

These missionaries from the ranks of the Brethren in Christ evidently remained in good standing with the denomination in North America even though they served with the Tabor-based group. Concerning Zook, the Kansas Joint Council declared: ". . . while we do not recognize Bro. David Zook as officially representing the Brethren in Christ as a foreign missionary, we hold him in loving confidence as a Brother in the Lord, and wish him Godspeed in his work abroad."[32]

Another indication of confidence and continued fellowship was the inclusion of reports from these brethren in the *Evangelical Visitor*, the denominational magazine. Various articles were written to the church from 1896 to 1907 by David Zook, Jeremiah Long, Mary Long and F. L. Smelser. Smelser wrote to the Brethren for the first time after he and Mary Long were married in Yokohama in September of 1901. He indicated that both of them felt that the time had come for them to be "more closely united in the work."[33] Prior to joining Smelser in Yohokama, Mary had been engaged in children's work in a fishing town of thirty thousand called Choshi, about one hundred miles to the north. It is not clear whether or not Mary initiated the work there, but she reported that one hundred forty to one hundred seventy children attended meetings in the missionary home on main street. She also worked with Sunday schools in other villages.[34]

David Zook indicated that the mission in Yokohama was primarily among the Chinese living in Japan.[35] Zook opened his heart to the Brethren at home concerning what he felt were careless attitudes and lack of stewardship among Christians in relation to missions. He noted that so many had settled down in their easy nests and were content with driving to church on Sunday in their splendid carriages. They dress in all the finery demanded by Dame Fashion, he lamented. They throw a few pennies into the mission box while the congregation sings "rescue the perishing, care for the dying" and then feel that they have done God a good service. He then is so bold as to add, "Such are some of you, dear readers."[36]

Jeremiah Long still identified himself with the Brethren in Christ as he signed one report, "Your brother in the field."[37] And some of the Brethren must have considered him one of them, for he acknowledged an offering of $35.55 which he had received after about nine months in Japan. He informed the readers that the Zooks had moved on to India when he arrived in Yokohama and asked the home church to pray especially on October 30, 1898, for "the awakening of Japan."[38]

From these reports, we can see that Japan had been on the hearts of some Brethren in Christ from a very early date, even though the church provided no official channel for carrying out that concern.

The Decision

We cannot be sure that the people who were looking toward Japan in the early 1950's were aware of their forerunners. The Foreign Mission Board had been discussing the possibility of opening a third field, now almost fifty years after beginnings in India. The Orient was one of the areas under consideration.[39] Interest then focused on Japan prior to and following the gospel team thrust by Youth for Christ.

We may list in summary four reasons why Japan was finally chosen. First, Samuel F. Wolgemuth had stopped in Japan to minister as part of a 1950 world tour. His reports of spiritual need coupled with the announcement of plans for the 1951 crusade excited California Bishop Jesse F. Lady and lifted his faith. Lady's enthusiasm in turn spilled over into the California church and particularly the Men's Fellowship group.

Second, Peter Willms had made his call known to the Canadian church as early as 1947. Evangelist Marshall Winger, a firm believer in the young man, began to promote Japan. His appearance at Upland in 1949 created the awareness of Japan in the California church which Wolgemuth later stirred into action.[40]

Third, personnel had now become available to the Foreign Mission Board for a particular place. No one else had expressed an interest in a field and offered himself for it. Peter Willms was available and his call was Japan. This fact largely settled the issue.[41]

Finally, Royce Saltzman, Gordon Johnson and Pete Willms came back from their summer 1951 evangelistic activities in Japan and reported to the church.[42] Their excitement was contagious and their challenge convincing. There is little doubt that these emissaries helped to move the church toward decision.

The action of the 1952 General Conference seems somewhat tenuous or hesitant. It voted to "give favorable consideration to entering mission work in Japan by approving further study . . . with the understanding that work may be opened if . . . details . . . are of such a nature as to recommend the opening of a work."[43]

The conference of the following year however, evidently considered the earlier resolution sufficient. It very simply approved the workers to fill the opening.[44] Prior to the conference, of course, was the Foreign Mission Board's definite decision to open work in Japan and to send the Willmses.[45] This decision was confirmed with detailed plans as they met on Conference grounds just before the general sessions began.[46] No doubt this action was amply explained in the sponsorship of the resolution on the floor of Conference.

Samuel Wolgemuth, anticipating approval of the new venture, expressed his delight in greetings from Japan to the Conference of 1953: "As you bid Godspeed to our first full-time workers for this opportune field, I challenge you to so cover them with the artillery of prayer, believing prayer, that they themselves will be amazed as they see God work."[47]

The Choice of Hagi

It was evident that Carl Ulery had been strongly impressed by the Japan Sea coast area of Yamaguchi Prefecture. It seemed that the Holy Spirit surely had led in a remarkable way by bringing Ulery into contact with three strangers, all of whom suggested Hagi and its environs as a location for the new mission. The Foreign Mission Board heard Ulery's report about his trip and his description of Hagi in their meeting of January 1953.

They acknowledged the possible direct intervention of the Holy Spirit. But their discussion brought out additional reasons why they should consider Hagi.

First, Yamaguchi Prefecture showed little missionary activity within its borders. Later information was to show it one of the areas most in need of a missionary presence.[48] Although two small churches were discovered in Hagi, there seemed to be no concern for outreach in either. In addition, there was no missionary to be found on the entire back coast from Shimonoseki to the neighboring Shimane Prefecture on the north.

Second, the country areas of Japan were generally ignored by foreign workers. The Japan Sea coast area, which includes Hagi, although dotted with several population centers of thirty thousand or more, was considered "country" by the Japanese. The reason was that it lay on the "back" side of Honshu, away from the transportation arteries which ran through the bustling Inland Sea cities on their way to the larger population centers. Missionaries were much more ready to settle in or near Kobe, Osaka, Nagoya or Tokyo. Those centers provided more cultural benefits, better education facilities, more opportunities for fellowship and more convenient transportation.

Third, Hagi's location and fame[49] made it ideal as a center for outreach into fishing towns on both sides and into mountain villages to its east and south. Ulery and his colleagues envisioned Hagi as the hub of a wheel on whose spokes and rim would be scattered many churches.

Perhaps the board's decision grew out of a concern for the principles of fairness and service instilled in their minds by their Anabaptist and Pietistic background. At any rate, they reasoned that, although there were far greater numbers of people in the large cities, at least there was some witness already there, while no witness at all existed in large areas of rural Japan. If the believers in the cities accomplished their mission, those places would be evangelized. But how would the country people hear the gospel if no one was willing to take it there?[50]

It must be admitted at this point that it would have been much easier for the missionary personnel to function in the urban areas. It is likely that some of the personal stresses resulting from numerous cultural tensions in the country could have been avoided. It is also possible that more converts could have been won more quickly in the cities. Larger population centers were made up mostly of people who had been removed from many of their restricted, traditional ways of thinking. Church growth is usually much more encouraging in such places.[51] Whether or not the board wavered in their choice because of these factors, we do not know. The fact is that they chose to focus on one of the most neglected areas. Their motivation was a concern for what they saw as the greatest need. In later years, the mission personnel would, for the most part, concur in this decision and rally to the task with a marked degree of commitment and disregard for personal comfort.

People and Issues

The Holy Spirit seldom moves in a vacuum where he has work to be done. God has committed the ministry of reconciliation entirely to people. Incredibly, he has determined that the desire of his own heart for all people to be saved is subject to the willingness of believers to take that desire seriously and make it their own at any cost.[52]

Missions is a partnership of people with the Holy Spirit. It is the expression of believers' hearts beating with God's. We must pause at this point to consider the kind of people God used to inaugurate the mission in Japan. We will look also at some of the issues with which they began to grapple in their desire to communicate the gospel effectively.

Carl J. Ulery's part in the new work has already been discussed at some length. Ulery is an example of the kind of dedicated service that characterized those involved in the opening of the Japan mission. His term on the board began in 1943 and ran for thirty-five years until his retirement in 1978.[53] Ulery is an example also of the attitude of total reliance upon God for direction and strength which characterized the board members.

In Ulery's case, reliance on God was expressed in a deep prayer concern. The responsibility of finding a location for the mission weighed heavily upon him. He turned to his only source of help, the Lord. He often lay awake at night praying for direction. We have seen how God answered his prayer for guidance in Hagi. But his reliance on trust as well as prayer is illustrated by an incident which took place immediately following his visit to Hagi.

Instead of returning to Tokyo by way of Shimonoseki, he and Samuel Wolgemuth tried to find a bus that would take them the much shorter route through the mountains of Ogori. They knew no Japanese, and no one responded to their questions in English. Finally, Ulery determined to trust God and get on the next bus that appeared. On the bus, they kept asking people for confirmation of their direction, but they received only smiles. On the outskirts of a mountain town, they suddenly noticed a U.S. military sign in English. Looking at their map, they discovered that the town was indeed on the way to Ogori.[54] They returned to Tokyo, rejoicing in their Guide.

It should be noted also that Ulery helped to prepare the way for new awareness of the flexibility needed in cross-cultural communication of the gospel. He was deeply committed to his church and willing to abide by its interpretations of Scripture. But he was also open to new insights and ready to replace old ways with new. Careful to guard against compromise with God's Word, he was at the same time willing to move with the times. His attitude of openness and gentleness was to give the missionaries much encouragement as they struggled between the pressure of church traditions and the demands of the new culture.

Samuel F. Wolgemuth must be acknowledged as a representative of the Brethren in Christ in Japan during the years just prior to the opening of the mission. He was a member of the Foreign Mission Board from 1955 to 1968. Although he increasingly moved toward the position of director of Japan Youth for Christ, he kept the needs of Japan before the church through his messages and articles.[55] He functioned as Japan's representative in greetings to Conference in 1952.[56] He was also designated as field counselor to the Willmses by board action.[57]

One observer of Wolgemuth's activities during the 1953 World Congress on Evangelism declared him an "outstanding administrator." His success in organizing sixty gospel teams that summer to spread over Japan's forty-seven prefectures is adequate confirmation of this fact.[58] Each Congress team included an evangelist, an interpreter, musicians and counselors. Team members were for the most part strangers to each other and assembled in Tokyo from a variety of backgrounds. Team schedules called for ministry in hundreds of different locations in city and country. Wolgemuth roamed Japan far and wide talking to leaders and arranging campaign sites. His wife, Grace, followed his effort with concern.[59]

The effort was not without its cost for the entire family. John N. Hostetter, editor of the *Evangelical Visitor* at this time, noted the considerable sacrifice on the part of Grace and the children in order that such a special service could be rendered. He declared that this sacrifice was an evidence of genuine consecration.[60] In this sense Grace and the children were missionaries to Japan.

Wolgemuth alerted the denomination to the urgency of the Congress:

> Your hearts would be deeply moved if you could but hear the prayers of pastors and missionaries ascending to the throne pleading that 1953 shall be a year of great spiritual revival in Japan. There is a note of expectancy in the hearts and upon the lips of those who share in preparation for the Congress. We covet the prayers of our dear folk at home that God will answer and that we shall see a great moving of the Spirit of God in this strategically located country of the Orient.[61]

The challenge added to the growing interest among Brethren in Christ in the new field of Japan. Leaders responded to the challenge not only with prayer but also with participation. Norman and Eunice Wingert, John and Nellie Hostetter, Erwin Thomas, Mark Wolgemuth, Henry Ginder and Eber Dourte joined the Wolgemuths and the Willmses for the World Congress. Charles and Kathryn Engle added their support, coming from India instead of taking a much needed rest.[62] It was thus appropriate that Peter Willms would later declare that the Brethren in Christ officially began its work in Japan in connection with the Youth for Christ World Congress on Evangelism.[63]

Wolgemuth's purpose for the World Congress teams was clearly evangelism. He was not calling Christians together for fellowship, nor was he interested in challenge without action. This purpose was clear also in the teams that campaigned in the summer and fall of 1951, two years earlier. Brethren in Christ representatives Saltzman, Johnson and Willms were first of all intent on calling people to decision for Christ. It was after their plan began to unfold that two other purposes gradually emerged. The first was that of stimulating the home church to renewed evangelistic concern. In this regard, the involvement of the three young men did, indeed, become a rallying point for a new emphasis on mission. The second was that of searching out likely places for Brethren in Christ mission involvement. Although these two were later added to the main purpose of the team,[64] we can nevertheless acknowledge they also were used of God in moving the church toward decision.

Henry N. Hostetter joined the Foreign Mission Board in 1949. He was to play a key role in the development of the new mission. In 1952 he became executive secretary for the board and held that position until his retirement in 1970. Hostetter too approached issues with an attitude of gentleness. He exhibited concern first of all for people. The Japan missionaries considered him a man of integrity. They were never disillusioned by his actions. They felt a genuine love for him even at times when they did not see eye to eye on some issues.[65] He was affectionately called grandpa by the children in the mission, with whom he used to laugh and romp.[66]

Hostetter saw two characteristics of the Brethren in Christ as crucial in its mission program. These were a deep commitment to God and a genuine concern for others. By a deep commitment to God he meant a determination to hear God and obey him. It is this commitment that saves us from many unfortunate incidents, he felt, especially where strong personalities are thrown together. If our commitment is deep, he declared, God can help us work through any situation.

Hostetter provided a steadying influence during the development of the Japan mission. He was in leadership during the time the denomination began to change from a rigid, traditional interpretation of Christian life and practice to a more relaxed, open attitude. Church practice had been particularly rigid in the area of plain dress, including the prohibition of the necktie for men and requiring the wearing of the prayer veiling for women. Hostetter saw the church begin its struggle toward greater freedom in these areas and in other issues as well, and he concurred in its attempts to move toward that freedom.

Hostetter was deeply concerned for the stability of the church. But he also recognized that unreasonable and restrictive practices in the home church created obstacles to the mission entering new lands. There is value in regulations, he noted. Regulations provide a sense of safety or protection. But when protection is gained, something vital is lost. The thing lost is the potential for evangelism.[67]

This was a remarkable insight for the 1950s. It was to aid the Japan mission in making adjustments to the new culture and at the same time in maintaining integrity with the church. Contact with other cultures was forcing the church to realize that some of its interpretations were culturally derived. Changes had to occur in the church in order for the maximum evangelistic potential to be realized on the foreign field.

Hostetter insists that the change in church practices at home actually began from a concern for the mission fields. Church leaders began to see that the church could not demand of young churches in other cultures the same applications of doctrine that it promoted at home. Cultural forms accepted in America could not necessarily be transferred abroad. According to Hostetter, adjustments made in the African church, in particular, were instrumental in urging changes upon the home church.[68]

Peter A. Willms was caught in the period of transition from rigidity to a more flexible approach in doctrinal interpretation. He had seen the dangers inherent in insisting on traditional approaches in changing times. He recognized that some church interpretations were products of the church's culture and thus were not to be considered sacred.

Willms was not given to compromise. Even at an early age he had shown strong convictions. After completing high school at Ontario Bible School, he returned to his home in Leamington and entered grade thirteen, the first year of college in Canada. Just then, military training became required for all public schools. Willms objected to the school principal and refused to participate. He was expelled. Inwardly crushed, he returned to Ontario Bible School for grade thirteen. It was that year when he received his call to Japan.[69]

Willms' level of commitment can be seen also in his attitude toward his mission in Japan. He was determined to become a citizen in Japan, if that would aid in communicating the gospel. He was even willing to die there. To that extent he was willing to identify with the people. And to that extent he stood firmly for what he felt was right.

Willms was committed to the principles of Scripture that the Brethren in Christ held dear. But he was not willing to accept applications of Scripture merely for the sake of human tradition. He was evangelical, but he was not conservative. He spoke out firmly when he saw what he thought were inconsistencies. He was one of the first to reject the church's prohibition on neckties. This made him suspect in the eyes of more conservative brethren. He also had serious reservations about the form adopted by the church for the prayer veiling. Though assenting to the principle of modesty and subjection which it represented, he and Mary gradually drew away from the particular form chosen by the church. Perhaps this was due in part to the fact that the

California church, of which they were members, was moving toward more flexibility on the issue. But Pete was concerned personally also that the church be able to adapt its forms to changing cultural patterns and still preserve the meaning of Scripture.

A significant event confirmed this feeling in Willms's mind just before he left for Japan. While studying in Pasadena, he met Eugene Nida, well-known Bible translator and anthropologist. Nida told the story of the Mennonite lady who returned to the United States from her mission field. One of the brethren in the church asked her, "Sister, do you teach the doctrine of plain clothes in Africa?" She replied, "Well, brother, we're lucky if they wear any clothes at all!"[70]

Nida also told of missions that took opposite approaches on the matter of whether a converted polygamist could be accepted as a member. One mission determined that no national with more than one wife could be a member. It thus relegated such a person to the status of a second-class Christian. The other group, while affirming that monogamy is ideal, allowed a man who already had more than one wife at the time he was converted to be a full member of the church. The first approach was unyielding, the second willing to adapt. Willms was moved by the non-legalistic approach, and was elated to realize that he was not alone in his thinking concerning the modification of certain forms in relation to the communication of the gospel.

It was because of issues of this kind that some questions had been raised about the Willmses. Even the board members, though sympathetic with the Willmses, were not at all certain that Conference would approve them for work in Japan. We have seen that their fears were not confirmed. But we must note here the far-reaching implications of this struggle within the church and the concern on the part of some about issues which were crucial for the cause of missions.

Henry A. Ginder also had a unique role in the mission's beginning, but the benefit was reciprocal. Ginder's participation, in turn, profoundly influenced his own thinking and his future ministry in the home church. Previously pastor of the Manheim, Pennsylvania, congregation, in 1953 Ginder was serving as bishop of the Rapho District.

Ginder states that his involvement in ministry in Japan helped him see the dynamics and implications of cross-cultural ministry as he had never seen them before. God worked on him in a fashion similar to the experience of Peter in Acts 10. Ginder acknowledges that if he had not gone to Japan himself, he likely would have been critical of the others who went. He admits, "I couldn't have understood their changed perspective if I had not been there myself."

Ginder notes that the Lord sent Peter himself to Cornelius' house. If Peter had not gone, he never could have understood the reports that the others brought back. He probably would have objected strongly to their views. But God changed Peter's mind by putting him directly in the situation. Ginder confesses that the Lord has had to handle him this way sometimes. This was true in the case of his experience in Japan.

Reflecting on the Brethren in Christ in the 1950s, Ginder notes, "We were pretty staid at that time. This was my first exposure to a cross-cultural situation." He declares, "My traditionalism was shattered. My horizons were pushed back culturally." He adds, "If it had not happened to me, I would not have understood it in others. I know myself well enough to know that."[71]

From the above descriptions, we are able to glimpse how God was at work through people. He was not only giving direction through his Spirit but he was also bringing the right people together for his purposes—people to whom he could suggest a new perspective and who could be free to see new possibilities in the way he might want to work.

One last observation needs to be made here about the roles of the Canadian and California churches. We have seen that Peter Willms went to California for study, married Mary, and joined the Upland church with her. Jesse F. Lady personally adopted the 1951 gospel team project and urged its support upon the California churches. Later Pete and Mary, having pastored at Pasadena almost a year, were given their send-off by those same churches. In this way the new Japan work was seen by many as being the child of the California conference.

But we need to be reminded that the vision for the work in Japan was born and nurtured first of all in Canada. It was Dorothy Sherk who helped Pete change his direction scholastically. Pete was then in a position to enter grade thirteen, where he heard God's call. Pauline Herr and Phyllis Pye were used of God to confirm Pete's inner stirrings. Marshall Winger carried the vision for Japan to the Upland church. Thus it was appropriate that Conference approval and the blessing of the church for the new mission took place on the grounds of Niagara Christian College in Canada.

This footnote is not intended to give glory to individuals. Nevertheless God uses people to carry out his work. How many others might have been used of God in equally dramatic ways, perhaps behind the scenes, we do not know.[72] Truly, to paraphrase Scripture, "One tills, another sows, still others water— and God brings into being" (1 Cor. 3:6).

With this background, let us now return to our friends in the Tomoe Inn.

The Sun Rises

The travelers were awakened by a cheery "*Ohayo gozaimasu!*" (Good morning!) The sound seemed distant to Mary. She stirred, then awakened abruptly as she heard the *shoji* slide open and realized that someone was coming into her bedroom. The maid proceeded to place a pot of steaming tea on the low table which had been removed to the corner of the room, bowed sweetly and inquired, "*Yoku oyasumi ni narimashita ka?*" (Did you sleep well?) Mary thought that the sleep might have been better if allowed to go longer. But a glance at her watch told her that it was already eight o'clock.

The maid pushed open the *shoji* on the garden side of the room. The sun was well above the nearby hills on the east, and sunlight was cascading over the tips of the manicured trees and bushes in the garden onto the wooden corridor that bordered the room. The cool air suggested that autumn might be nearing.

Pete finally began to stir after deciding that the intrusion was no longer to be denied. The maid left the room, allowing the visitors to get into their clothes for the day. Soon she returned to fold up the thick comforters and stack them once again in their special cupboard.

There was hardly time for the three travelers to step down the hall to wash the sleep out of their eyes before the maid appeared again with bowls and chopsticks for the morning meal. Breakfast was much simpler than supper had been—just white rice, brown *miso* soup with chunks of *tofu* breaking the surface, tiny bits of pickles and a raw egg. One was supposed to break the egg over the very hot, steaming rice or mix it into the hot soup. Henry Ginder chose a third alternative—ignore it. He wasn't quite ready for the idea of a raw egg for breakfast.

The dishes were cleared away and the adventurers were once again left alone. Quietly, each pressed closer to the table as if ready to reach out to the others. They began to ask God's help for what lay ahead. There was no time to lose. Many arrangements had to be made for the special campaign. Other team members would be coming from various parts of Japan in a day or two.

The three had already experienced precious times of fellowship around God's Word. Now Henry opened his Bible and began to read: "I have taken you by the hand and kept you. I have given you as a light to the nations, to open the eyes that are blind, to bring out the prisoners from the dungeon, from the prison those who sit in darkness."

Pete and Mary listened in utter amazement. Ginder had read the words of Isaiah 42:6-7. These were the very words that had been impressed so strongly upon Pete's heart just three months earlier. Pete had included them in a letter during the time of final preparations for Japan. In the letter he had added:

> It is not just an accident that the fields are ripe. They are ripe because some 'corn of wheat has died' and the Lord of the harvest has ordained that when a corn of wheat dies there shall be fruit. That fruit is now ripe and ours is the season of harvest. How thankful we are that God has called us to labor during the harvest season![73]

Three pilgrims bowed their heads in the solemnity of that moment. Tears began to well up from three hearts who were suddenly very much aware of the presence of their Lord.

After plans for the day were discussed, the trio stepped out of the room and filed down the hall toward the front of the inn. Hearing their movement, the maid hastily appeared and, opening the tiny cupboards under the polished threshold, she drew out their shoes and lined them up carefully on the concrete floor.

The air was fresh and the sky clear and warm. They moved through the gate in the wall, only to step back again as one of those three-wheeled trucks with a front end like a motorcycle clattered around the corner and honked its way among the bicycles and dodging pedestrians.

It was a beautiful morning. They didn't know then that God was beginning to work unexpectedly in some other adventurers. In just two years another couple would witness the sun rising upon the land of Japan, this time from the railing of a boat, and would be welcomed by the young couple who now moved out into the streets of Hagi for the ministry that God had prepared.

Chapter Three

Early Evangelistic Efforts

A feeling of excitement added spring to the steps of the three missionaries as they moved out into the narrow streets. They were glad to be together—they knew they were a special team. Each had the same thought: "This is it! This is where the work begins!"[1]

Pete and Mary were glad Henry Ginder had come. With him along, each moment seemed filled either with inspiration or laughter. Their business was serious, but days with Henry were always exciting.

Ginder had arrived at the World Congress delighted that the church had approved a new mission field. As a church leader, he felt he must see the place on which the attention of the church would now be focused. He determined to make every effort to get to Hagi. He was willing to leave the Congress group flight and pay an extra fare, if necessary. He approached Sam Wolgemuth one day during the Congress. "Now, Brother Sam, you understand that just because you and I are both Brethren in Christ, you are under no obligation to me. I have no right to ask you to put me on the team to Hagi. But I will tell you that I'll not return to the United States until I have been there!"[2] Wolgemuth grinned, restraining a chuckle. Ginder was assigned to Hagi.

Ginder knew no more than a few words of Japanese. One day on the trip to Hagi he was driving the Carryall. Shortly after crossing a railroad track, he was stopped by a policeman. He was puzzled as to why he had been stopped. And he couldn't understand a word the man said! Pete and Mary sat absolutely still, fascinated. Ginder racked his memory for something to say. He thought of *sayonara* (goodbye!), but somehow that didn't seem quite appropriate. He became more and more uncomfortable. Finally, in desperation, he managed a cheerful smile and blurted out, *Arigato gozaimasu*! The policeman stared at him. And he waved him on! An enthusiastic "thank you!" had done the trick![3]

The Hagi Campaign

There was reason to feel optimistic about the planned campaign. A number of people, including several city officials, had expressed interest in the mission venture on Pete's earlier visit. One of these was the police interpreter who assured Pete of a warm welcome in the city. Another was the police chief himself. He promised Pete that street meetings would be permitted and then asked him to explain the Christian faith. Pete did so through the interpreter.

The chief then opened his drawer and took out a New Testament printed in Japanese. He explained that he had read it three times but could not understand it well.

The mayor also offered a warm welcome. He felt the new mission would be good for the city. He stated that he had listened to a Christian radio broadcast just the night before. Pete felt that these expressions were a sign that God was preparing a harvest.[4]

On the other hand, there were also indications that the work would not be easy. Pete was already aware that the Hagi area was extremely conservative. This meant that it was feudalistic, Shintoistic and intensely Buddhistic. In addition, two of Japan's three communist leaders had come from Hagi. Pete recognized that Satan's forces were arrayed against them. But he took the words of Hezekiah as his battle cry: "With us is the Lord our God, to help us and to fight our battles."[5]

The last two members of the team arrived in Hagi. They were Vincent Gizzi of the Oriental Boat Mission and the interpreter, Takahashi, a Southern Baptist. Gizzi shared the speaking load and contributed music. Several members of Shimonoseki churches came to serve as counselors.

Preparations for the meetings included securing permission for holding open-air services and for announcing the meetings with the Carryall's loudspeaking system. The requests were readily granted by the police department. At the city hall, the small auditorium was secured for the final night of the campaign.

The team moved up and down the streets each day in the van, announcing the evening services. It was not difficult to attract attention. People stared at the spectacle of the huge American car and the strange-featured passengers. The group stopped at busy corners to pass out tracts and leaflets which gave directions to the meetings. Mary attracted children at various locations with her flannelgraph stories.

The Lord worked with the evangelists in a variety of ways. On one occasion the loudspeaker system stopped functioning. All attempts to restore it were futile. Finally the group laid hands on the equipment and asked God to heal it. They turned on the switch, and immediately it began to work.[6]

There was some anxiety about what the attendance might be. Takahashi suggested that perhaps twenty to fifty might come. He warned that Hagi was very conservative and strongly Buddhistic. The first night, however, more than one hundred gathered on the street corner that had been selected. The next night there were close to one hundred and fifty. Mothers came with babies on their backs. Each night a few people remained to inquire further of the counselors.[7]

A bond of mutual appreciation developed between Ginder and Takahashi during the week. Each day Ginder explained the general direction of the message for that night. The two men then prayed. And they preached as a unit.

John and Nellie Hostetter and Mark Wolgemuth arrived for the final meeting from campaigns in Beppu and Shikoku. Charles and Kathryn Engle had hoped to be present, but their arrival in Hagi was delayed one week. The climaxing service was held in the city hall auditorium. It was a plain room with a sloping concrete floor. Fans suspended from the ceiling circled lazily in the warm air. Ginder's text for the last service was John 1:29: "Behold the Lamb of God, which taketh away the sin of the world." He poured his heart out, and Takahashi echoed his fervency. A small group remained for counseling and prayer.[8]

The day for Ginder's farewell arrived. Mary was totally unprepared for the feeling which suddenly came over her. Ginder was her last tie with America. All of a sudden, she wanted to be back home! Just before Ginder's departure she broke down: "You're going home! I'm stuck here for another five years!" Ginder opened his Bible to Psalm 37: "Trust in the Lord . . . so shalt thou dwell in the land, and verily thou shalt be fed . . . Delight thyself also in the Lord . . . Commit thy way unto the Lord . . . He shall bring forth thy righteousness as the light . . . Rest in the Lord, and wait patiently for Him." Comforted, Mary and Pete said goodbye to their friend and companion in adventure.[9]

A Small Beginning

A fascinating account of the appearance of the foreigners is found in the *Hagi Residential News*. This was a small newspaper published every three weeks by the real estate broker, Takeshita, whom Pete had met on his first visit to Hagi. The article was entitled, "Self-sacrificing Young Missionary Couple Do Evangelistic Work."

> We bow our heads as we watch the august figures of young Rev. and Mrs. Peter Alfred Willms preaching Christ's message at various street corners of Hagi with a shapely dark-green car and a loudspeaker. They have come to purify the minds of the people. . . . This couple is planning to devote their whole lives to the evangelization of Hagi . . . We citizens of Hagi welcome them heartily, as we hear such a lofty determination. Here is Mr. Willms' message to citizens of Hagi: 'Jesus Christ told His followers to go everywhere and preach the Gospel . . . My wife and I came to Hagi . . . to tell you about Christ and give you the opportunity to decide whether you will accept Him or not. The Bible says that those who accept Christ will receive the eternal blessing of God . . . We pray that you will trust Jesus. We plan to buy a house and live in this wonderful place permanently . . . I am very glad if you will accept us.[10]

The Willmses were gradually accepted by the town. And a few of its people accepted the Savior whom they proclaimed. Many others showed an interest in their teaching, or at least in the foreigners themselves. Pete wrote to the church in America that the immediate response of the Japanese people was heartening. He acknowledged that foreigners approaching a cultured and religious people of another faith can ask for nothing more than a courteous reception. This was graciously extended. He declared that some had placed their faith in Jesus and were growing remarkably in spiritual matters. He said, "There is every reason to believe that they know the meaning of the new birth."[11]

Time was to confirm Pete's evaluation. A small group of converts from this first meeting became the early leaders of the Brethren in Christ Church in Japan. Most of them remained faithful over the years in fellowship and in witness.

Pete and Mary made the Tomoe Inn their home for about one month. For several weeks following the campaign they could not find a suitable place for meeting with those who had responded. They invited the seekers to a follow-up meeting in their room at the inn on Thursday, September 3. The next meeting was the following Sunday morning. India missionaries Charles and Kathryn Engle had arrived from their World Congress involvement. Five young ladies met with the four missionaries. On the next Sunday there were ten adults.[12]

Finally they were able to rent a house on the main street of Hagi, some distance south of the center of town. It was near the Hashimoto bridge that Pete had crossed on his first long trek from Hagi station. The Charles Engles provided encouragement for the younger missionaries by helping them move into their first residence.

On September 15 Pete sent a letter to those who had responded during the meetings. The letter was translated into Japanese by a high school boy who had professed faith. It began: "You are one of the many people who have decided recently to become Christians . . . or at least . . . to learn more about Jesus Christ. The angels in heaven are very happy about your decision." Pete reminded them that he had promised to invite them to Christian meetings when he and his wife found a place to live. The place they had found would serve both as residence and meeting place. He informed them that the meeting would consist of prayer, Bible reading, singing together, and answering questions. He added: "Many Christians are praying for you that you will become very good and very happy Christians. God bless you."[13]

The new Hagi believers met in their first church location on Sunday, September 20, at 10:00 a.m. The place was No. 28 Hashimoto. Twenty-one people gathered for the meeting, including the police interpreter. Others appeared at subsequent weekly meetings. Six new faces were seen on September 27, and sixteen others appeared on the next four occasions.[14]

The building where the first meetings were held had once been a store named Ogiya which sold cloth for kimonos. The Willmses were able to rent the front part of the first floor for an office and meeting room. They shared the downstairs kitchen and bath with people who lived in back. They slept above the old store. Interestingly, the building was originally the home of the doctor of the feudal Lord Mori. The *daimyo* himself had lived in the castle which stood at that time beside the bump of land called Shizuki mountain.[15]

In addition to the Sunday morning gatherings, Bible classes and English conversation classes were begun. An interest in English caused many people to seek out the foreigner in the first few months. Some of these contacts turned into lasting personal relationships. Some became fruit for the Kingdom.[16]

Three of the first seekers who became closely attached to the Willmses were Tomoichi Sakamoto, Emine Katsura and Uno Ichikawa. Mr. Sakamoto was an intelligent, eager high school student from a poor fishing family on the west side of Hagi. He showed remarkable ability in the English language. He immediately began to help Pete with follow-up letters and with visitation. He also became one of Pete's interpreters for the church services. Pete was to develop a deep concern and love for this young man. He was also later to suffer much grief on account of him.

Miss Katsura had worked on one of the American military installations following the war. She now lived with her mother in Hagi. In time she became the housekeeper for the Willmses and was to provide great help during times of busyness and illness.

Mrs. Ichikawa was in her sixties. She and her husband had no children, much to their disappointment. However, she always had a merry twinkle in her eye. She made a firm commitment to Christ and was one of the first to be baptized the following year.[17]

Others soon became a regular part of the fellowship. One was Ritsu Iwakura. Now in her fifties, she had been baptized as a young woman while attending a small school in Osaka operated by Disciples of Christ missionaries. Classes were in English, and she gained skills in translation and typing. After working in Kyushu during the war years, she returned to Hagi to care for her aging mother. She opened a private school in her home where she taught English grammar and typing. She became a faithful supporter of the ministry and served on many occasions as interpreter.[18]

A curious fact began to emerge in relation to the early converts in Hagi: Most of those who responded to the gospel had either lived in a foreign country during the days of Japan's expansion or had otherwise been removed from their traditional environment for a time. This was true of Koichiro Sugiyama. Sugiyama grew up in Manchuria where he had the tragic misfortune of being treated by an incompetent eye doctor. He almost lost his sight, and was never able to get a job or make his own way in life. He became bitter and very lonely. He later declared, after an evening of relaxed fellowship and hot chocolate with Pete in the Willmses' home, "This has been the happiest moment of my life."[19]

Sugiyama had a brilliant intellect. He taught himself German, Russian, and English which he spoke and wrote almost flawlessly. He was self-taught also in higher mathematics. He had a critical mind, but he responded readily and simply to truth when he saw its reasonableness.

Sugiyama said that his father was a die-hard Buddhist. He brought a priest to their home every month, and Sugiyama had to attend the meetings. But he was very perceptive. He saw the illogicality of the Buddhist teaching on reincarnation. He saw also the inconsistency of other Buddhist teachings and of the hypocritical life of his father. Consequently, he rejected Buddhism.

Sugiyama admits that he went to the city hall meeting for two reasons. One was sheer curiosity. The other was that he wanted to hear some real English![20] That night was the beginning of a close relationship with the mission. It also was the beginning of a changed life that soon led him to baptism. He interpreted occasionally for the mission and served as treasurer and leader in the Hagi church.[21]

God was working to form the little flock in Hagi. Another man appeared on the scene through some unusual circumstances. He was to become a source of joy and encouragement to the missionaries and a loyal servant of the church. His story deserves to be told in some detail.

Seiichiro Aburatani had been working in the local tax office. One day he noticed an advertisement in the *Hagi Residential News* which stated that a Rev. Peter Willms was in need of an interpreter in English. To Pete's surprise, Aburatani appeared at his door applying for the job. Pete was surprised because he had not placed the ad. It turned out that Mr. Takeshita, the real estate broker, had written the notice. Aburatani gives his view of this first meeting with the missionary in his own unique style:

> One afternoon probably in the month of September, 1953, this writer made his first visit to the said missionary's evangelical meeting place inside the old but pretty spacious Japanese second-story house, and he could exchange a customary polite greeting with Rev. and Mrs. Peter and Mary Willms in English and he informed them about his true intention to visit here frankly and without conservation. The young couple was very pleased to hear that and they frankly persuaded him to come and help them through his good English speaking, reading and especially writing very well. This was the first encounter between this writer and the young missionary couple, namely, Rev. and Mrs. Peter and Mary Willms here in Hagi City.[22]

Pete hired him for occasional help on written material and in interpreting. However, a serious stomach disorder, brought on in part no doubt by the pressures of his work, hospitalized him for almost a year. It required major surgery. Pete visited him in the hospital and prayed for him.[23] Weakened by the surgery and faced with a long recovery, Aburatani quit his job. Pete encouraged him to open a private English school in his own home. It was a hard struggle at first. It took a long time for word to get around to students who needed extra help in their studies. Aburatani was later greatly encouraged by the coming of the first voluntary service worker, who helped draw many students to his classes.

Church in the Home

Meetings continued in the front of the store for almost three months. The situation, however, was far from satisfactory. It was difficult to heat the old house whose walls were full of cracks. There was little privacy; not only did the front of the building face a bustling street, but the back part of the house was shared by two other families. The one bathroom and the kitchen were shared by all three parties.[24]

On Pete's first visit to Hagi, it was evident that suitable facilities were not available for rent. But a house had been discovered for sale. It was on Tokaichi Street in a quiet residential area. Although somewhat far from the main streets of town, at least it was in a different part of town from the other two churches. Pete wrote the board immediately upon his return to the World Congress, stating that the property would wonderfully meet their needs and asking for permission to buy. He included drawings to show that the house was large enough to provide both meeting rooms and family privacy. A two-deck storage building and a one-room cottage adjoined the main house. The U-shaped building complex enclosed a traditional Japanese garden with ornamental trees, a fish pond, and huge moss-covered rocks. The back of the lot was an open piece of land, about fifty by fifty feet. This was unusual for a residence in Japan.

Pete assured the board that the 250 *tsubo* property with 40 *tsubo* in the main house was an exceptionally good buy at $3,200.[25] The board agreed, advanced the money from emergency funds, and appealed to the church for support for the project.[26]

The transaction for the house was not completed without some obstacles. The promised money did not arrive on time and, when it did arrive, the local banks hesitated to handle a check which represented such a large amount of foreign currency. Furthermore, when it came time to sign the documents, Pete discovered that the owner was asking him to sign a receipt for much less than the actual purchase price. The owner's intent was to save a great deal of tax on the sale by reporting the smaller amount. Pete refused to comply. He declared that he could not sign an untrue statement because he was a Christian. He waited, wondering if his refusal might mean the end of the negotiations. Finally, the owner acquiesced. On November 24, 1953, the Brethren in Christ Church became the owner of its first property in Japan. The missionaries moved into the house by the end of the month.[27]

The building had been a restaurant named *Akaishi* (Red Rock). Most of the inside walls consisted of the white *shoji* and other sliding partitions which were covered with a heavier, patterned paper. These were called *fusuma*. The partitions could be removed from their grooves, thus enlarging the meeting space. The Sunday morning services and the various classes immediately began meeting in the mission residence.

Pete reported to the board that, during December, twenty-five to thirty adults met regularly for service. He indicated that attendance should increase visibly since they had settled into a new meeting place, were initiating a more aggressive program, and were able to heat the rooms to a comfortable temperature. Mary had begun a Sunday school in the rented Hashimoto house on October 4. Miss Katsura served as her interpreter. Seventeen children had attended the final Sunday in that location. Since moving to Tokaichi, however, at least forty children were attending.

He went on to report that an English Bible class met on Thursday nights with an attendance of fifteen or more. Colored slides on the New Testament were used for this class, and interest was high. On Sunday evenings during September and October, Pete and Mary attended the Presbyterian Church on Tamachi Street. Since the church had no pastor at that time, Pete was usually asked to preach. The lawyer, Takeda, who had helped in the purchase of the property, interpreted. Pete noted that Sunday night attendance increased during this time. The church people spoke appreciatively of his help. After the new pastor arrived, the Willmses began their own Sunday night Bible study. Nine people attended the first service on November 1. A regular midweek prayer meeting was started on Wednesday, November 25. Eight came to the first service, and the average soon increased to twelve.[28]

It soon became evident that very few seekers remained from the Ginder meetings of the previous summer. But a faithful core of believers had formed out of that campaign. Several reasons for the drop-off in attendance seemed evident. First, many of those who responded did not claim to be making decisions; they were only expressing interest. Second, lack of a ready place to hold meetings and lack of a capable interpreter for follow-up made people lose interest. Third, many addresses which had been collected were incomplete, and follow-up information sent to those addresses returned unopened.[29]

The services were always led through interpreters. Miss Katsura had helped in the very beginning. Miss Iwakura then became available. Sakamoto, Aburatani, Sugiyama and Yasuo Miyamoto all helped at times. Pete gave much of his attention to the training of these and other leaders, urging them gradually into positions of responsibility for the services and the activities of the church. He worked much with the student Sakamoto. He was sure that young man would develop into an excellent interpreter and, perhaps, into a pastor. Pete and Mary considered him their "Timothy."[30] Sakamoto responded to Pete's guidance and became the interpreter for the next special evangelistic meeting.

The Visit of John Z. Martin

With the sending of the missionaries in 1953, the board had also acted to provide adequate guidance for the new mission. A committee was appointed to counsel and advise the Willmses. Carl J. Ulery and Henry A. Ginder were appointed to the committee, and John Z. Martin, president of Upland College and member of the board, was also asked to serve. One of the committee's duties was to consider doctrinal issues in relation to the new culture. Martin, who served on the board from 1950 to 1958, worked closely with the Willmses in certain areas such as the purchase of equipment.[31]

In the summer of 1954 Martin went to Japan to encourage the Willmses and to discuss with them the formation of a policy for the field. Pete joined him in Tokyo, and the two men proceeded to visit several missions in various parts of the country. Their main purpose was to try to discover insights that would help in formulating a policy for their own mission. They first interviewed leaders for the Japan Inland Pioneer Mission, whose work they visited near Tokyo. They found that the mission depended largely on a Bible school for training converts. Martin noted, however, that the school was not doing well, even though the mission offered to provide all expenses for those who wanted to attend. He also observed that congregations could not be built on students because they were too unstable. Positively, he noted that the mission emphasized indigenous church principles by turning the leadership of the churches entirely over to the Japanese.

Martin and Willms then journeyed north to Hokkaido where they visited with Mennonite missionaries and toured their churches. They found that the missionaries tried to identify with the people in modest housing and by sending their children to Japanese schools. They were told that the mission explained to the church the biblical teaching on certain doctrinal matters, such as the prayer veiling, and then left the application of those doctrines up to the church itself.[32]

Following the Hokkaido visit, the men stopped briefly in Osaka for talks with Mennonite Brethren personnel who were just opening mission work in that city. Later, after a time in Hagi, they traveled to the southern part of Kyushu where the General Conference Mennonite work was located.

Hoping to utilize Martin's visit in the most effective way, Pete had planned an evangelistic campaign in Hagi. He purchased a 30- by 16-foot war surplus tent that was equipped with new poles, ropes and pins. The cost was just over one hundred dollars.[33] Some wooden benches were made, and permission was secured to pitch the tent on a vacant lot in Shinkawa, just north of the center of town.

The Chevy van was once again put to good use in broadcasting news of the meetings and in distributing tracts. The unusual size and shape of the foreign vehicle, together with the fact that unheeding pedestrians often had to be honked out of the way, caused no little embarrassment to the missionaries. They felt like intruders under the curious stares of the people. But the believers joined enthusiastically in the effort. Little Mrs. Ichikawa sang over the loudspeaker in her quavering voice. She passed out tracts and information about the meetings to children and instructed them to take the material straight to their mothers. The Carryall, though embarrassingly conspicuous, continued to be an aid in outreach and a great blessing to the Japanese Christians personally.[34]

The meetings with John Martin continued from July 6 to 13. Each evening, music and testimonies in Japanese were broadcast at 7:20 from the Carryall which was parked beside the tent. The time for the meeting was set for 8:00 p.m. in hope that farmers would attend after finishing their work. From 8:00 to 8:30 p.m. pictures of the life of Christ were shown. Explanation of the pictures was given in Japanese by the young Sakamoto who evidenced the gift of teaching. The pictures attracted many children, but adults also gradually entered the tent. Martin began preaching by 8:30. Each night the tent was jammed with close to 130 people. Many responded to the invitation to enroll in the Navigator's Bible study course. Fifteen of these declared that they wanted to believe in Christianity and receive more information.

Approximately one week later, a second meeting was held in Nago, a fishing town north of Hagi. It took thirty minutes each day to travel the ten miles of country road which wound among the rice fields and squeezed through crowded villages. The meetings were held in the town's recreation hall. Martin describes the building as resembling the old one-room school houses of Pennsylvania. The wooden benches used in the Hagi meeting provided seating for adults. The children were asked to sit on mats similar to those which cover *tatami* in houses. Adults were very slow to enter the building for such an unusual occasion. The children, however, eagerly filled the space on the mats and listened to the Bible stories. Sakamoto and Katsura taught them. A Sunday school was formed in Nago which was carried on for several years by Katsura and other members of the Hagi church. Eighteen young people and adults expressed some interest in Christianity. In his report to the board, Martin expressed hope that a church might also be founded in Nago.[35]

During the week between the two meetings, John and Pete took a group of the Hagi young people seven hundred miles south to Miyazaki. There they participated in a youth camp sponsored by the General Conference Mennonites. The bulky tent was taken along for their nighttime shelter. It became shelter, however, for the Kyushu group also as rain poured down during much of the conference. The Hagi people benefited greatly from the fellowship and teaching. This fact stimulated Pete to plan similar activities in the Hagi area as soon as possible.[36]

Martin's report to the board concerning his Japan experiences included a number of recommendations for formulating a beginning policy for the Japan mission. One recommendation outlined the concept of "two distinct types" of Brethren in Christ witness in Japan. One type was the mission which should be the outreach arm of the church, should nurture the Christians, and should train leaders to take over the church as quickly as possible. The second type was the church composed of the Japanese themselves. This group was to carry on evangelism, conduct worship and fellowship meetings, and provide education through Sunday schools and other types of teachings.

Although the idea was similar to policies on the denomination's other mission fields, Martin felt that it needed to be developed more clearly. He also suggested that the American church should put very little money into church buildings initially. It should rather encourage Christians to stress evangelism and pastoral support and to rent a hall for meetings.[37] The beginning policy which emerged from these and other suggestions will be considered in more detail at a later time.

The faithful nucleus of believers which met in the Tokaichi house slowly began to grow. Pete listed twenty-eight names as "decisions" of the Hagi meetings with Martin. Sixteen of the names had special marks beside them, perhaps an indication of special interest. On July 31, 1954, he sent a letter to the people on the list. He informed them that almost thirty had come to Christ, or, at least, "began coming to Christ." He urged them to come to a special meeting on Sunday, August 1, at 8:00 p.m. He pointed out the necessity of continuing in the faith so they would "not be moved away from the hope of the gospel." This letter was followed by a similar one on October 23.[38]

Some came in response to the follow-up, and a few remained, growing in the fellowship of the gospel. New faces began to appear also. Many of these were high school students. Attendance of students was boosted by the work of Yasuo Miyamoto, an English teacher in one of the city's high schools. Miyamoto had been baptized some years earlier and occasionally attended the church on Tamachi Street. He became very warm toward Pete and Mary and began attending services with his wife, Kikuyo. He told many of his students about the English and Bible classes and urged them to attend church.

Jihichi Oba also began coming to the fellowship. An older man, he kept himself busy with odd jobs and with his favorite activity, fishing for eels among the holes in the rock walls that bordered Hagi's rivers and ocean front. Oba was always cheerful and willing to help in any task. He was later to render invaluable assistance in the incorporation of the mission and in the purchase of the Nagato property.

October 3, 1954, marked a day of special significance. Happy missionaries celebrated the first baptismal service of the little church. Those who testified to new life in Christ were Mrs. Ichikawa, young Sakamoto and a young lady, Tomiyo Kawakami. Miss Iwakura interpreted in the regular worship service and Mr. Miyamoto assisted Pete in the baptismal service which followed at the seashore.

Pete recorded the events of that memorable occasion in a letter to those who had received baptism. He said that he thought they might want to remember the details of their special day. Among other things, the letter indicates that Pete spoke on forgiveness from Psalm 32. The group sang "O Happy Day" from the Japanese hymnal, then moved toward the beach in the van and by bicycle. On the way to the beach, rain began to fall. The rain stopped, however, upon their arrival at the beach, and the warm rays of the sun broke through the clouds, lending cheer to the occasion. The sea was surprisingly smooth for October. The group sang, "Lord Jesus, I Long To Be Perfectly Whole." Mr. Miyamoto then read Mark 1:9-13, the story of the baptism of Jesus. Pete spoke of the death of the old life and newness in Christ. He warned of temptations which may come. After the last candidate rose from the water, the believers sang "My Jesus, I Love Thee." As the service closed, it began to rain once again.

Pete closed the letter by expressing his personal joy on the occasion. He regretted that he had not been able to instruct them or pray for them in their own tongue that day. In spite of this lack, their response to God, he declared, was proof that the Spirit of God was mightily living in them.[39]

Helpers in the Task

It seemed that the Willmses had no sooner arrived in Japan than they began calling for more missionaries. Even before 1953 had ended, Pete urged the board: "You can send them anytime. We need people to do more or less what we are doing, and before too long we'll need a well-qualified Bible teacher." Pete asked the board to "lay it on the hearts of the folks at home" to give diligently so that more personnel could be added. Perhaps he was also trying to whet the appetite of new prospects as he added: "This is thrilling work! Because God is 'the God of all grace' we have lived much more happily and more victoriously the last five months than we have ever lived."[40]

One of the reasons for requesting more personnel was that so many opportunities for witness lay all around. In particular, Pete was concerned about the fishermen gathered in their own villages up and down the coast. He wrote to Henry Hostetter:

> The villages are opening up to hear the gospel much faster than we can handle the open doors. We are concentrating on training Japanese workers to eventually do the evangelizing but at the same time we feel the responsibility to reach hungry hearts now. These two aspects, training and evangelism, together with Bible study, personal Bible study and correspondence make for more work than we can handle.[41]

Pete pointed out that the fishermen were largely neglected all over Japan. He declared that in order to reach them it would be necessary for one man to devote himself to their needs alone. The response was likely to be discouraging at first, he warned, but nevertheless "they also have souls . . . and are desperately idolatrous and needy." His plan was to let one couple take over the mountain areas and another the sea coast and islands.[42]

A second reason for sending more workers was that both he and Mary were in desperate need of formal language study. They had come to Hagi intending to combine study and ministry. They tried various methods to learn the language. They offered help in English to a local high school teacher in exchange for tutoring in Japanese. They also studied for a time with the police interpreter, Sueda. Finally, they secured a set of books used in the Kobe and Tokyo language schools for missionaries. They were able to make some progress with these books. But they still had to study by themselves, and the many interruptions made discipline difficult. Pete reported to the board that the ministry was now being hindered by the lack of language training. People now expected them to be able to converse, he felt. Such people, he regretted, have no idea how little time there really is for language study. Even the better textbooks were no substitute for a time of concentrated study away from the many pressing duties.[43]

Two further reasons for requesting workers soon began to emerge. One was the problem of increasing demands for teaching English. Pete was lecturing regularly in Mr. Miyamoto's high school and appearing on occasion in other schools and in some private classes as well. It was extremely difficult to refuse the many requests. They were coming from people among whom the missionaries now lived and wanted to win. A second reason was a growing health problem in Pete. A worsening stomach condition sometimes left him tired and in pain. It was clear that the work load was too heavy.

Pete's appeal for more workers was finally answered. At first, it seemed to be answered only in part, for the couple who came planned to stay only two years. Nevertheless, the two who arrived in 1955 were followed by another couple in 1957, and a third arrived in 1963.

The Books

Doyle C. Book and Thelma Heisey lived next door to each other across from the old Upland Brethren in Christ church on Third Avenue in Upland, California. Thelma's parents, C. Ray and Lista Heisey, had responded to a call from Upland church in 1940, moving from the pastorate at Pleasant Hill, Ohio. After completing seven years of service, the Heiseys remained in Upland. This gave their four children the opportunity to attend the denomination's high school and college located there. Thelma was active in gospel teams during her years in school and participated enthusiastically in sports. She also served as editor of the school paper and yearbook. She was graduated from Upland College in 1950 and received her M.A. in English literature soon after.

Thelma encountered Jesus Christ in a personal way at the age of six. During an altar call, her mother almost stopped her as she began to move forward from the pew. She was sure that the little girl could not understand what the invitation meant. But Thelma knew that Jesus had entered her life.

From that time she became aware of an inner desire to be a missionary. At first the interest was something like that of a child wanting to be a nurse or a fireman. As she grew older, there was no particular sense of a specific call nor an urging to prepare in any special way. But when the opportunity later presented itself to go to Japan, there was no hesitation whatsoever.

Doyle had moved to Upland from Kansas as a second-grader with his parents, John M. and Delilah Book, and one brother. He, too, received Christ into his life at the age of six. He was graduated from Upland College, where he was active in various sports, edited the school's yearbook, and participated in musical groups, including the Conqueror's Quartet, which traveled widely in the denomination.

After Doyle and Thelma were married, on June 17, 1951, they were asked to join the staff at their alma mater. Doyle taught high school English and drama and coached various sports. Thelma taught literature on the college level.

During this time, a strange event occurred which was to alter their future radically. In order to supplement their meager salaries, Doyle took summer jobs. He had registered as a conscientous objector to war in response to the military conscription program which continued after World War II. His 1-W classification under this sytem required him to give two years of alternate service in lieu of military training. He was deferred, however, because of his ministry in a religious school. During the summer of 1954, a questionnaire from the draft board asked for his activity as of July 1. The only answer was, driving a truck. He was immediately summoned to fulfill his two years of required service. An appeal to the effect that he was only between years of teaching was to no avail. He and Thelma together made application to the Mennonite Central Committee for alternate service in Germany among war refugees. Arrangements were made for them to sail in the summer of 1955.

At that point John Z. Martin, president of Upland College and member of the Foreign Mission Board, asked the Books if they would be willing to go to Japan instead of Germany. He explained that Doyle would assist the missionary in Hagi by teaching English in various schools. This type of service would fulfill the requirements of the U.S. government. The goodwill, cultural contribution would also relieve the missionary of much pressure from the many requests for teaching English. Within one month the direction of the Books changed completely.

Standing at the railing of the *Hikawa Maru* at dawn on August 17, they peered through the haze and mist for their first glimpse of Japan. The coastline gradually became visible in the light of the rising sun. Approaching the pier at Yokohama, they suddenly spied two figures which stood out from the black heads of the welcoming crowd. One was Pete Willms. His companion was Norman Wingert, who, with his wife Eunice, was director of the Mennonite Central Committee work in Tokyo. Pete left immediately for Kobe, and the Books went to be with the Wingerts at their home in Tamagawa. The next day they continued to Kobe where they were welcomed by Pete and Mary. The Willmses had come to Kobe to snatch a few precious months of language study. They had left the Hagi members in charge of the church. The Willmses now returned to Hagi with the Books to help them begin their work.

It was dark when Doyle and Thelma arrived at the house on Tokaichi Street. A train had taken them from Kobe to Ogori, where they boarded a bus which rattled heartily over the rock-hard, chuck-holed mountain road for almost two hours. Leaving their shoes in the *genkan*, they moved through the Willmses' front room to the back porch. They noticed how the *tatami* cushioned their steps. They donned some wooden slippers and clattered over the flat stones which marked the short path to the little one-room guest cottage. Just before dawn it rained hard. It was a typical late-summer storm. They awakened to look out of their east window upon a garden drenched and glittering in the morning sun. The cicadas buzzed happily in the sultry, but freshened air. It was August 31, 1955.

They thought they had come for a short term of service. They did not know the surprises God had in store for them.

The Graybills

John W. Graybill and Lucille Hoffsmith grew up in the fellowship of the United Christian Church in the small Pennsylvania town of Annville. Lucille's parents, Paul and Anna Hoffsmith, provided a warm home atmosphere for their five children. There was, however, no particular interest in the home concerning missions. The parents had not become Christians until well into their adulthood and thus had heard very little about the subject. Furthermore, the United Christian Church had no mission work of its own. Two of its members had gone to Africa under the Brethren in Christ Foreign Mission Board, but contacts with them were infrequent so far as the Hoffsmith family was concerned.

Lucille opened her life to Jesus on December 3, 1939. The focus of family life was the church. Lucille's father was a deacon, and the family attended services faithfully. The small denomination was very conservative in its doctrines and practices. There was a very strong group consciousness among the few churches of that area. Church life provided a close-knit fellowship and a feeling of security. Thus Lucille never had reason to venture very far outside her home community.

Most of John's friends, like Lucille's, were farmers and community people who knew one another. John's parents, M. Wesley and Margaret Graybill, required the five children to attend the frequent camp meetings sponsored by the church. This was their "vacation." At the camp meetings, John heard many missionary presentations which aroused his curiosity and sense of adventure. Some of the stories were quite exciting. One visiting missionary, Elwood Hershey, spoke of adventures in Africa which included encounters with lions.

John was graduated from Millersville State Teacher's College and secured a position in Derry Township High School as vocational arts instructor. He and Lucille were married on June 23, 1951. But he was still uneasy about his future ministry. His mind had been opened to various kinds of service. He was particularly moved when there was a missionary challenge. He was drawn to Africa because of the other United Christian members, Anna Kettering and Anna Graybill, who were there.

In a dream one night he thought he saw some dark-skinned people, perhaps Orientals, gazing at him. Was this a call? he wondered. The next day he asked God to confirm whether or not it was. That day at the Cleona camp meeting an acquaintance, George Shaud, laid his hand on John's shoulder. Suddenly John felt something "unusual." There was a "strange sense of anointing." He felt urged to express this to George, but he hesitated.

A short time later, George died. Still feeling that God had somehow used George to speak to him, John decided to seek out George's grave and there wait upon the Lord for his direction. The cemetery was covered with snow. Desperate, John asked God to let him know where George's grave was. He discovered one grave which was free from snow. It was George's.

John felt that surely this was a second confirmation of God's leading. He decided to seek one more. In August 1956 he approached the Foreign Mission Board and offered himself. The reply was immediate: We need you in Japan.

Now fully convinced of God's call, John quit his job and entered Messiah College in 1956 for one year of Bible training.[44]

The *Evangelical Visitor* records a service of farewell for the Graybills on July 7, 1957, in the chapel of the Messiah Home in Harrisburg. The five members of the supporting United Christian Foreign Mission Board shared in the service with those of the sending Brethren in Christ board. Messiah College students who had learned to appreciate the Graybills' sincerity and cheerful natures were among the many people who attended. John spoke of being "laborers together with God" in planting and watering (1 Cor. 3:5-9). He also declared that God has spoken to him through an African brother, Jonathan Muleya, also a student at Messiah College at that time. In answer to the question, "What is the secret of reaching hearts in a foreign culture?" Jonathan had said, "No matter how eloquent or good-looking you are, or how much money you have, you must *love* them."[45]

John and Lucille arrived in Japan with their three children on August 19, 1957. Their call to that land, however, was not yet fully secure. They were to face a struggle that would threaten their stay there.

The Zooks

Marlin E. Zook and Ruth Mann began to realize that God was bringing them together while they were singing in a hospital staff chorus in Cleveland, Ohio. Ruth was reared in Africa, along with one brother, by missionary parents Roy H. and Esther Mann. She was one of those children referred to as "third culture children." She responded to an altar call at an Ohio campmeeting at age nine. Her exposure to missionary activity helped create in her a natural desire to be a missionary herself sometime. This desire was in turn reinforced by a missionary challenge one day while she was attending Messiah College. She felt compelled to respond to the challenge. She dates her call to missionary work from that time.

Marlin was born in Hannibal, Missouri, of Mark Twain fame. His parents, A. LeRoy and Naomi Zook, took him regularly with his four brothers and one sister to their Mennonite church. Marlin's parents had moved to Hannibal in order to help establish the church as a home mission outreach. Seemingly unable to have children, they prayed for a baby. Marlin came as a true Samuel for a modern-day Hannah. His parents informed him at an early age that he, like Samuel, had been dedicated to the Lord's work.

Evangelistic meetings were held frequently in the area, partly in support of the mission outreach. Myron Augsburger, George Brunk, Merle Good and other Mennonite preachers kept the vision of evangelism alive in the church and home. Marlin received Christ at age seven and dedicated himself for ministry at fifteen.

Thinking that he would like to be a missionary doctor, he entered the pre-med program at Goshen College in Indiana. 1-W service interrupted this study after one semester. He fulfilled his required term of two years at several hospitals connected with Western Reserve University in Cleveland. A men's chorus was formed by alternate service personnel assigned to the hospitals. Soon the men decided that a mixed chorus would be much better. Some brought their wives, and nurses in the hospitals were also invited. Ruth was in training to become a registered nurse. She joined the chorus and met Marlin. They were married on July 18, 1959.

Marlin finished college at Goshen and in 1963 completed a Master of Divinity degree at what is now Associated Mennonite Biblical Seminaries. The Zooks' thoughts were directed to Japan by the many Mennonite missionaries who had returned from there for continued study or who were planning to go there. It seemed as though half of Marlin's graduating class were headed for Japan. Furthermore, there was no opening in Africa just then for him to pursue his interest in Bible teaching. Henry N. Hostetter urged him to consider making use of his talent in Japan. Sensing an inner peace, Marlin and Ruth responded. They arrived in Japan on August 30, 1963.[46]

The Team is Formed

In this way, God brought together a team for his work in Japan. There were to be many adjustments to the culture and to each other over the years. With their varied backgrounds and personalities, there would be many tensions, and misunderstandings would have to be resolved. But they were a special team, as was the one that had earlier moved uncertainly out of the comfort of the Tomoe Inn to begin the mission in Hagi. But before we continue the story of the four missionary couples, let us consider the kind of culture to which they had come. Let us look at some of the surprises they faced and some of the adjustments that had to be made.

Pulling up rice shoots from the seed bed for transplanting.

Planting rice shoots in even rows.

The city of Hagi, where the Brethren in Christ began mission work in 1953.

Stephanie Book "exploring" a wayside image, around 1965.

Neighbors, friends, and families gather at the temples and shrines to pray for success at New Year's time.

The family god shelf in a home.

Praying at a shrine (above) contrasted to an Easter sunrise service in Hagi in 1960 (below).

Yaeko Kaneshige and Noriko Matsuura of Hagi holding children's meetings for the beginning of a new church in Senzaki in 1958.

A moment of prayer in Hagi, 1958.

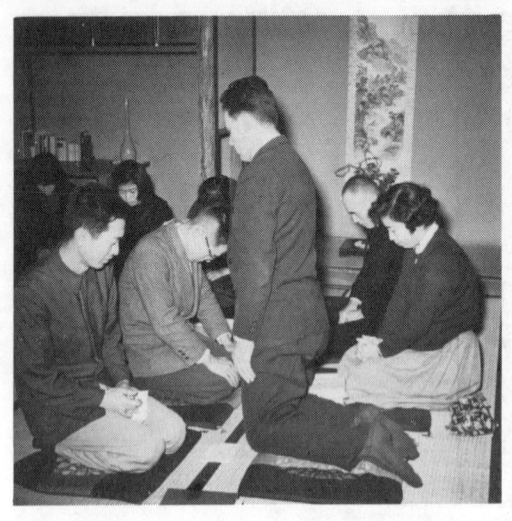

Pete Willms praying for two church leaders: Sugiyama (left) and Aburatani. To Pete's right is "Kay San" Kanakubo (now Mrs. Hataya) and blind evangelist Takaichi Hada. (About 1957).

Taken at the celebration of Hagi's fifth anniversary in 1959.

The mission staff in December 1963. From left to right: Marlin and Ruth Zook, Doyle and Thelma Book and Charity, John and Lucille Graybill, and Pete and Mary Willms and Kenneth, together with Henry Hostetter, then the Director of Overseas Missions.

Henry Hostetter and Charity Book enjoy a rice lunch on the train in 1963.

A men's English Bible class in 1972. (See the Prologue.)

A 1971 ladies' Bible class in Shimonoseki enjoys a time of refreshment.

Chapter Four

A New Home

Strange Ways

It did not take long for the missionaries to become sharply aware of contrasts between their own country and the land to which they had come. Many of the customs at first seemed almost quaint. Some of them were enjoyable and would later be carried back to America at furlough time. One of these was the privilege of leaving one's hot or muddy shoes outside the entrance of the house and stepping up to the cool, cushioned comfort of the *tatami*.

There was a haunting fascination about some of the sounds—the flute that signaled the little cart passing on the cold, dark street and beckoning the hearer to a bowl of hot broth and steaming noodles; or the stringed *samisen* vibrating forth its plaintive notes under the hand of the artist. There was the delight of new taste discoveries—the hot, fat sweet potato dispensed from the cart with the raspy steam whistle and inviting the buyer to peel it and plunge his teeth deep into its moist, golden goodness; or the chewy *mochi* rice cake roasted over blazing charcoal and dipped in tangy soy sauce. The wonder of sounds and tastes like these attached itself to the hearts of the missionaries and their children with a deep nostalgia that brought a feeling of loneliness when they were later away from their adopted land.

The foreigners soon felt the graciousness of the Japanese. There were the polite bows, the delicate turn of the hand as a bowl of tea was being prepared, the thoughtful gifts that came as expressions of appreciation for small favors. Many times a total stranger would go out of his way to show the newcomers the best path to their destination.

The missionaries felt secure in their new surroundings. Often while shopping they produced a piece of money far too large for the purchase simply because they could not understand the price involved or the value of the Japanese currency. They were always given the correct change.[1] They noticed that items left outside the house, such as a bicycle, or along the street, such as firewood for sale at a nearby store, were never stolen. One of the missionaries could not help but notice some disturbing contrasts between the new land and his own. In Japan there was the delicate, caring touch of the flower shop proprietor who tied a ribbon around every rose stem. In America there was the crudeness of the waitress who vigorously chewed gum while serving her customers and of the bellboy who blew bubbles with his gum while he carried the guests' bags.[2]

There were, however, some disturbing contrasts within the new society also. Some of these were perplexing to the foreigners. People who were so kind in a face-to-face situation where personal relationship already existed, or might soon develop, would be seen crowding up to the post office window in disregard for the line that had already formed or rudely pushing others aside to get a seat on a crowded train. Although their own gardens and paths were always swept clean of debris, it appeared that they would not hesitate to drop trash along the front of someone else's house or on the floor of the vehicle in which they were riding. Perhaps even more paradoxically, the people who were such lovers of nature and quiet meditation failed to see the necessity of a day of rest, but drove themselves at their jobs seven days a week.

Some of the perplexities became sources of irritation. And irritation often turned into frustration and, on occasion, even anger. Very early in his missionary life, Pete wrote that "Japan is known as the land of frustrated missionaries." He indicated that "missionaries who have broken down or are breaking down" are a constant source of concern.[3] He had earlier declared buoyantly to a group of missionaries: "If there is any hardship in mission work in Japan, I haven't met it yet." A more seasoned missionary commented to an observer, "It's good to catch again the feel and fire of youth." The observer noted that Pete and Mary were then running with urgency, soaring with wings as eagles, and knew little of weariness in those early missionary days. He later noted, however, that the Willmses, although not complaining about hardship, had, nevertheless, made its acquaintance. The meeting had not been sudden. It was rather "a growing realization of obstacles previously overlooked."[4]

Some differences in the culture were readily visible. Such surface things seemed innocent enough and could hardly be considered obstacles. Most foreigners could adjust rather quickly to driving on the left side of the road instead of the right, to pulling a saw and plane instead of pushing them, or to eating with chopsticks instead of forks and knives.

But other differences lay below the surface of the society. They came from vastly different ways of thinking or from presuppositions that were hidden to the uninitiated. The missionaries did not yet fully understand that each culture is governed by a set of perspectives, and that these perspectives dictate responses to various situations. The responses are, in turn, culturally approved and meaningful to the people of the culture, but perplexing indeed to the one coming from the outside.

At first the missionaries were not aware that tensions were building within them because of encounters with different ways of thinking. They did not realize in many cases that they were subconsciously trying to compensate for customs which did not fit into their own perspectives. They were not aware that the effort involved in such compensation had a wearing effect on their emotions. They tended to evaluate quickly "strange" customs as "bad" or "backward." They had not been taught that the customs of each culture are to be evaluated only on the basis of their acceptability within their own culture and the cohesiveness they bring to it.

Eventually they began to sense the subtle tensions that arose from their encounters with new perspectives. They were experiencing the cultural differences that tend to keep the newcomer "off balance." They were finding that, in a new culture, one spends most of his energies just trying to maintain an emotional equilibrium.

At first, the practice of giving and receiving gifts seemed pleasant enough. The missionaries were frequently overwhelmed by the thoughtfulness and generosity of their Japanese friends. Gifts came to them for favors that they had passed off as insignificant. Often a returning traveler would bring a box of special sweet cakes or crackers which were unique to the place he had visited. A caller would usually open his colorful, square carrying cloth called a *furoshiki* and present a gift before stepping over the threshold for his visit. It was extremely difficult to receive a gift from one who, the missionary knew, could ill afford to give it. But to deny the feeling of goodwill and kindness behind it would have been rude and hurtful.[5]

The missionaries' children, of course, were delighted at the flow of trinkets and sweets which made the entire year seem almost like Christmas. However, the adults found themselves faced with some awkward situations. In some cases an *orei* (expression of thanks) was expected of them. They were under obligation to respond to a favor, and offense could be caused if the response was not appropriate. They were never sure when to give a gift or how much. They resented the awkward position forced upon them. Gifts which came from others also sometimes left them very uneasy and even upset.

One day a woman approached the Books with a request for lessons in English conversation. The Books were in Tokyo at the time for a period of intense language study. They knew they could not find the time to teach her. However, along with her request, the stranger had already presented them with a lovely and expensive vase. The Books recoiled inwardly from what seemed to them like a bribe. Resenting the obligation being forced upon them, they explained their circumstances and refused the vase. The lady insisted they keep it, however, and, avoiding their protests and efforts to return it to her, retreated through the *genkan* door. The Books later gave the vase away because of the unpleasant memory its presence evoked.

Another area which caused the newcomers a great deal of frustration was that of the meanings behind words. They could not necessarily take words at their face value. The commonly used word for assent was "Hai!" But it was gradually discovered that this word did not necessarily mean "Yes, I agree," or "Yes, I will," even though accompanied by vigorous nods of the head. Instead the person responding might merely be indicating, "I hear you," and, in some cases, "I am considering what you say."

In any face-to-face situation the Japanese would be most polite. Later, however, the foreigner might find that things were not carried out as agreed or that the impression he received was not entirely correct. The newcomers gradually learned from older missionaries that, where disagreement might be involved, it was customary for a person to say what he thought the listener wanted to hear, rather than what the speaker actually felt. The Japanese desired at all cost to avoid a confrontation which might produce a strain in relationships or cause disappointment in the hearer. In situations of this kind, the Americans could not help feeling insecure and wondering how they could get close to the people.

It became evident that some traditional perspectives were fraught with grave spiritual implications. One such was the Japanese concept of God. The missionaries were dismayed to find that the Japanese seemed almost totally unaware of the idea of one, living, Creator-God. God was the "presence" that was said to be in the sun or the sea, or in a rock, tree, or stream. God might also be one of the hundreds of noble teachers who had exerted a positive influence on society and who were usually commemorated at one or more of the Shinto shrines.

They learned that the Shinto religion was represented in almost every home by the *kamidana*. This was a small shelf attached high on one of the inner walls of the house. It usually held a tiny vase with a few flowers, a piece of dried mochi rice and perhaps a wooden tablet on which had been inscribed some Chinese characters. Many homes also contained the more ornate Buddhist altar. This resembled an open cupboard with a gilt image of Buddha, a piece of fruit, a bowl of rice and a small urn where incense was kept burning.

It was difficult for the Japanese to comprehend the idea of a holy God who was, in himself, truth and righteousness. It was even more difficult for them to understand that each human being is personally accountable to him. Since there were many gods already, one could add one more to the list of those already revered. Therefore, a Japanese, after attending church a time or two, might think of himself as a Christian in addition to being a Buddhist and a Shintoist.

Closely aligned with the Japanese idea of God was their concept of sin. Since there was no God to whom one was ultimately accountable for his actions, sin was understood to be a crime against society. And since very few people were guilty of stealing, murder, or other similar criminal acts, sin was thought to have no relationship to the average person. The greatest "sin" in the Japanese mind was usually considered to be a breach of group solidarity or shaming the family through disobedience or a careless act. One Japanese author declared, "It might even be said that the Japanese word 'disloyalty' is the nearest synonym for the Christian concept of 'sin'."[6]

The idea of obligation to one's family was instilled in every Japanese child. This sense of obligation often created problems for Christian young people when it came time for them to be married. Marriage partners were usually suggested to them by their parents through a go-between who negotiated with another family. To reject a potential partner because he was not a Christian might be an affront to the negotiator, the parents and the other family and could create a great deal of tension among family members.

Describing one such incident, Thelma Book noted, "In Japanese society there is no absolute standard of right and wrong. Everything is judged by what people think; and so to do anything contrary to accepted opinions becomes 'wrong' and disgraceful."[7] This sense of obligation to the family was evident also at times of commemorative ceremonies for dead family members. Although some of these rites appeared to be a kind of worship, it was very difficult for a new Christian to stand against such customs and declare his allegiance to God alone. Such a stand might suggest that the family was no longer important to him.

Whenever possible, the missionaries endeavored to adapt themselves to the accepted practices of the country, even though at times they could not understand the perspectives which lay behind them. They observed that people seldom touched each other intentionally. They would, of course, press against each other in crowded busses and trains. Furthermore, they appeared to think nothing of bumping each other, with no word of apology, while hurrying along a crowded sidewalk. Occasionally they would use a western handshake in greeting. But they never embraced or expressed affection or emotion through physical contact. The missionaries soon realized that they must avoid any public demonstrations of affection. An innocent kiss might be extremely embarrassing to any Japanese nearby. The Willmses once cautioned the newly arrived Books that linking arms as they walked down the street would suggest to the onlookers an immoral relationship.

In later years this hesitation to allow physical contact changed somewhat, especially among younger people in the cities. But in general, and in rural areas in particular, the Japanese continued to show great restraint in intentional touching or in expressing affection through physical contact. One of the missionary children who returned to her former home many years later noticed that this part of the culture had changed very little.[8]

Did this physical aloofness in the society suggest an inner desire to keep a safe distance emotionally? Were the Japanese expressing even among themselves that it is better not to get too closely involved—that there is safety in being wary? The visitors began to see the significance of the word for foreigner—*gaijin*. It meant "outside person." And they became aware that they would forever be, in some sense, an outsider.

In these ways, the missionaries began to experience the fact that "the threshold is very high" indeed. It was high socially—it was difficult to be fully accepted in the society. It was also high emotionally—it was hard to find an opening into the heart of the Japanese and to understand their true feeling.

Personal Struggles

The foreigners were often naive and ignorant of what was proper behavior. They did not know that one is not supposed to sit on the edge of a desk or table. In America they could sit almost anywhere they wished. Likewise they did not realize that one must sit on the *tokonoma*, the floor of the alcove which was a few inches higher than the *tatami*. This kind of blunder, however, was readily overlooked by patient and understanding hosts. After all, foreigners could not be expected to understand such things! Often the missionaries themselves had to laugh at their blunders.

There were many adjustments that had to be made to the new land and its ways. There were also adjustments that had to be made to each other. In addition to cultural and inter-personal adjustments, there were also spiritual battles to be faced. These adjustments produced struggles with emotions and relationships. The struggles were sometimes intense because the missionaries were very ordinary people. They were no more saintly—nor any less—than anyone else.

The new living conditions brought the first challenge. Some adjustments here were easy and pleasant. Among these was the delightful experience of climbing into the steaming *ofuro* and soaking up to one's neck. If one stayed in long enough, it might not be necessary to light the kerosene heater for the rest of the evening. Enough clothes would keep one warm until bedtime. Another easy and pleasant adjustment was eating with chopsticks. The foreigners were often praised for their skill in manipulating these. After learning to use chopsticks, they found that without them Japanese food did not taste quite so good.

Other adjustments to living conditions were not so pleasant. One was the public restrooms designated "for men and women only," as Thelma once described them.[9] Another was the little creatures that roamed about in garden and house. Mary, Thelma and Lucille all loathed the tiny, red or gray land crabs that scurried sideways, glared up at them with beady eyes and threatening pincers poised, and sometimes found their way into the shoes that were parked under the eaves of the porch. There were the miniature frogs that croaked in shrill chorus all night and sometimes ventured into the house with their slimy feet. There were also the mosquitoes, "The bane of our existence," and the "large, crackly cockroaches" about which Thelma wrote: "Nasty creatures. I abhore them utterly, but . . . I cannot bring myself to squash them properly as they deserve!"[10]

Some of the missionaries found it very difficult to get used to being stared at. They tried hard to remember that most of the people in the "country" towns of the Yamaguchi coast had never seen a foreigner before. They tried to accept the fact that they were real curiosities. Nevertheless, they felt at times as if they were living in a zoo, so unabashed and lingering were the curious stares of children and adults alike.

John and Lucille declared an open house one day soon after they had moved into the newly remodeled Nagato mission house. They thought the people would like to see what an American kitchen looked like and perhaps would want to look at some picture books of the United States. Lucille was diapering baby Debra when the twenty-seven neighbors entered as a group. They had never seen a baby like that one or the way Americans took care of their babies. From that moment the gleaming kitchen and all the other American decorations were totally ignored. The baby literally "stole the show."[11]

Doyle noticed two little boys gawking at him one day on a Hagi street. His first thought was, "Don't they have any better manners than that?" Then he remembered that he was in a different place where staring was not considered rude. Trying to be friendly, he smiled at the boys and waved at them. To his surprise they came running up to him with big eyes which seemed to say, "Yes, what is it you want?" He found out later that he had beckoned the boys with his American gesture. In Japan, one waved by moving the hand from left to right instead of extending it in front.

No doubt one of the most difficult adjustments in living conditions was the penetrating cold of the coastal winters. The temperatures were not so low— the thermometer hovered only around 35° or 40° in January and February. But the skies were usually dark and gloomy, and the wind constantly moved among the houses in its thrust from the chill ocean toward the hills.

The Willmses and the Books both had the opportunity to adjust to the country weather patterns by arriving in Hagi in late summer. But the first exposure of the Graybills to Hagi was in January. Since arriving from America several months earlier, they had been studying language in reasonably mild Kobe. They were used to low temperatures in Pennsylvania. However, "the very day the Graybills came over the mountains into the beautiful delta of Hagi City, the icy winds began to blow and one of the coldest winters that had been felt for a long time in this area set in. Thus they were initiated quite thoroughly to some of the less desirable qualities of 'paper-and-wood' house living."[12]

"Paper-and-wood" house living meant that the sliding room partitions and the windows and doors which moved on rollers offered many inviting cracks to the wind currents. Curtains swayed as drafts moved freely through the rooms. It was impossible to heat the house efficiently. As kerosene heaters became available, one room in the house would be designated for the heater and the spaces around the sliding partitions would be taped shut.[13]

Paper and wood houses were delightful at other times. In the spring and fall, all the "walls" could be opened to allow the warm breezes to flow through the entire house. But Japanese construction was less desirable during the winter for those used to warm American houses. Because of this, questions were later raised among the missionaries about the kind of house they should buy in the future. Some wondered if they shouldn't buy vacant lots and put western style houses on them. But the board affirmed an earlier policy that the mission should use Japanese style homes and remodel them somewhat "to provide the necessary minimum comforts." They were concerned about two things: identification with the people among whom the missionaries lived and property disposal when the mission moved on to new locations.[14]

Another major adjustment for the foreigners was the language. Communication is often an intricate and fearful process even when one is at home in his own country. Individual perspectives, personal feelings and inadequate knowledge color meanings of words and also affect the way one listens. This often results in misunderstandings or costly errors. The missionaries found that in cross-cultural situations the dangers of error and misunderstanding were multiplied greatly.

In the 1950s many missions lacked sufficient awareness of the urgent need for cross-cultural orientation. The Foreign Mission Board possessed no specialists who could give training in cultural perspectives and principles of language learning for missionary candidates. Schools which specialized in world mission courses were almost unknown. Furthermore, the church in general had the idea that the most important thing for mission work was a special "call." May felt it was the only necessary requirement. As a result, mission candidates were often sent out unprepared for the cultural shocks awaiting them. The board recognized in some measure the lack in orientation. In the case of Japan, they felt that the time in language school would provide this orientation. Language learning would serve as a "buffer" for entering the new culture.[15]

Of course, even earnest language study does not eliminate the possibility of error. But the Willmses had hardly any study prior to beginning their work. They were in Hagi five months before they were able to break away to Kobe for a brief term of language training. Although they studied as well as they could by themselves in Hagi, there were many embarrassments as they blundered their way through some situations.

Mary still flushes red as she recalls one incident. She had been informed that heart was one of the cheapest meats available. She looked up the word for heart in the dictionary. She assumed that the word she found included the physical organ as it does in English. She proceeded to the meat store and asked for *kokoro*. She got her meat from a very perceptive—although, no doubt, amused—butcher. Mary had actually asked for "the seat of the will and emotions." Much later, a visiting Japanese friend inquired about Mary's meat dish that evening. When Mary informed her that it was "kokoro," the friend quickly pointed out the mistake. Appalled, Mary asked her housekeeper why she hadn't corrected the error earlier. The helper meekly replied that she didn't want to embarrass her!

Another butcher shop experience was to make Mary realize the immediate need for careful study in the language. Her dictionary did not reveal any particular word for "ground meat." But she had seen the grinder in the butcher shop. So she pointed to some beef in the case and cranked her arm at the butcher. From that time, whenever Mary came into the shop, the butcher would grin broadly and crank his arm at her! She quickly set about to learn the right word![16]

Relying on English for communication purposes also proved to be precarious. We have mentioned earlier Seiichiro Aburatani, who was encouraged by Pete to begin his own private English school. Aburatani was a gentle, loving man who truly desired the life of the Lord Jesus to be manifested in him. But for a long time he was troubled by the habit of smoking. One day in an attempt to show him his part in being set free, Pete "challenged" him to give up his habit. Aburatani heard only "challenge." He was crushed. He knew that the word involved a declaration of war. He felt that his relationship with Pete was now doomed to a win-lose confrontation, depending solely on his own success or failure in overcoming his habit. Pete was later able to correct the error in perception, and Mr. Aburatani became a faithful friend of the mission. But in this way the missionaries became aware of the assumptions people bring into the communication process and of the perceptions that motivate people in their relationships.

If the missionaries were frustrated without sufficient language study, they were equally frustrated with it. The experience of concentrated language study was a demanding and difficult one. They often despaired of huge vocabulary lists and perplexing Chinese characters. Japanese was considered by some experts to be one of the world's most difficult languages. It caused some missionaries to give up their ministries. Others settled for using an interpreter in their communication of the gospel.

The spoken language was difficult enough with its confusing levels of politeness. But the main source of frustration was the Chinese picture-symbols called *kanji*. The strokes of these characters had to be memorized in the proper order. This was achieved only by endless practice. Fully half of the missionaries' study time was spent in trying to remember the meanings and various pronunciations of these symbols and how to write them. John Graybill admits that he, too, would have quit except for two things: he knew he was called of God, and he was too proud—he couldn't return to Pennsylvania as a quitter![17]

Disappointments in ministry also weighed heavily upon the missionaries. While Mr. Aburatani refused to allow his wounded feelings to keep him away from the fellowship of the church, this was not the case with one or two others. These would periodically stop coming to church simply because they were not recognized for positions of honor or responsibility. Fortunately, such times were rare. Most of the church leaders grew in genuine humility and in caring for one another, "esteeming others better than themselves" (Phil. 2:3).

The falling away of promising seekers was part of the disappointments in ministry. So many people would eagerly receive a tract.[18] Others would give evidence of an eagerness to hear the gospel message, responding with what seemed to be an open heart. Still others seemed to assent personally to the call of God and join the fellowship for a time. But so few remained, it seemed.

The glowing reports of success which were taken home by crusade speakers became a sore trial to Pete. He knew that some of these reports often misled the churches in America. He struggled under the pressure of feeling that Brethren in Christ churches at home were eagerly waiting for similar reports of overflowing meetings and mass conversions.

The Willmses and the Books often talked together about such misleading reports and misguided expectations. Thelma noted in her journal: "It is true that masses may turn out for a tent meeting and that a large percentage of decisions for Christ may be given, but the actual fruitage from such an effort is extremely small. . . . This is far from glamorous work. There are no mass movings to Christ in this work." Even in the case of those who came regularly, she noted, there seemed to be so little understanding of the duty of the Christian to put Christ first. Some of them could say "no" to other Sunday activities, letting it be known that they go to church that day. But so few were willing to do this.[19]

One of the greatest disappointments in ministry for Pete and Mary was the drifting away of their "Timothy," young Sakamoto. Sakamoto wavered in his Christian life between the cares and pleasures of life and times of repentance and eager service. He was brilliant, but he lacked commitment. After vacillating for two years, he finally left the fellowship and moved away from Hagi.

To add to the Willmses' hurt, two leaders in the church misunderstood Pete's motives in handling Sakamoto. They were also ignorant of some of the facts involved in the situation. They thought that Pete was grooming Sakamoto to be a pastor and that the mission should send him to Bible school, paying all expenses. Letters were written and conversations took place behind the scenes. However, a more discerning member of the church perceived that Sakamoto was not of the spiritual quality to receive mission support. She sensed that such encouragement would only bring embarrassment to the mission later and declared that Pete had handled the matter very well indeed.[20] Many years later, the other two leaders acknowledged the unworthiness of Sakamoto and the wisdom with which Pete had handled the young man.[21]

Illness also brought severe struggles to the Japan team. It took a toll on their emotions as well as on their bodies. Pete's stomach disorder became worse. The change in diet no doubt contributed to the problem. No milk was available. Instead of milk, much tea was consumed. But the concerns and pressures of the work also played their part in the illness. Pete's temperament at that time was "hurry," and he pushed himself too hard. In time he began to mend, and was able once again to put himself wholeheartedly into his work, although more cautiously.

With Pete's recovery, the Willmses saw an opportunity for an extended time of language study in Kobe. Suddenly misfortune struck again. Mary came down with tuberculosis. It was a heavy blow. Mary was hospitalized in Osaka. The doctor suggested that perhaps the Willmses should return home. Two little girls needed Mary's care, the one just five months old. But restoration of health demanded Mary's total removal from the cares of the family. The young parents were severely tested. But they gave the whole situation to the Lord. And God worked in this situation also for good.[22]

The necessity to return to the United States was forestalled by the offer of Mary's sister, Anna Haldeman, to go to Japan and take care of the children until Mary was well. This quiet sacrifice of Anna and her husband, Bill, allowed Pete to remain on the field during a crucial time when his experience in Japan, his vision, and his overall view of the work were essential to its progress.

John Graybill was also hit by physical testings. One day John was hunched over in the luggage space of a station wagon. The car hit a bump in the road and John was thrown against the ceiling. His back was severely injured. Because John was a man on the move, his hospitalization was a severe trial. He was depressed and asked God repeatedly, "Why?" But the third day in the hospital brought victory as the Spirit of God ministered peace to him. On the seventh day he felt a peculiar touch of the Lord. He was sure God had healed him. But he had to wait patiently two more months until the doctor was willing to remove the cast. The examination revealed that his back had fully mended.[23]

Not all of the missionaries' struggles were caused by factors from without. Some arose out of their own personality traits or emotional makeup. Others occurred because of hasty reactions or self-interests. Personal attitudes and responses of the workers were well-tested through periods of living under the same roof. These times came at points of transition such as furlough or the opening of a new phase of the work. The Willmses and the Books shared the same house at various times for a total of about two years. Both Graybills and Zooks shared households on different occasions with the other two couples for periods which varied from several weeks to several months.

Missionaries are not beyond temptation to self-pity, defensiveness, or resentment. These temptations came, sometimes with force, to the little team of workers in Japan. Pete and Doyle were close together in age, were sports enthusiasts, and had been good friends in college. They were glad to be together once again in Japan. Doyle idolized the New York Yankees as a boy. Furthermore, the impressions gained from the exploits of Babe Ruth, Lou Gehrig and others remained with him as an adult. But Pete couldn't stand the Yankees. To him they were big bullies. When Pete and Doyle talked about baseball their feelings clashed. Pete lived near Detroit. The Tigers usually lost to the invading Yankees. Pete was concerned about fairness. The Yankees, he thought, had too much money. This helped them gain a monopoly on the player market. Doyle was brought up in California, which had no professional baseball team at that time. There was no reason for him not to be a Yankee fan. So he rose to the defense of his childhood idols when Pete attacked them.

Other tensions began to surface. As Pete's stomach problem grew worse, he became more and more in need of rest and quiet. Since Doyle and Thelma's cottage had only one small room, they had been given free access to the main house. A work desk for Doyle had been placed on the opposite side of the partition from where Pete had his desk. Gradually, Doyle's and Thelma's entering the main house, with the sliding open of the partitions and their walking across the floor, began to disturb Pete. Their conversations about letters home and incidents in their work made it increasingly difficult for Pete to concentrate on his studies.

Some of these difficulties were expressed, and tensions began to grow. Some of the things Pete said made the Books feel that their coming had merely been the cause of more work for him and that they were more of a burden than an encouragement in the ministry. They felt that their suggestions for lightening his load had not been adequately considered, possibly because they were thought incapable of performing the tasks.

Pete, on the other hand, was trying to express the fact that some kind of change needed to be made in order to assure periods of strict quiet for the sake of his study and rest. And so one day he informed the Books that he and Mary had decided to move Doyle's desk over to the cottage. He added that it had really been their plan from the beginning for the Books to live over there. Doyle and Thelma were non-plussed. Because Thelma had come down with a bad cold the day before, she was physically weak. Satan came in like a flood. The moving of the desk became a symbol of rejection, of their inability to be co-workers with Pete and Mary.

At last the two couples opened their hearts to each other. Doyle and Thelma shared their feeling that they were being treated like children rather than as equals. Pete and Mary explained that they had felt that the Books wanted to take over in certain areas. Pete admitted that Doyle's free time beyond his 1-W work had tempted him greatly. He said that he and Mary had sensed that something was wrong after the moving of the desk, but they didn't know what to do about it. Then the two couples together allowed the Lord to break through into the situation. They confessed to each other and were melted together in forgiveness and love. They confessed before God that they had allowed the devil to gain inroads in their lives. They were restored and healed in spirit. That night, as if in confirmation of their victory and oneness, one of the believers dedicated his life to the Lord for his service.

Both couples later agreed that in no way was that year a bad one. Christmas together that year was exciting. They shared recreation and enjoyed many good times together. Living together was almost always a positive experience. God had removed every vestige of wrong feeling.[24]

At one point Lucille, because of a combination of circumstances, was locked in a severe battle with loneliness. Thelma noticed her struggle. Hoping to be an encouragement, Thelma suggested that Lucille should just let the Holy Spirit help her through these problems. The words brought a sense of guilt to Lucille. She felt bitter toward Thelma. She thought, "Oh, you're so spiritual. You don't know what I'm going through." But Lucille and Thelma loved Jesus very much. And because of that, they could truly love each other. Lucille opened her heart to Thelma one day about her feelings, and Thelma responded with sympathy and apology. Fellowship was restored.

Later the Books and Graybills lived together on two separate occasions for a total of seven months. On the second occasion, each family had a new baby. The weather was cold and children and adults alike were besieged by a virus. Lucille was once asked, "How can you live together like that?" She smiled as she recalled, some years later, "Those times together were good times. And we appreciate each other more because of them."[25]

In this way the missionaries became aware that God wanted to work in them perhaps as much as he wanted to work in others. They also began to see that before he could work fully through them, he must be able to work freely within and among them.

Loneliness also brought struggles. Most of the workers faced this problem more than once. Mary had to face days and nights alone when Pete journeyed into the mountains for ministry or went to Tokyo for conferences and other business. But she also testified to victory over loneliness and eagerness to support the work.[26] The Zooks quickly recognized the need for fellowship with others and took advantage of the various conferences provided in Tokyo. They also promoted a fellowship of missionaries while they were in Yamaguchi. In order to avoid feelings of loneliness, Marlin frequently listened to tapes when driving long distances, and Ruth did the same when remaining at home alone. The mission's purchase of two small cabins at Lake Nojiri provided fellowship with other missionaries and fun for the whole family.

The Graybills, however, were thrust into a situation that was totally unexpected. Satan attacked Lucille, in particular, through a combination of difficult circumstances, almost destroying her ministry in Japan.

Lucille had not felt a special call to missions. She felt called to be John's wife. She struggled with the idea of going to Japan, for she had never been far from her home community. Her family and their many church friends formed a very intimate fellowship. But she could not refuse John's call. The Graybills were pressed into immediate service because of Mary's illness. The board thought that the Willmses might have to come home, and they wanted Graybills to enter language school as soon as possible in preparation for taking over from Pete and Mary.

The Graybills landed in the port of Yokohama en route to Kobe. To a girl used to farmland and forest, the smells of the harbor were disgusting. There was a stench about everything, it seemed. The sight of the open gutters made Lucille feel sick. She became very thirsty, but was afraid to drink the water. Pete had found a house for the Graybills on the western outskirts of Kobe. He did not know that earlier tenants and their dogs had left the place littered or that it was overrun by rats.

Pete took the Graybills to the General Conference Mennonite house for three days while they got their baggage through customs. He noticed that Lucille was not eating. Thinking that a western meal in a good restaurant might help, he took the Graybills downtown. There Lucille was shocked to find that men and women used the same restroom. She became nauseated. Pete had to leave for Hagi. He explained how to board the electric train for Shioya and said goodbye, still unaware of Lucille's inner turmoil.

There was now no acquaintance for Lucille to talk to. The house was indescribably filthy. John shopped for buckets, and Lucille cowered in fear of the rats. The Books were preparing to move to Kobe for language study at the time. Thelma came early, accompanied by Miss Masae Saito who had agreed to serve as Graybills' helper. The four adults worked together for several days until the house sparkled. Lucille's spirits rose after the house had been scrubbed clean and the rats had been driven away. She asked the Lord for help concerning her attitude.

Then three months later another blow fell. An apartment in the Mennonite house had become available. It was close to downtown and much nearer the language school. Transportation costs could be cut. In addition, the rent was much less. Pete asked the Graybills if they would mind moving. Lucille determined, "If I move again, it will be clear across the ocean!" She looked longingly at the ships in the harbor and thought of home. Then waves of guilt swept over her once again, and she asked the Lord to forgive her.

Language school was difficult, and the children were homesick. Summer provided a welcome respite in one of the mission cabins by Nojiri Lake. For two more years Lucille struggled alternately between feelings of resentment and repentance for her unwilling heart. Then two incidents occurred which changed her life.

At the new mission station in Nagato, Lucille was once again overcome by her disgust for the open gutters and the unkempt appearance of the laboring class of neighbors. One day in the front room of the house God spoke to her: "Look out the window to the north, south, east and west. Don't you see the people out there who are dying without Jesus?" Lucille was changed. She became friends with her neighbors who formerly had seemed so nosey.

One test remained. The birth of Barbara brought joy to the Graybill home once again. But the baby soon became very ill. For six months she gained no weight. Lucille was in despair. One day, she laid baby Barbara on the big bed. With tears of anguish she prayed, "Lord, here she is. She's yours. Take her if you wish." In that moment Lucille was totally free.[27] Soon Barbara was well again. And Lucille's ministry grew in fruitfulness and joy both within the mission and outward to others.

There were other struggles in the Japan mission. By the time the Books arrived in Hagi, few indications of animosity toward the American conquerors remained. Doyle and Thelma never felt any resentment expressed toward them personally. For the most part the Willmses also were graciously welcomed. On occasion, however, there was some indications of bitterness and suspicion toward Americans. On several nights, some drunken men passing by the Willmses' house called out derogatory remarks. In nearby Susa, one man was so bold as to confront Pete and say, "We lost the war, but not on intelligence. It was only on technology. We'll get you next time!"

The Americans were involved in the Korean war at this time. Many GI's made their way to Japan for rest and recreation. Since Hagi was the point in Japan closest to Korea, some of them took an overnight ferry from Pusan to Hagi. In addition, some occupation personnel were stationed on a radar base on Mishima Island, just off the coast from Hagi. These troops also appeared in the town at times. Whenever he had the opportunity, Pete was quick to explain to his Japanese friends that he was Canadian, not American.

Pete gradually became aware that he was under suspicion by the Hagi police. He found that they assumed he had a link with the CIA. They thought this for two reasons: first, he received so many letters and, second, he constantly rode around town on his bicycle taking pictures![28]

Of somewhat greater concern was the communist agitation which was sometimes directed against the mission. Pete informed the Books that the communists considered all of them part of the occupation forces. They pointed to the mission property and car as signs of capitalist greed. They ignored the fact that nothing belonged to the two couples personally. At times Pete wondered if the missionaries should give everything away and live just like the people. But he realized that as soon as they did this, the outreach would be confined to a smaller area and the resources for giving the gospel would be greatly limited.

Pete realized that the average person could not comprehend that the missionaries were sacrificing—giving their time without salary—because of a burden and love for the Japanese people. They probably thought that the job carried great prestige and opportunities for selfish gain. He assumed that the propaganda against the mission kept some people from drawing close. The thought came often, "What's the use of it all; we might as well pack up and go home." But there was always the conviction that this place was where they belonged. In this firm conviction, the Books joined them.[29]

The Missionary Heart

Thus it was that the road into the hearts of the people lay through many struggles on the part of the missionaries. Some of these struggles were with the culture. Some of them were within themselves and with each other in interpersonal relationships. But two things always carried them through the struggles. They were the attributes Henry Hostetter had found in the Brethren in Christ: a deep commitment to the Lord and a genuine concern for others.

Norman Wingert observed about the Willmses what he might have said about the other three couples also:

> In all these testings they did not faint. The faith and strength that had buoyed them up on eagle's wings now helped them to endure. . . . I found Pete and Mary well conditioned to their new environment. Lonely 'foreigners' in a sea of differing customs and traditions, they had adjusted to the new way of doing things: Living in a Japanese style house, speaking the new language, manipulating chopsticks, eating Japanese dishes, observing the niceties of what is proper and what isn't . . . Pete and Mary, although still 'one of us,' have become 'one of them!' And Hagi has accepted them . . . Herein lies both responsibility and opportunity for Christian witness, for little that they do or say goes unobserved.[30]

There were many challenges yet to be met. But there was also a great deal of soaring to be done.

Chapter Five

The Family Grows

The Willmses, Books and Zooks had no children when they arrived in Japan. The Graybills went there with three little ones. In a few years—or so it seemed—the mission families had thirteen children among them.

Children were an asset to missionaries in Japan. Typical of oriental culture, the Japanese thought it quite strange that some of the missionaries did not have one or two children during their first few years in Japan. They would sometimes probe, "How long have you been married?" The presence of small children would quickly open the door to conversation with any Japanese mother. It might also draw questions from men. The American mothers were quite surprised when a Japanese man would inquire, "Do you have enough milk for the baby?"

The missionaries were aware that they themselves provided good advertising for the Christian church or for a planned evangelistic meeting.[1] But whenever their children were with them, all eyes were firmly fixed on the little ones. The curiosity of the Japanese knew no bounds on matters of child care. They were totally surprised to discover that American mothers usually didn't sleep with their babies. They were also amazed that the foreigners would feed the babies vegetables and meat at an early age.[2] Metal pins in the diapers were unheard of as was the practice of putting babies to sleep on their tummies.

Although children were an asset, they also required much of a busy missionary's time. Pete was sometimes envious of missionaries who had no family responsibilities. He saw that language study could be so much more effective without children around—one might live with a Japanese family and thus immerse himself in the spoken language along with formal study. If this were done, progress would be faster and skills would also be increased.[3]

Children's education demanded much attention and time. Without a doubt it was the greatest single item of concern in the Japan mission. Ruth Zook commented that the children's education was the most difficult issue their family had to face. She and Marlin constantly wondered, "Are we doing the right thing for them?"[4]

Not only did the parents have to adjust to the new culture, but so also did the children. In some ways the children were more Japanese than American. They learned the language quickly and naturally. Japanese sounds seemed easier to form than those of English. Both the Willmses and the Books found that the children would have preferred to speak Japanese all of the time. In order for them not to lose facility in English, the parents made a rule that only English would be spoken at home.

In a sense the children were not part of either culture. They were a product that lay somewhere in between. At school the Japanese children recognized them as foreigners. But on furloughs they didn't quite fit into American schools either. They were, in a very real sense, "third culture children."[5] The smaller children were not aware of any differences between the two kinds of people they associated with. Without thinking they would address a Japanese person who came into the room in his language, and then they would quickly and naturally switch to English when their attention was drawn to an American. They considered themselves fully Japanese or fully American, depending on whom they were with. The realization that they were really different came for some as a very rude awakening.

One day Charity Book came home from first grade sobbing as if her heart would break. Thelma had never seen her so distraught. In spite of her mother's expressions of concern, she continued crying. Finally she stammered, "Today they called me a 'gaijin!' Mommy, I'm not a 'gaijin!' " There was no indication that the children had been teasing Charity. But she had been referred to as an "outside person." She sensed the feeling behind the word *gaijin*—"You are not one of us." She felt that she was being excluded from the deep, heart acceptance of those who were her only friends and playmates.

Thelma took Charity into her arms and tried to explain that her family were in fact different in some ways from the people around them. Even though Charity had been born in Japan, her family belonged to a different country. To help her understand such differences, Thelma called her attention to the color of her hair and eyes. Charity was finally consoled. She made the emotional adjustment and continued in school as "one of them," but not quite.[6]

The obvious differences in the foreign children naturally attracted much attention. To people who saw nothing but black hair and dark eyes around them every day, the foreigner's features were fascinating. They were amazed at Bonnie Willms' sky-blue eyes. One boy was heard to wonder if she could actually see with those eyes. The Willmses discovered that some Japanese had the idea that people with such strange eyes might actually be a bit weak in the head!

The children's hair also caused much amazement. Little Kenny Willms had curly blonde hair. This was too much for some of the Japanese. They had to touch it. Mary couldn't help but wonder what the hands had handled before patting the baby's head. Older sister Margy must have had similar thoughts. One day after Kenny had received a curious patting she exclaimed, "Mom, how can you stand it!"[7]

Perhaps the children's hair attracted the most attention because it was touchable. Barbara Graybill couldn't understand that people reaching for her were only curious. She screamed, "They're trying to take my hair!" The children became very self-conscious about their blonde and light brown locks. Charity Book wanted to dye her hair black. Brian Zook was even more uncomfortable. He covered his head with a cap and refused to take it off. He finally consented to remove it in his own house, but for some time he would wear it even when among a group of foreigners. On the other hand, Elaine Zook, adopted in Japan, one day asked if she could have brown hair like the rest of her family.[8]

Charity expressed her feelings quite emphatically one day about having the only brown head among hundreds of black ones. Thelma often made Japanese breakfast for the family. The *miso* soup, which accompanied plenty of white rice, was very nourishing. Little sister Stephanie loved both the soup and the rice. Chari liked the rice, but didn't want to eat the soup. One day Thelma said to Chari by way of encouragement, "Just think, this morning we are having the same breakfast that all your Japanese friends are having." Doyle added diplomatically, "When you eat your soup, you are really being a good Japanese." Chari looked up apathetically, "It's no use trying to be Japanese when your hair is brown!"[9]

"The Cutest Little School"

Most third culture children have the capacity to adjust to various situations. The children of the Japan mission were no exception. They were not fully aware of the concern their parents felt as to the best way to meet their educational needs. Individual families wrestled with the problem as they contemplated moving from one work to another. Mission meetings often included long discussions on the best ways to work out the children's schooling. The board also showed much concern in the matter. They wanted to provide adequate care in the way that suited each family best. They recognized the need for enough schooling in English so that the children would not be handicapped when they returned to the United States. They assented to making use of the Japanese public school system where that was preferred, but they kept constantly in mind the eventual return to America.[10]

Until 1963, the work of the mission was located entirely in Yamaguchi Prefecture. Private schools which provided instruction in English were available only in the large cities. The missionaries spent periods of time in Kobe and Tokyo for language study, but either there were no children at these times or else the children were very small. As the children approached school age, the mission considered the use of the city schools. Kobe was 250 miles away from Yamaguchi and Tokyo was 500. Dormitory facilities were available for older children, but care for younger boarding students was not provided. For a time the mission considered cooperating with the General Conference Mennonites and the Christian and Missionary Alliance in a children's hostel in Kobe.[11] That plan was later canceled when a teacher appeared on the scene, volunteering her services to help the Japan mission. She arrived in July of 1960.

The teacher was Edna Wingerd. Edna joined the Willmses who were studying language in Kobe. She attended language school until the end of August. She then journeyed to Hagi where she began what was later termed "the cutest little school in the world."[12] Edna felt that God had called her to this special service.[13] The Graybills had moved to the new Nagato station earlier in the year. Lucille had been teaching Michael, but the load proved too heavy with the responsibilities involved in the new work and with adjustments to the culture still to be worked through. Brenda Graybill, Eddie Graybill and Margy Willms were now ready to begin school.

The new teacher immediately became known as "Miss Edna." She stayed in the little cottage attached to the Willmses' house in Hagi. Each day Michael and Brenda boarded the train from Nagato for Hagi where the little school convened. John Cunningham, son of Lutheran missionaries in neighboring Shimane Prefecture, also became a part of the school. he was welcomed into the Graybill household. Each weekend he returned to his home in Masuda. The mission charged the Cunninghams only the actual cost of his board and room.[14] Eddie Graybill and Bonnie Willms joined the school in its second year. Eddie was delighted to take the train each day to Hagi. Sometimes he was invited to ride in the engine with Takashi Takamura, an engineer and member of the Nagato church. For many years following this experience, Eddie was sure that he wanted to be an engineer.

Happy children and parents were convinced that the "cute little school" was also one of the best in the world. Miss Edna proved to be an asset to the mission in many ways besides sharing her gift of teaching. She helped redecorate the Hagi house. Her music ability was put to good use as she conducted Christmas and Easter choirs for the Hagi and Nagato churches. She taught some English and helped in youth activities. She assisted Mary after Kenny's birth. She encouraged and helped Lucille while John lay in the Osaka hospital for two months with his back injury.[15]

Miss Edna's term of service came to an end in June 1962. The mission recorded its heartfelt appreciation for her devoted ministry in teaching the children. It recognized her as "a mission worker who has been one with us in the battle for souls in Japan." It asked the board to open the way for her to return to Japan as a member of the mission staff. Sixty Hagi young people attended two farewell meetings held on her behalf. Church people joined the mission in expressions of appreciation for her fellowship and service.[16]

Public Schools

With the conclusion of Edna's service, Margy and Bonnie Willms enrolled in Meirin Primary School in Hagi. They studied, cleaned the rooms and halls, and participated in school activities as if they were Japanese children. Later on, the Books and the Zooks enrolled their children in the public schools also. The Graybills left for America on furlough after the Hagi school closed. They returned the following year to open a new Brethren in Christ work in Tokyo. Their educational needs were thus supplied by local kindergartens and by the Christian Academy in Japan (CAJ), formed by six missions who shared educational concerns. Ninety percent of the students enrolled at the school were from missionary homes. John contributed to the school by teaching courses in industrial arts, two days a week for nine years, thus reducing costs for the mission.

The mission children in Yamaguchi developed rapidly in the Japanese language as they attended the public kindergartens and grade schools. They learned to write the simple phonetic symbols of the pronunciation system and memorized some of the more difficult Chinese characters. Other adjustments were somewhat more difficult. The missionaries informed the schools that they would like their children treated in the same way as Japanese children. They pointed out that they wanted no special privileges. They found, however, that their children were singled out from the others on some occasions. One day a picture which Bonnie had drawn was given special attention even though another child's picture was better. In the class grading system five points was the highest grade possible. This score was limited to five pupils. One time Bonnie achieved this recognition. After that, however, the teacher sometimes pointed out to the children that, if a foreigner could get five points, they should be able to also.[17]

For the most part the foreigners were well accepted by their teachers and schoolmates. There were times, however, when they were soundly teased. Barbara's classmates thought they had never seen anything so strange as raw carrots and celery for lunch! Everybody knew such food was for animals! Stephanie Book opened her lunch one day to reveal a special treat of peanuts and raisins. The children roared with laughter, and Stephanie cried with embarrassment. All the children wore canvas shoes in the school building. One day Charity appeared at school in new blue ones. She came home vowing never to wear them again. Blue was for boys, she declared. All girls wore red shoes!

There were other problems of adjustment. Since classes in the public schools met through Saturday noon, special events were often scheduled on Sunday. To be a part of the school meant that the mission children were expected to participate in these events. They begged their parents to attend also. This sometimes created a conflict with the church service. To deny the children the opportunity to participate with their classmates would create deep disappointment in the children and raise many questions in the minds of their peers and teachers. For the parents to avoid attending the events meant that they would miss vital contacts with other families at functions which were extremely significant to the culture and enjoyable to the people. Usually the missionaries allowed the children to attend the special occasions and, after the morning service was over, joined them as quickly as possible.

Another conflict in the minds of some of the parents concerned the value system of the culture. They realized that their children were being taught the prevailing "morals" of the society, and they knew that this excluded any idea of absolute standards of right and wrong. School excursions sometimes included visits to a local shrine. Such an event was looked upon purely as a cultural experience by most Japanese. However, such visits also included the children's lining up and bowing together toward the inner part of the shrine as a sign of respect. The missionaries felt that this came dangerously close to an expression of worship. Yet, as Thelma Book once pointed out, even if one of the mission children were to be aware of the deeper issues involved in such an act and decide not to bow, it was doubtful that there would be even one more Christian pupil to back him or her up. Each stood alone in a sea of people who had no concept of God-revealed absolutes.[18]

Since the mission children had to be prepared to function in two cultures, their studies in Japanese schools had to be supplemented with work in their own language. This meant that mothers had to teach children at home, especially in English reading, writing and spelling.

As the children moved closer to junior high age, the dual study load became more and more difficult. Homework increased markedly in the public schools, and other school activities demanded more time. In the case of the Books, a choice had to be made between the two systems. With furlough only two years away and with the realization that Charity would most likely have to function primarily in American culture in the future, they decided to withdraw her from the neighborhood school during her fifth year. The principal opened the way, however, for her to graduate with her class one year later. With his permission, she attended art, music and Japanese language classes on Saturday mornings at the school and completed other basic requirements at home in English.

Teaching one's own child at home was not easy. Children seemed to react against the idea of mother functioning also as teacher. Thelma taught Charity each day for three of her five hours of study. Tensions began to build until Doyle and Thelma began to wonder if they were under Satanic attack. They remembered that Japanese homes were dedicated to the "gods" at the time of their construction and that a symbol of this dedication was always sealed in the attic. It seemed probable that the false altar was directly above the study area where Thelma and Charity had their desks. Parents and pupil talked together, reminding each other of their authority in Jesus Christ to overcome the powers of evil. They rebuked Satan in Jesus' name and walked through the house, cleansing it by the power of the blood of Jesus. Charity cut a cross from a paper and pasted it upon the ceiling above her desk. From that day there were no more serious problems in the little schoolroom.

Family Life

The missionary parents tried to be sensitive to the needs of the children. They knew that the children were aware of their isolation from relatives in America and from other foreign companions. They were careful to provide some of the material things the children saw in other homes. This was sometimes difficult on a personal allowance of only $15.00 a month for an adult and $7.50 for each child.[19] But they did not want the children to grow up feeling, as the Graybills expressed it, that they were deprived on the mission field. They hoped that the children could feel with them that being a missionary is a wonderful privilege.

John and Lucille later declared that the mission field provided a special opportunity for a family to grow closer together. Family relationships were more meaningful because no one else was available for support and encouragement. For the Graybills each Friday night was family night. Parents and children played games together—or did whatever the children wanted to do. These nights were carefully guarded from all intrusions. John also made himself available to the children each day for an hour just before supper.[20]

The Willmses maintained a similar policy regarding a family night. They knew that it was not the amount of time spent with the children that was important, but the quality of the time spent. The children were assured that they could have the full attention of their parents at the time designated. Pete also planned occasional camping trips for the family. Furthermore, Pete and Mary were careful to keep any promise they made to the children. On one furlough they sensed a reluctance in the children to return to Japan. Their attitude changed, however, when they were assured that the family would get a television set when they got back to Japan. On the day of their arrival, Pete bought the TV.[21]

Furloughs presented the biggest challenge to the family.[22] Being entertained in people's homes was pleasant. Church contacts, however, were more appreciated by the parents than by the children. The children often complained about being dragged around to strange places. They resisted standing in front of audiences and being asked to sing. They got tired of the presentations of their parents. However, it was meaningful to the entire family when a church or group within the church took the missionary family as their special project, writing letters to the children and sending occasional gifts.

Lack of material things usually presented no problem so long as the family was still in Japan. But once back in the States the children began to be aware of many things they did not have. Pete and Mary tried to be very open with the children in the areas of finances and what they could and could not afford. The children thought that anyone with wall-to-wall carpet must be very rich. Occasionally they asked, "Why do we have to go back to Japan?" Pete and Mary explained carefully that they did not have to go, but they wanted to go so that they could share the good things which they have with others. The children usually accepted this explanation.[23]

The families of the Japan mission had to face these and other stresses. But each of them came through the stresses with a sense of family solidarity and mutual appreciation. Most of the children felt a genuine fondness for the land of Japan and its people. Upon her return to Japan following a furlough in America, Charity Book was heard to declare, "I'm glad to be back home!" Brenda Graybill was even more emphatic. "I love Japan and its people. Japan is my home!"[24] Debbie Graybill once told her parents: "I wouldn't trade my years in Japan for anything." And her sister Barbara wrote to her parents at graduation time:

> Japan is a beautiful culture, and that made my life there worthwhile. I would never want to change my upbringing for anything. I now view American culture from a different perspective and I feel that this is a

privilege. Japan will always be my home, if not in reality, at least in my heart. I would never exchange my eighteen years in Japan for anything.[25]

Most of the children did very well in the schools in Japan. Upon their return to America, those who had been in the more advanced Japanese public schools felt themselves well prepared for further study. CAJ graduates expressed similar feelings about their education.[26] As the older children began to enter college and seminary in the United States and begin families of their own, they showed a high degree of success in adjustment and in achievement. Some of them used their almost-native ability in the Japanese language to work as interpreters in business negotiations.[27]

Supporting Each Other

Not only did the mission family grow in numbers as children came along, but another kind of growth was taking place also. This was a growth within both the life and the activities of the mission. It was a growth of the spirit that produced a sense of teamwork.

There were encouraging signs in the growth of the church family also. The second baptism service in the Hagi group took place on September 11, 1955. The newly arrived Books joined a dozen worshippers on the Hagi beach as three believers testified to new life in Christ: Seiichiro Aburatani, Koichiro Sugiyama and Mrs. Kikuyo Miyamoto. Plans for the service had been made while the Willmses were in Kobe for their first, brief term of language study. Some members of the church, including those baptized just one year earlier, began to emerge as leaders of the little flock. Miss Ritsu Iwakura took the main responsibility, especially when the Willmses left for Kobe in January. Mr. Aburatani and Mrs. Ichikawa faithfully assisted her. The advisability of leaving leadership mostly in the hands of women was questioned by some onlookers. Pete's feeling, however, was to entrust the work to whomever the Lord had given the church at that time.[28] These leaders conducted the services with appropriate songs, prayers and messages. The messages usually consisted of simple Bible studies or testimonies shared by the believers themselves.

Indigenous leadership had been developing for some time. One year earlier, John Z. Martin had noted that the group of Christians had conducted its own worship services and prayer meetings on several occasions. It had elected its own treasurer, Koichiro Sugiyama. Some of the group had shown definite interest in helping others find the way of salvation during the special evangelistic meetings. They also invited non-Christians to church, saw that they were comfortably seated, and chatted with them after services about the Christian faith.[29]

Shortly after the Willmses first arrived in Hagi, word of the foreigners' coming had reached the ears of an old, blind evangelist in a mountain village. Takaichi Hada had visited the United States many years earlier. He witnessed among Japanese people living in the San Francisco area. He now lived on a tiny farm in Yadomi, an hour's drive from Hagi over winding, bumpy roads. He maintained informal ties with the Presbyterian church in Hagi. Delighted that missionaries had at last come to his area, Hada called on the Willmses one day to get acquainted. A close friendship developed between the missionaries and the saintly man of God.

Hada sometimes visited the Hagi church and spoke in their services. During the Willmses' study period in Kobe, he came regularly to encourage the believers, accompanied on the long bus trips by a nephew who served as a guide. Pete often joined him with the Chevy van for circuit visits to tiny groups of believers scattered from Yadomi in the mountains to Susa on the coast. On Christmas in 1955, the Hagi Christians journeyed to Yadomi by chartered bus for a joint worship celebration in the town's public hall.[30]

There were other encouragements in the growing family. The Nago Sunday school, a fruit of the Martin campaign, continued under the leadership of Miss Emine Katsura. Now, in early 1956, almost eighteen months after the meetings, most of the original twenty children were still attending the classes. The Miyamotos began a Sunday school in their home also. Mrs. Miyamoto taught the children enthusiastically.[31]

Many years later, a young woman testified that she had often observed the class as she passed by the house. The singing sounded so good, she said, and the gathering looked so inviting. She later became a Christian and a member of another church.[32] Mr. Miyamoto's mother, who had been saved earlier in the year, now voluntarily decided to burn her god-shelf. She became a candidate for baptism a year later.

The arrival of the Books brought joy to both the Willmses and the Hagi believers. They had been praying together for more workers. In addition to the Books, however, God sent another worker. She became a great encouragement to both the mission and the church. Her name was Hiroko Kanakubo.[33]

"Kay San," as the missionaries soon came to call her, began attending a Bible class in April 1955 at the MCC center of Norman and Eunice Wingert in Tokyo. She was very good in English, and the Wingerts soon began to make use of her skills in interpreting. Pete, who had finished his term of language study in Kobe, went to Tokyo to attend the International Open House sponsored by the Wingerts in August. He was asked to baptize a group of six young people following the Open House, of whom Miss Kanakubo was one.

Pete was so impressed with the young woman that he asked her to join the mission in Hagi. She consented and joined the Willmses and the newly arrived Books in Hagi on September 18. The Willmses had been hoping for someone to serve as interpreter for Thelma and as language teacher for them. Kay filled both these needs most capably. She served willingly for two years, receiving only her board and room and an allowance of 1000 yen ($3.00) a month.[34]

With Kay San's help, Thelma took the responsibility for the three Sunday schools that had already been operating. She coached the teachers in Sunday school administration. She began weekly children's Bible classes in several mountain villages and a ladies' Bible class in Hagi. She also assisted Mary in the various kitchen and household duties.[35]

Kay San and Thelma became close friends as they rode the bus week after week to the little mountain village of Sakura or took the train down the coast to Muneto. They shared past experiences and fellowshipped in the Word during the cold night hours spent on hard benches while waiting for a train back to Hagi. They ministered as one and often shared tears of joy or disappointment as they saw people respond to the Holy Spirit or reject him. Late one night as the pair crossed Hagi's Hashimoto bridge, Kay San confided, "You know, sometimes I feel that I have not been speaking at all. It is as though the words are not my words, but Someone else is speaking through me. It was like that tonight. I forgot about myself."[36]

The two were invited to Muneto by Hisako Yamazaki, a poor widow with five children. She had appeared at the mission home one day to express her gratitude for the Mennonite Central Committee food package she had received. Weakened by tuberculosis, she began attending church at considerable cost of money and time for the one-hour bus trip. Her home was an old storage shed through which the winter wind passed freely. But she gathered the neighborhood children faithfully, and the message of the gospel began to take root in their hearts. One girl wanted to have prayer at supper time in her home. When her mother insisted that she didn't know how to pray, the little girl said, "You listen. I'll pray, and you just say 'Amen!' "[37]

The Word began to have its effect in Mrs. Yamazaki's heart also. The local Buddhist priest warned her that she had better not believe the new religion. But she had a dream in which she saw her dead husband telling her not to worry about it. She reported this to the priest and said that she thought the two religions were warring within her. The priest then responded that, since Japan permits freedom of worship, she may do whatever she wished![38] Mrs. Yamazaki was baptized in the third baptismal service held by the Hagi church on September 2, 1956, along with Mr. Jihichi Oba, Miss Yaeko Kaneshige and Mrs. Yasuko Miwa.

From 1-W to Missionary

With the help of Yasuo Miyamoto, Doyle soon found himself busy with appointments in teaching English. He was welcomed to Hagi High School as guest instructor in English conversation for several classes. He was also introduced to other schools in the city. English teachers requested his help privately. He was called on for lectures on American life and culture and was frequently asked to judge English contests. On numerous occasions before school audiences and other groups, he was asked to explain why he had come to Japan. The audiences listened attentively to his testimony concerning the Prince of Peace who could replace hatred with love for one's enemies.[39]

He also began to assist Mr. Aburatani in his private English classes. The struggling teacher was greatly encouraged by the help of the young missionary "with his brotherly love in Christ Jesus."[40] Enrollment in the English school began to increase as it became known that instruction and practice in English conversation were available from a foreigner. One of the early church leaders reported that the figure of the English teacher riding his bike all over town was familiar to many of the town people. He said that the name "Book" had become quite famous.[41]

The two-year period of service included coaching students for English contests and an increasing number of appearances in Hagi schools and elsewhere. But another event occurred which changed the plans of the Books radically.

By the end of their first year in Japan, Thelma was feeling a desire to remain in the work. Ever since she was a little girl, she had always thought that someday she might be a missionary. This simple childhood dream now turned into an inner urging. She felt an exhilaration in her work with Kay. She was glad with the prospect of giving her life to the people she had come to love. One day she gently asked Doyle how he felt about the idea of staying on as missionaries, and then she waited patiently.

At first Doyle didn't share his wife's interest. He felt that he had been involved in a very noble service before coming to Japan, and he looked forward to continuing that teaching ministry. He also looked forward to getting back into sports competition in the city and church leagues. He didn't feel rebellion toward what God's will might involve, but he resisted the idea of a change of his plans. He felt that one could surely serve God in important ways other than in foreign mission work.

But he recalled that he had always told himself he was willing for whatever God would show him. While Thelma waited, deeply concerned, he finally became willing to pray about the matter. He began to sense that God had caused the draft board to refuse his appeal so that he could bring him to this particular place. One day the words of John 12:24 spoke forcefully to him: "Except a corn of wheat fall into the ground and die, it abideth alone; but if it die, it bringeth forth much fruit." Suddenly he realized that, even though he might serve God in very noble ways, if he missed God's desire for him, his service would be meaningless. He realized that God was asking him to be willing to die as a seed in the land of Japan.

The decision was made to remain. So clear was the inward response of the Holy Spirit to the decision that he never doubted that God had called him to Japan. This deep conviction was later to carry him through some very difficult times. From this experience he formed his own definition of a missionary: "One whom God takes to a strange place so he can go to work on him!"

The Books applied to the board for status as regular missionaries. They were accepted[42] and remained in Japan for three years beyond their 1-W commitment, thus completing a full term of five years. They entered language school in Kobe upon completion of the 1-W term of service. At this same time Miss Kanakubo, her main work with Thelma now completed, returned to her home in Tokyo.[43]

A grateful church and mission bade Kay goodbye with reluctance. In a letter from Pete, the mission members expressed their gratitude. They noted that in addition to rendering assistance in the language, she had been an "unfailing help and blessing in the struggles of everyday Christian living." They acknowledged her attitude of servanthood and the inspiration of her conscientious life. The letter continued:

> Soon after we came to Japan we were told that, in trying to teach converts, the first necessity is a Japanese Christian who will be an example of what the word 'Christian' means. You have been this example, a living letter 'known and read by all.' It will take greater insight than we have now to know all the good that you have done, but it is obvious that your work and witness to Jesus has borne rich fruit. We are indeed thankful that, in answer to our prayers for a co-worker, He sent you to us.

The letter invited Kay San to return to Hagi again as a part of the mission staff. It assured her of her co-workers' love and the firmness of God's promise: "I will go before you and level the mountains . . . that you may know that it is I, the Lord . . . who call you by your name (Isa. 45:2-3)."[44]

Teamwork

A curious fact began to emerge concerning the first seven years of the work in Japan. Pete reported to the Foreign Mission Board that, in spite of the fact that the board had been supporting one couple for seven years, two for five years and three for three years, "the middle of 1960 marked the first time that more than one couple has actually been in the work." The reasons given for the phenomenon were the long periods of language study that were necessary for all six adults and the times of illness which came to some. In addition, the Willmses completed their first term of five years in 1958 and returned to the States for a furlough. Thus it was that "these first seven years represent the equivalent of one couple's time as contributed, however, by three different couples."[45]

One characteristic of the Japan mission was its teamwork. The couples exchanged places with each other or filled in for one another whenever circumstances required such an exchange or whenever it seemed good for the mission or the churches. Decisions were made whenever possible by the mission group as a whole, and the good of the work was considered above personal comforts.[46]

The *Handbook of Missions* recorded the fact that in 1957, "with Books changing from 1-W to 'professional missionary' and the Graybills coming, the missionary staff trebled!"[47] With the increase in staff, the need for decisions also increased. There were now six regular missionaries, and they agreed that the mission should convene in business meetings on a regular, yearly basis.

The first official business meeting of the Japan Brethren in Christ Mission was held on September 7, 1957, in Hagi. The Graybills had come from Kobe and Pete from an Osaka suburb where Mary was recuperating from her bout with TB. The Books were working with the Hagi church in preparation for the Willmses' return and in anticipation of a year of formal language training. The purpose of the coming of the three from the Kansai area at this time was twofold. First, a baptismal service was to be held on Sunday, September 8, and Pete was scheduled to officiate. Second, it was felt that Graybills should be introduced to the Hagi church and, in turn, receive their first glimpse of the city of Hagi and the work there.

The first business meeting consisted of a Saturday evening time of discussion. A typhoon was approaching the city, threatening to disturb the baptism service the next day. Pete read from Job 26:12: "By his power he stilled the sea; by his understanding he smote Rahab." Pete pointed out the implications of the first part of the verse for their particular situation. The word "Rahab" in the second part of the verse was taken to mean the forces of evil. It had been reported that these forces were bringing discontent to one believer about the weather and had caused another to withdraw because of family antagonism. The group "offered earnest, unhurried prayers." Sunday morning dawned clear and bright with the sea quiet enough for the baptism.[48]

It was agreed that Pete should serve as chairman of the mission. The remainder of the discussion centered on which household items should be considered as personal expenses and which should be paid for by the mission. It was suggested that personal items could be determined as follows: (1) whatever a person could get along without and (2) whatever one would want to take with him when he moves.

An earlier letter from the board was discussed. The letter indicated that "your personal allowance is to cover such items as clothing; dentist bills, unless major; toilet articles . . . in other words, items of a personal nature that would not be used in operating the house."[49] One of the group suggested that they all needed the kind of vision that would give the mission the benefit of the doubt in such matters. It was decided that things definitely of a personal nature were: toiletries such as toothpaste, clothing, and photographic items. Pete said that he asked the board for permission to consider all necessary medical items as mission expense. Although the board's reply had not yet come, he was suggesting that such items be recorded in this way.[50]

The next official gathering for business was just two months later. The Books were now in Kobe for language study along with the Graybills. The Willmses had been living in the Osaka suburb of Takarazuka following Mary's hospitalization. Mary had recovered sufficiently from her illness to attend the sessions. The little group met on November 7-9, 1957, in the large Shioya house where Graybills had settled for their first few months in Japan. The Books had joined them in the house by moving into the upstairs rooms. The mission minutes record the gratitude of the group upon the occasion which marked "the first time that all of us, as mission personnel, met together for business and mutual Christian fellowship."[51]

Following this meeting, the Willmses returned to Hagi to take up the work there once again.

Pete had earlier expressed what all six of the workers now felt:

> As you think of us in our work here, we would like you to think of us as servants who consider it a tremendous privilege and who find it a real joy to minister in this land. When you pray for us, we would that you would ask God to give us greater discernment of His will and a quicker obedience to it . . . We have come to see in a new way that whether we live or die, the only thing that really matters is whether or not God is using us. In . . . Exodus 33:14 . . . God promises Moses, 'My presence shall go with thee, and I will give thee rest.' What more can we desire?[52]

Chapter Six

Methods in Mission

The primary purpose of the Japan Brethren in Christ Mission from its beginning was to plant churches and nurture them. There was never any intention to become involved in institutions. Such involvement was unnecessary. The Japan public schools were well-advanced academically. Hospitals and medical care were geographically within reach of everyone. Bible schools and seminaries for the professional ministry were available in the larger cities.

In the early years of the mission, the evangelistic campaign was seen as a necessary tool for establishing a foothold. We have already traced the story of the two initial Hagi meetings with Henry A. Ginder and John Z. Martin. Each of the campaigns involved about one week of meetings. One was conducted on the streets of Hagi with a concluding rally in the public hall. The other was held in a tent on a vacant lot near the center of town. The work in Nagato was also begun by tent meetings. One was held in the part of the city called Senzaki in August 1958. It produced an initial core of believers. A second tent meeting was held near the Nagato train station for ten days in the summer of 1960.

The tent meeting approach was questioned by some. One Japanese leader considered it an "American method" not appropriate to the Japanese.[1] Henry Hostetter was uncertain about its value for Japan because of its emphasis on decision first and study later. He felt that lasting decisions would be more likely to occur after a deliberate and prolonged time of Bible study. Since the Japanese needed time for intellectual orientation, evangelistic campaigns with their call to immediate decision were little more than advertising.[2]

There can be no doubt that the tent meeting did attract a great deal of attention. Such an event was a curiosity in Hagi and Nagato. Many people came who would not otherwise have been contacted. A few responded to the call to discipleship. But it soon became evident that the curiosity and novelty that surrounded the work in Hagi had faded. The missionaries found themselves face to face with the need of presenting the gospel message without such continuing attractions.[3]

There were several general concepts that underlay the Japan mission's approach to church planting and nurture. The first was that the church should be made available to the people where they were. This meant that, instead of an emphasis on a centralized worship location to which everyone would be encouraged to come, an attempt would be made to establish small pockets, or cells, of believers wherever an interest in the message was shown. Such cells would be nurtured in the hope that each would grow into an established, self-sustaining church. Hagi was envisioned as the hub for a great complex of these cells.[4] With the cell approach, church buildings were to be deemphasized. Until a group came to the point where a building was clearly needed for continued growth and for outreach, the believers were to be encouraged to meet in homes and rented halls.[5]

The second general concept under which the Japan mission operated was that each of the churches established should be autonomous, community-type churches. Denominational ties were not to be emphasized. It was recognized by the mission that churches established under the same mission might naturally develop ties of fellowship, mutual encouragement, and idea exchange. However, such churches should not encouraged to declare themselves formally a denomination, thus adding to the confusing maze of church names which already confronted the Japanese public. The mission was to instill in the believers a consciousness of their relationship to all Christians. The name Brethren in Christ was not to be displayed prominently on a local church. Instead the church should be called by the name of the community in which it was located.[6] All of the church groups accepted this policy regarding the name of a local body, following the example of the Omotomachi Christian Church in Hagi and the Fukagawa Christian Church in Nagato.

A third general concept of church planting and nurture was that the Japanese churches were to be encouraged to become self-sustaining as quickly as possible. The indigenous principles of self-support, self-government and self-propagation were to be strongly encouraged among them. Impressed by the writings of Roland Allen and others, Pete and Mary Willms deliberately left the new Hagi church alone and went to Kobe for language study in January of 1955. Pete made occasional visits to encourage the little flock. The experiment was successful as the believers responded to the challenge of leadership.[7] The church moved steadily toward complete control of its own affairs. The American church was informed concerning the goal of the mission in this regard and was asked to pray for the national leaders.[8]

Lay Leadership

The fourth concept relating to church planting and nurture was foundational to all the others. It was that the churches should be led by self-supporting members of the church rather than by paid, "professional" pastors. Pete was convinced that if rural Japan was to be reached with the gospel, it would have to be done by Japanese Christians who were self-supporting and who worked as lay people, probably unordained. This conviction was agreed to by John Z. Martin and was approved as beginning policy for Japan.[9] Pete noted that this concept was compatible with the idea of "two separate, autonomous and yet interdependent organizations—church and mission."

It was a revolutionary concept so far as Christianity in Japan was concerned. The mission felt pressure from other missionaries and older national Christians to conform to the traditional, western idea of supported pastors. However, this approach was causing some of their own missions and churches many difficulties. The lay leadership approach was seen as the only way in which all villages could have their own witness. The Hagi believers had seen the reasonableness of this concept and were moving with the mission in it.[10]

The lay leadership concept was further articulated in a 1961 paper written by Pete. The paper made clear the fact that "lay leadership" did not stand in opposition to "trained leadership." In fact, training was crucial for lay members of the church in order for them to function effectively in leadership and evangelism. The term was rather to be contrasted with "professional leadership." The word "lay" was to be best understood as "self-supporting." "Leadership" meant "taking the lead" in the local assembly in outreach, visitation, entertaining visiting brethren and functioning as shepherds for the general welfare of the flock (Acts 20:28). The paper declared that the New Testament knows nothing of a special sacerdotal caste distinguished from the laity. It does not divide Christians into orders described by the words "clergy" and "laity." Instead, all Christians are seen as priests and, as such, have the right to administer the sacraments and teach in the church.[11]

The paper listed a number of advantages for the lay leadership approach. First, it declared, the concept fits the situation in Japan. Because of the small number of Christians and the antagonism of the culture, the situation resembles that of the early church much more than the church in America where the clerical system seems to meet the need. The indigenous "non-church" movement (Mukyokai) has flourished because of its lay approach. Furthermore, the paper noted, the lay approach makes possible the planting of many more congregations since it is not limited by the availability of personnel and finances. It allows rapid planting of congregations and provides leadership the moment a church is born.

In addition, the lay approach emphasizes the priesthood of all believers. It aids in the discovery and development of gifts, whereas the presence of a professional often causes such gifts to remain buried. It effectively combats the attitude of "let the pastor evangelize and visit the sick—he's paid to do it." It promotes a sense of voluntary service which is necessary for effective evangelism. And also, the lay approach is ideally suited to give the kind of training most needed in Japan. "It allows people to be trained while they are interacting with the real life of the people they seek to win. Thus meaningful training and soul winning are accomplished at the same time." It is almost impossible for schools to provide this kind of training.[12]

Other advantages were also cited in favor of the lay leadership approach. It promotes growth both in numbers and in quality. It enables the local church to handle its own finances, thus avoiding dependency upon a foreign church through financial subsidy. It does away with problems inherent in importing leaders from outside the congregation, especially that of salary and the notion that others also should be paid for service in the church. It promotes a more harmonious and mutually sympathetic congregation. It avoids the tendency to control by one person which is stifling to spontaneity. And it avoids the difficulty and misunderstanding so often present in handing over leadership from the mission to the church.

Some drawbacks to the lay approach were also acknowledged. A congregation might not progress as rapidly as it would under professional leadership. It may make many mistakes. It may develop an inferiority complex because of the pressure from neighboring churches which are under the clerical system. The believers may struggle with the thought that theirs is not a "real" church because it has no professional pastor. They may also struggle with the prevailing view that a layman cannot speak and lead with as much authority as a seminary-trained pastor. Education which is so crucial for the layman may be difficult to work out. And, finally, it is necessary to provide an outside authority who can give guidance and bring encouragement to the group.[13]

These concepts of church planting and nurture had begun to form in Pete's mind before he left America for Japan. They developed in his thinking in the first few years of the work and were acknowledged by the board as worthy of implementation. They also found ready soil in the hearts of the other mission members as they arrived one by one in the field. These concepts were developed and applied further by the mission group during long hours of discussion in the annual business meetings. They became part of the working policy for the Japan Brethren in Christ Mission.

Mission and Board Relationships

Various matters of policy were developed in the mission business meetings. Early meetings were usually led by Pete Willms, who had been appointed chairman of the mission at the first business meeting. In 1965 Pete asked to be relieved of the chairmanship. The mission expressed its thanks for his service and asked the board to appoint another chairman. In response, the board created the title of Field Superintendent, and John Graybill was asked to serve in this position.[14]

Mission meetings were held, whenever possible, in conjunction with visits by various board representatives. The mission staff were grateful for the fellowship and interchange provided by these representatives. They asked that the board try to send delegations to Japan at least every two years. The first board visit, following the 1954 trip of John Z. Martin, took place in October 1961, when Henry N. Hostetter and Carl J. Ulery arrived. Other visits came during the next ten years, in December 1963 (Hostetter); December 1965 (Hostetter and Richard Royer); October 1967 (Hostetter and Eldon and Harriet Bert); October 1969 (Hostetter and J. Earl Musser); and October 1971 (Musser).[15]

Mission meetings were times of special fellowship even when board members could not be present. They were highlights of any year and were anticipated by adults and children alike. The families took turns entertaining the others. Mealtimes were always special because of the relaxed atmosphere and the unending stream of chatter. They usually produced some special treats also—a can of olives that the Books had been hoarding or chunks of milk chocolate shared by the Graybills from a ten-pound Hershey Bar. Ice cream was a must whenever the mission met in Kobe or Tokyo. The host family would secure a two-gallon restaurant-pack from a friendly wholesaler and everybody would eat his yearly fill.

Henry Hostetter's coming meant special fun for the children. They had learned that "Grandpa Hostetter" always came ready to play games with them. The favorite game of the smaller ones was one in which Grandpa slowly and mysteriously touched different parts of the anatomy and chanted a special rhyme. "Head bumper," he said as he tapped the forehead a few times. "Eye winker"—he peeped into one eye by lifting the eyelid. "Tommy Tinker," brought a peep into the other eye. Then "nose smeller, mouth eater, chin chopper," he chanted in succession. The children shivered in anticipation, then squealed with delight as he cried, "Gully, gully, gully . . . !" and his quick but gentle hands tickled their chins or ribs. They rolled on the floor in laughter, then, half afraid, came back for more.

Business discussions often dealt with complex, difficult matters. Solutions were sometimes long in coming as the team struggled to work through the implications of issues or to formulate minute points of policy. At times opinions were voiced strongly and disagreements were expressed freely. Sometimes the discussions got too "warm" for Lucille. She was not used to such bold, open exchanges. She would quietly slip out of the room and busy herself with something in the kitchen or take a short walk outside.

The board watched the mission team with interest. They recognized that there were strong personalities present in the group and that this could be dangerous to its harmony. But they saw that the missionaries desired to work together. Each respected the sphere of labor of the others and tried to complement it.[16]

Suggestions for policies were usually initiated in Japan. The policies were then formulated in consultation with the board. The general attitude of the board was that decisions should be made as much as possible by the Japan staff itself. They should come primarily from the needs that the staff felt on the field. The board indicated to the mission that they were always available to give guidance, but they felt that the Japan mission was able to see issues that related to the local situation much better than they. This attitude freed the missionaries to pursue plans which they deemed beneficial. Minutes of the mission meetings were always sent to the board for perusal and further suggestions.

The discussion over what items should be considered personal and which should be mission expense was not resolved quickly. The staff was very much aware that the board had little money at its disposal for missionary support. They knew that in 1957 the amount necessary to support a missionary "fully" was considered to be $1,500 a year, an incredibly low figure for that time. This figure was arrived at "by dividing the total Foreign Mission expenditures by the number of active missionaries."[17]

The board paid all expenses necessary to maintaining the mission. This included most household items. Clothing, toothpaste, and normal dental care was to be taken care of by the individual missionary from his personal allowance. These allowances were set originally at $150 a year for two. This was later increased to $10 a month per adult, then to $12.50 and finally to $15.00. In 1966 the mission voted to divide revenues from the teaching of English among the regular staff, up to a limit of 10,000 yen ($28) per quarter. Finally, in 1975, the board acted to put the missionaries on an individual salary basis similar to the system in practice for American pastors. Among other things, this system did away with the detailed reports from each family which listed the amounts spent on items such as food and utilities.[18]

With rising costs in Japan, the mission was forced to assume financial responsibility for some items which had earlier been considered personal. Normal dental care became a mission expense. One prayer letter per year was allowed in the amount budgeted for each family, and vacation allowances were also included in the budget.[19]

The establishment of a church building policy was a significant step. In 1959 a summary of policies for Japan had been formulated by the board, including suggestions for an approach to church buildings. In was felt, first of all, that "it will be to the best interests of the work if nationals assume primary responsibility in providing worship places, be they in homes, halls, or other locations." The policy encouraged Japanese Christians to build churches only after they had first gathered together an adequate nucleus of worshippers. Should they desire to buy land and build a church, they could request assistance of the Japan Brethren in Christ Mission after they had gathered one tenth of the cost of the property. The mission could then submit a request to the Foreign Mission Board and assistance, if granted, would be, first, a gift "matching the property fund" already gathered or "one tenth of the purchase price" and, second, "a long term loan to be repaid on a matching fund basis."[20]

The Japan mission took issue with the idea of a donation of only ten percent. It suggested that the mission should donate at least fifty percent of the price of the land or even buy it outright for the church. Land was expensive in Japan and had to be purchased quickly, the full amount being paid in one lump sum. The mission could encourage the church a great deal by assuming this responsibility. Once the land was secured, the church could then gradually collect funds for the building.[21]

Shortly after this action, the earlier policy was revised to reflect some of these concerns. It was decided that a church could request assistance of the mission when it had gathered ten percent of the estimated cost of the entire project, including "the actual price of the land, transaction costs, and the cost of the proposed building." The Japan mission would then consider the request and make its recommendations to the board. A building fund was to be established, from which assistance would be granted. A loan would be issued from the fund to cover the remaining ninety percent of the proposed project. The loan would be repaid into the fund on a matching basis, "that is, the mission matches the payments of the church." In effect, this meant that a church would pay fifty-five percent of the church building project and the mission would assist the church with forty-five percent of the costs.[22] This was to prove over the years a workable policy for which the churches were very grateful.

Doctrinal Issues

Both the mission and the board recognized the fact that, in order to maintain the enthusiastic support of the home church, the confidence of the church in the mission would need to be cultivated. At the time the Japan mission was inaugurated, the home church was struggling internally with some of its interpretations of Scripture, particularly in the area of dress and the prayer veiling. Pete Willms was one of those who saw that changes must take place in the church in order for it to maintain an effective witness in society. Some of the more conservative brethren, however, were concerned about his views on some issues, and a few questioned his suitability for service abroad. It was decided that he should appear before the Examining Board of the denomination. The dreaded interview was changed, however, to nothing more than "a time of fellowship."

The Willmses were relieved, but nevertheless wanted to make sure that they were not out of harmony with the Examining Board's thinking or that there would be misunderstandings later. Their concern was not only for themselves but also for the peace of mind of those on the board and others in the church. They inquired as to what church practices would need to be applied in Japan.[23] One of the members of the Examining Board, Elam Dohner, exhibited sensitivity and tolerance in his reply: "We are not interested in specific practices. We are concerned first about the direction, or spiritual tone, of the church in Japan." The other members agreed with his statement.[24]

The Foreign Mission Board also was characterized by an attitude of tolerance. It tried to maintain a policy of openness and flexibility. The board had appointed a special committee to "hold hearings" with the Willmses "with a view to formulating a doctrinal policy for Japan."[25] They had also dispatched John Z. Martin, obviously not only for the purpose of evangelism but for "the study of other problems that relate to the establishing of a work."[26] But their action at Conference in 1953 seemed to set the tone for their considerations of doctrinal matters relating to the new work. They affirmed the principles of modesty, simplicity, non-resistance, prayer veiling, feetwashing, etc., and agreed that they should be "promoted and emphasized." But, they declared, these principles shall be "adjusted to the Christian's life in Japan." In the concern to express these principles in actual practice, they added, "we are deeply conscious of the need of their being adapted to the people whom we are going to serve."[27]

Perhaps they were not aware that their concern for flexibility had its precedent in the denomination as many as fifty years earlier. India missionaries faced the question of whether or not to require the same style of head covering as that worn in the home church. The board decided with them that the culturally approved *sari* could function just as well. Amazingly, the board even went so far as to approve receiving into church membership in Africa those who were still living in polygamy, providing that there be "convincing evidence of salvation" and that the "matrimonial relation was contracted and completed while in ignorance of Scriptural teachings on this subject."[28] This action exhibited a remarkable degree of scriptural understanding and cultural insight, one that was absent from the policies of most missions for the next fifty years.

In the case of Japan, the primary issue was the prayer veiling. Attempts to find the best way for all concerned continued for the first ten years of the mission's existence. Shortly after arriving in Japan, Pete expressed his feeling that the prayer veiling as discussed in 1 Corinthians 11 was an expression of the particular culture of that day. He noted that such a practice was absolutely foreign to the Japanese culture and that to try to teach it would be to actually promote a particular part of western culture that had adopted it.[29] The board replied that, because it shared the Willmses' concern on the matter, it had left the issue open for further discussion. It asked only that Mary wear some type of head covering during worship and assured them that it did not wish to indicate what type that should be. It noted that biblical interpreters were still not agreed on whether or not the Corinthian passage did, in fact, indicate the particular culture and had no universal implications. It declared the church's willingness to make adaptations but not to set aside what it felt was proper interpretation of God's Word.[30]

One of the board members suggested that the African church had successfully adopted a head covering, seemingly in opposition to its culture. Pete responded that circumstances between Africa and Japan were vastly different. In Africa the Brethren in Christ were quite isolated from other denominations. In Japan the believers were surrounded by other churches. An insistence on a head covering there could cause offense to members of other churches and add to the division that already existed between denominations. He warned also that Japanese respond all too readily to regimentation. They are willing to submit to outward rules which suggest a way to work for their salvation, but they find faith a hard concept to grasp. He assured the board of his own deep concern over the delicate issue and of his prayers for the right kind of solution.[31]

The board members wanted a solution that would keep the confidence of the church at home and yet open the way for an effective witness in the new culture. They were committed churchmen who saw the need for respect of the traditions and practices of the church. At the same time they realized that few people in the home church had any awareness of the dynamics of cross-cultural ministry. On his first trip to Japan, Henry Hostetter was shown some of the implications of differing cultural perspectives. While accompanying John Graybill one day in Nagato, he was told, "Watch what happens." John approached a lady who was working nearby and greeted her. Immediately she reached up and removed the protective scarf that was draped over her head. The implications were clear: respect and submission in Japanese culture was shown by *removing* the head covering.

Because of obvious cultural difficulties of this kind, the board chose to be patient in problems that related to doctrinal interpretations, keeping them as "low key" as possible in the American church. They assented to the principle that any interpretation which would create an impediment to the gospel must be approached very carefully. Where such an impediment might occur, it was more important to adapt to the culture of the unbeliever for the sake of the gospel than to cater to the tradition of the church.[32]

Discussion on the question of the prayer veiling continued for some time within the Japan mission and between the mission and the board. The matter was discussed with the Mennonite missionaries in Japan and was a subject for study at conferences with the Mennonites. Although he was unable to comply with the request, Carlton Wittlinger was asked to prepare a study paper on the history of the practice in the American church.[33]

The problem was finally resolved not by a policy decision but by the changes which gradually occurred in the American church itself. The period of most intense struggle with the dress code was from 1942 to 1952, just prior to the opening of the Japan mission. Attitudes softened somewhat around 1957 and changed considerably after 1962. By the early 1970s the dress code was no longer a crucial issue.[34] But, as Carlton Wittlinger said concerning an earlier generation, ". . . the brotherhood demonstrated that it was at least making an effort to grapple with the realities of proclaiming the Brethren message in cultures differing radically from that of the homeland." Early missionaries often attempted "to reproduce in the mission settings models of their faith and life-style as formulated in rural North America." However, the mission movement itself "forced the Brethren in Christ, both at home and abroad, to reappraise their value system and, in the process to open their movement to possibilities for change."[35]

Country and City

According to the original plan, the missionaries stationed in Hagi reached out to establish and nurture various preaching points or "cells." The main cells were Nago and Susa, on the coast north of Hagi, and Yadomi and Kawakami, in the mountains to the east and south. The Nagato station was opened in 1960 when the Graybills moved into the new mission residence in the Fukagawa section of town. The believers in Senzaki were encouraged to attend Sunday worship services at the Fukagawa church. Senzaki was made a midweek preaching point. Other cells gradually developed. One was Furuichi, about twenty minutes down the coast by train. Another was Takibe, forty minutes beyond Furuichi.

The cell meetings were usually warm in fellowship. Yadomi's blind leader, Hada, once declared that he would like his little group to become a part of the Brethren in Christ.[36] When he died in 1968, however, the Presbyterian church in Hagi assumed the responsibility for the believers in Yadomi because of a previous connection of some of them with the church.[37]

Most of the cells realized little growth. Some of them were eventually discontinued. Looking back in 1961 on the first seven years of the mission, Pete wrote that, although he believed that the brethren Ulery and Wolgemuth were led of God to this very neglected area, it had nevertheless turned out to be a difficult place to work. This was so "because of its stable, secure farmers, its conservative, tradition-bound fisherman, and its lack of industrial laborers." He reported that Hagi is known all over the nation for its adherence to the old ways. Furthermore, lack of a university and job opportunities in the area "takes away many of the mission's best prospects and is responsible for most of our membership loss which stands at twenty-five percent."[38]

It was for these and other reasons that the mission began to consider a station in one of the large cities. The likely choice for such a venture was Tokyo. First of all, most of the country people migrated there. In 1963 it became evident that about sixty people who had had at least some contact with the Yamaguchi churches were scattered over the city. Many of these were lonely, and few were attending church regularly. It was felt that this was adequate reason for the mission to be committed to a work there.[39]

The second reason for looking toward Tokyo was the education of the missionaries' children. It was felt that, as the families moved to and from furlough and from place to place within Japan, it would become more difficult for the children to maintain schooling in two languages. The Christian Academy in Japan offered the most appealing arrangement for junior high and high school levels especially. It was felt that the mission might even provide a hostel for all of its children who might someday need schooling there.[40]

The third reason for considering Tokyo was the possibility of joining forces with the Mennonite missions in Japan for evangelism in that city. It was felt that a cooperative effort on the part of the (Old) Mennonites, the General Conference Mennonites and the Brethren in Christ would conserve resources and make it easier to follow up those affiliated with the three groups. In addition, it was now generally recognized among the three that the big city was in itself a worthy target for evangelism and that there was potential there for much faster church growth than in the country areas.[41]

After returning from their furlough in 1961, the Books were placed in Tokyo for their second year of language study. They were asked by the mission to make contact with as many of the Yamaguchi people as possible. They telephoned and visited as they had time. During one three-month period they made twenty-six contacts. Sixteen Yamaguchi people assembled at the Tokyo airport to see the Graybills off for furlough. Meetings were called at other times at convenient places around the city.[42] When the Graybills returned from their furlough in 1963, they took up permanent residence in Tokyo suburb of Koganei, continued the cooperative effort of the three missions for a time, and began pioneer evangelism in their own area.

Training and Outreach

In its concern for evangelism and the nurture of believers, the mission embarked on some special projects that were to have far-reaching significance. One of these was in the area of training the Japanese believers. Pete's concern was that laymen have the opportunity to prepare for leadership in the church while remaining active members of their society. He had long dreamed of a special school that would provide such training.

One day he was approached by a young lady, Noriko Matsuura, who had wanted to go away to Bible school but for whom the doors had seemed to close. She suggested that a school be started in Hagi and offered to become the first applicant. The "opening ceremonies" for the Christian Evangelism School were held on Easter Sunday afternoon in 1961. The first class session was on April 7 with five students enrolled. Two discontinued soon after the school began, but Matsuura and two others, Hajime Onimura and Seiko Sugiyama, completed two years of study. In 1963 a new class of seven enrolled: Masaharu Okano, Kikumi Onimura, Kimiko Ueda, Michiko Furuya, Tasuko Yoshinaka, Hosaku Yamane and Emine Katsura. Five of these completed one year of study in March 1964, at which time the Willmses went on a six-month furlough.[43]

Classes met every Friday evening for three hours. Since discussion often continued much later, and since transportation was not available for those going to Nagato, all the students stayed overnight in the Willmses' house. They had morning worship together, ate breakfast together, and then left for their jobs and respective duties. Times of intimate sharing together, often until the early morning hours, were very meaningful to the students. They opened their hearts to one another in confession and expressions of burdens for their families and fellow workers. A survey course took them through the entire Bible. Other courses filled out the term of study. Upon the return of the Willmses from their short furlough, thirteen students enrolled for a semester during the winter and spring of 1965. Ten of these completed the course.[44]

The effort was a highly successful attempt at theological education at the local level. Most of those enrolled in the first two years became strong leaders of the churches and enthusiastic supporters of lay witness principles.

Several other special projects involved outreach. The first of these was summer camps for young people. The first camp was planned for high schoolers on August 13, 1955. An old, abandoned hospital along the river in Kawakami eight miles from Hagi was scrubbed from top to bottom for the event. Then the blow fell. Teachers would not give permission to their students to attend the camp. Since the Japanese schools had full authority over their students, even during summer vacation, the students had to comply. It was discovered too late that the opposition came from one disgruntled teacher.

Evangelist Hashimoto arrived, and it was decided to have special meetings for everybody in the mission home. The junior high camp followed without opposition. However, a typhoon struck with torrents of rain, and the campers were soon marooned inside the leaky building by the flooded river. A boat which had been used to ferry supplies to the campsite was in danger of being swept away. Doyle Book and a teacher friend had to rescue it by swimming with it across part of the swollen river. The campers had a wonderful time and were almost disappointed when the sun broke through on the final day. Several decisions were made during the camp that were to bear lasting fruit for the Kingdom.[45]

Youth camps became a yearly event. The school opposition was gradually overcome. Japanese evangelists were called in to serve each time. In 1959, twenty-five high school students met in the Kawakami public hall, sleeping on wood floors with only a blanket spread underneath. Four were later baptized. The following year twenty-four attended the junior high camp and twenty-six joined the high school camp. Many made decisions, and eight were baptized soon after. Three out of five baptisms in Hagi during 1962 were the direct result of the summer camps.[46] Several of the future leaders of the Yamaguchi churches made decisions for Christ during those early camp efforts.

Another special outreach project was radio. On February 14, 1958, "one of the greatest events in the history of our Japan mission and church took place." The gospel broadcast "Good News" was sent out over the air from Hagi for the first time. The weekly broadcast of thirty minutes featured "high quality Christian music, vibrant testimonies and appealing gospel messages." The messages were usually provided by Rev. Akira Hatori, a well-known Japanese evangelist. The programs were produced by the Tokyo-based Pacific Broadcasting Association and utilized a team of Japanese artists and technicians.[47]

Responses from the general public were few during the first year, but the broadcast brought great encouragement to the Christians. From 1960, followup was left to the Pacific Broadcasting Association offices, and listeners were directed to respond to that address. PBA supplied correspondence courses and other materials to those who wrote in. PBA recorded 187 responses from the Yamaguchi area during December 1962. The previous high was 57 in August of that year. It was determined that the cost of reaching one person with a fifteen-minute gospel broadcast was about one-fourth cent. This meant that radio was the least expensive method of seed-sowing.[48]

The broadcast tapes were often used in the Hagi and Nagato area fellowships for the benefit of those who could not hear the program on the air. This practice continued even after the broadcast was changed in 1965 to the fifteen-minute "Light of the World" and was aired from Yamaguchi City across the mountains. The tapes were sent to Hagi or Nagato and were returned to Tokyo after use there.

In 1966 the mission discontinued direct sponsorship of a local broadcast in favor of supporting a nationwide, daily broadcast arranged by PBA through area stations. The amount of support was initially 80,000 yen a month. This was decreased over the years to the amount of 20,000 yen.[49] Seiichiro Aburatani recorded 2,150 total responses which were forwarded to Hagi from PBA during the period from December 1, 1962, to January 31, 1970.[50] Many of those responding were supplied with Bibles and study materials, and some decisions were recorded.

The third special outreach project was the Christian bookstore. This project was another long-standing dream of Pete's. The store opened at noon on December 23, 1960, at the busiest corner of downtown Hagi. The location had been a liquor store. It was now "converted" to display free tracts outside and Bibles, song books, Christian greeting cards and calendars inside. The mission did not expect the store to make a profit, but considered the venture another seed-sowing opportunity.[51]

The store opening was made possible by an offering from Christ's Crusaders, the youth organization of the American church. The mission responded with joy to the splendid gift and the prayers of many which followed it. The gift covered total operations for one year and rent for the second year.[52] Emine Katsura was asked to take charge of the store, and some training for the task was financed by the mission. Mr. Jihichi Oba and Miss Yaeko Kaneshige assisted on a part-time basis. High rent costs forced the move of the store from Tamachi to Yoshida-cho the following year. It was later moved to Omotomachi, across the street from the present Hagi church location. It finally found its home in the upstairs of the church on June 10, 1967.[53]

The mission moved to place the control of the store in the hands of the national church as soon as possible. This was effected in 1970. However, the churches felt that they could not support it financially. A meeting of representatives of the mission and the various churches was held on March 21, 1970. Stock was offered to the churches at a discount and some materials were donated for evangelism. The remaining stock was disposed of by the Jordan Press.[54]

Inter-Mission Cooperation

In addition to programs which related directly to church planting and nurture, the mission also participated in various co-operative efforts with others. Most of these efforts involved the other Mennonite missions. Some of them reflected broader, ecumenical concerns and included attempts to reconcile the exteme theological positions among missionaries in Japan. The Mennonite-related missionaries, sensing a need for fellowship and understanding of each other's work, formed the Japan Mennonite Fellowship in January 1954, with an initial meeting in Osaka. This led to other "All-Mennonite" fellowships in Kyushu in 1956, Hokkaido in 1957, and Osaka once again in 1959.

The fellowships, in turn, gave rise to a variety of cooperative ventures. Some of these were directly related to the Mennonite Central Committee work which was led by Norman and Eunice Wingert. The Wingerts were Brethren in Christ who had moved the MCC work from Osaka to Tokyo in September of 1954. On one occasion, the MCC supplied the Hagi mission with surplus food packages for distribution to the needy. This distribution resulted in the salvation of Mrs. Hisako Yamazaki, whose story has already been told.[55] The MCC also offered Dr. Melvin Gingrich and Dr. Paul Peachey to the Japan missions as resource people for lectures and conferences on Anabaptism and the peace position.[56] Under the auspices of the Japan Mennonite Fellowship, a number of books of Anabaptist orientation were translated and published in Japanese. These included *These Are My People, Not Regina,* and *Coals of Fire.* Plans were made to establish a Mennonite paper. Thelma Book was appointed by the mission to the literature committee and served as secretary for the group.[57]

The Japan mission promoted the peace position of the Brethren in Christ Church in its nurture of the churches. This fact stands in clear opposition to an article that appeared in the *Visitor* following the General Conference of 1978. The article stated: ". . . the teaching of non-resistance has not been a distinct part of the initial message of BIC missions."[58] This is incorrect in the case of Japan.

The Doyle Books arrived in Hagi two years after the mission began for the express purpose of giving a witness against war and the Christian's participation in it. Doyle shared his testimony with the churches and with non-Christians in numerous appearances in schools. His two years of service "in the name of Christ" received many favorable comments from school principals and teachers. Melvin Gingrich visited the Yamaguchi churches for the purpose of correlating the peace message with other aspects of the gospel witness. His lectures found waiting hearts in the believers, who were still hurting from the memories of the recent war.[59] Paul Peachey made various contributions to the mission and the churches. These included an appearance at one of the summer camps.[60] He also brought into being, with the special support of the Brethren in Christ, the yearly Hayama Seminar, a study conference that brought together many missionary men from both the "evangelical" and "liberal" positions. This seminar was the means of bringing people together from the two camps for the purpose of dialogue. The topic for the first conference in 1960 was "Ministry of Reconciliation in a World of Conflict." In 1963 the group considered "Christian Discipleship."

In addition, the mission helped promote a peace seminar for Japanese pastors in Yamaguchi in December 1962. Pete and Doyle took several of the Hagi and Nagato leaders to the meeting which represented many denominations. Yamaguchi church leaders were also a part of the Japan MCC Consulting Committee and attended the Anabaptist Seminar in Osaka in 1964.[61]

The Brethren in Christ Mission hosted the All-Mennonite Fellowship in October 1960. The facilities of the Otani Sanso, a resort hotel near Nagato, were secured for the record attendance of forty-eight adults from the four missions. The speaker for the conference was Dr. C. N. Hostetter, Jr. He proved to be "a suitable 'doctor' for the tired bodies and discouraged spirits of the missionaries." They were inspired by his messages on "The Miraculous Christ." A spirit of oneness and melting together characterized the conference. Some of the visitors remarked that this conference was the high point in the series to date. The Graybills expressed their personal delight at having " 'the man of God' put his own two feet" under their family table. They declared that Hostetter had injected new life and spiritual encouragement into their spiritual veins.[62]

Voluntary Service

Without question, one of the most significant methods of witness used in the Japan mission was the teaching of English. The personnel for this program came from voluntary service people, who placed the support of the mission effort above their own personal ambitions for a period of two or three years.

As each of the missionaries arrived in Japan, they soon became aware of the intense interest on the part of the Japanese in learning English. They saw that this interest lay particularly in the area of conversation. Japanese students began to study English in the first year of junior high school. English was also required of them each year after that until they graduated from high school.

A certain measure of proficiency in the language was necessary in order to qualify for university entrance. However, learning English was approached almost entirely through memorization and translation. As travel and business opportunities increased, people became interested in spoken English. Thus whenever a "native speaker" appeared, he or she was deluged with requests for practice in conversation.

Pete Willms had more than enough requests. He could not fill them all and still be effective in his evangelistic work. Doyle Book came to relieve the missionary of this pressure. He was involved in approximately thirty hours each week of classroom instruction in local schools and private classes. In addition, he was asked to coach many students on both the junior high and high school levels in preparation for district recitation and speech contests. He was once invited to accompany two Hagi girls and their teachers to Tokyo for a national contest. For a newcomer, this was an exciting trip which included Japanese inns and food. It included also the privilege of sitting near the Crown Prince at a reception in honor of all the contestants.

Doyle also occasionally attended meetings for educational leaders. On one occasion he was part of the group that welcomed the United States Information Service chief to Hagi. The official, hearing of Book's purpose in coming to Japan, commented, "This kind of service has the potential to create much goodwill between the United States and Japan." The English teacher's presence in Hagi also helped to draw many students to the church services. It likewise encouraged the growth of a girls' Bible class, which was taught by Thelma and which bore much fruit in decisions for Christ.[63]

Edna Wingerd's contribution to the mission was also "voluntary service." However, she was busy as teacher for the missionaries' children and thus did not get deeply involved in an English teaching program. Therefore, after Doyle's 1-W service was completed, the missionaries once again had to reject many of the requests for English which came their way until voluntary service assignments for teaching English were inaugurated in 1967. At this time, J. Andrew Stoner joined the Graybills in Tokyo for a term of two years.

John Graybill described the teaching of English conversation as one of the most effective doors to witness. With Andy Stoner's arrival, he said, the potential of the missionary's ministry was greatly enlarged. Andy soon had a full schedule of classes. Small classes of five to eight people were held in or near the Graybill home and included neighbors, company people and church friends. He also taught some classes of forty-five to sixty people in downtown English centers. The mission had long before given up the idea of trying to render this service without compensation. Not charging for the classes meant that people would bring gifts, some of them out of proportion to the service rendered and some of them useless. Appropriate fees were established for the classes, and Andy more than paid for his living costs during the two years.[64]

At this time plans were being made to purchase land in Nishiichi and to build a residence for the Zooks. The Women's Missionary Prayer Circle contributed to the cost of the residence, but funds were still needed to pay for the land. The mission decided that Andy Stoner's surplus earnings should go to the purchase of the Nishiichi mission land. They also designated some of the funds for the remodelling of a house for the Books in Shimonoseki. The combined cost of the two projects was $3,500.[65]

As his term drew to a close, Andy offered several suggestions for a voluntary service policy for the future. One of these was that there be "an open policy toward indefinite expansion of the VS work in Japan." He suggested that, if the financial policy were revised somewhat, many couples as well as single people would undoubtedly volunteer to come to Japan. This would mean a "greater increase in contacts, more help for the missionary, fellowship for the VS people involved and, of course, much more income for the mission at no additional outlay of mission funds.[66] The suggestion was almost prophetic. The results suggested were to be fully realized during the next ten years.

Timothy and Nancy Botts took Andy Stoner's place in September 1969 and became the first VS couple in Tokyo. Because of the success of Andy's service, the mission decided to buy a small piece of land next to the Graybill residence at Kodaira and erect a VS building with a garage and classroom below and an apartment above. It was thought also that the downstairs part might some day be expanded to provide facilities for a new church. The building of the apartment was supervised by John Graybill and was completed in February 1970.[67] The number of classes taught by Tim and Nancy increased rapidly. The couple became a much appreciated addition to the Koganei church fellowship for their term of three years. Baby Andy was born to them during their stay in Japan and quickly became a favorite of the church people and the Graybills as well as the parents themselves.

Dwight and Carol Thomas arrived in Japan in September 1971, just one year after the Bottses. Following three months of language study in Tokyo, they joined the Books in Shimonoseki to set up a full program of English teaching. The Books secured a house for the Thomases and helped them organize the program.

The Thomases were willing workers, and in a short time were scheduled in Shimonoseki for a total of eighteen classes involving thirty-five class hours and 143 students. In addition to this heavy schedule, they took on five more classes in Nishiichi and its vicinity, under the supervision of the Zooks. These classes totaled thirty-five students. They also began an English meeting in their home with the purpose of sharing the Christian faith. They hoped that the fellowship would form a bridge to encourage students to attend the English and Japanese services at the Yamanota church.[68]

Other VS personnel followed these pioneers in rapid succession, as Andy Stoner had hoped. Rosalind Tarnowsky came as a tourist but offered herself for nine months of service in October 1972. Michael Graybill, John and Lucille's oldest son, offered himself with his wife, Holly, for service from July 1973 to July 1977. Beth Bearss arrived in August 1975 for a two-year term. Miriam Bowers offered herself to the mission in September 1977 after retiring from her position as librarian at Messiah College. She stayed for three years. Jay Smith served from October 1977 to July 1979. And in 1980 Mary Brubaker, Connie Lofthouse and Dora Myers arrived in Tokyo to help Marlin and Ruth Zook open a new English and evangelism center in the city of Fuchu.

Spiritual Contributions

The VSers made contributions to the mission and church in ways other than teaching English. Tim Botts used his skills in art to design a promotional pamphlet for a church member and to serve the Christian Academy in Japan as art teacher. Tim and Nancy together provided a Christian fellowship meeting in English in their home. One of those who attended became a Christian. They were approached on numerous occasions by their students with questions about the Christian faith.[69] Dwight Thomas provided times of hymn singing for the Shimonoseki church and gave guitar lessons to the Sunday evening participants at Nishiichi. On two Sundays each month, he and Carol traveled to the coast to Takibe, Nagato, or Hagi to fellowship with the believers and offer encouragement by their presence. They invited the youth of the Shimonoseki church on occasional hikes and picnics. They saw the potential of the Japanese youth and tried to draw them into the Christian church. Carol lightened Thelma Book's load considerably by teaching Charity one of her subjects.[70]

The volunteers testified to their own spiritual enrichment and cultural benefit during their service in Japan. Stoner listed as benefits the awareness that he was doing something important as a person in his own right, the satisfaction that his service was not less spiritual than other kinds of ministry, the opportunity to travel widely in other Asian countries, the satisfaction of seeing something tangible result from his labors—the Nishiichi property, and the certainty that he was *not* called to missions!

Bottses spoke of gaining an appreciation for the ways of others, experiencing the thrill of seeing Jesus Christ fill the empty place in the life of a person of a different cultural background and the acquiring of a heart for missions. Thomases indicated that they are now able to accept differences in people, that isolation made them draw closer together, and that they felt fulfilled in having set the missionary free to use his time in more direct evangelism. Miriam Bowers noted the delight of getting acquainted with some of the Japanese arts, the benefit of being asked, "What does it mean to believe" and having to rethink her Christian faith, the renewed appreciation for corporate worship through not being able to understand the church services, and the realization that she more than paid for her own support.[71]

There were common frustrations: not being able to communicate to the heart hunger of their students in the Japanese language, feeling that they were expected to be a missionary at times and "less than a missionary" at others, and the lack of assurance that they had made a significant contribution to the life of the churches.

John Graybill once estimated that more than six percent of the members in the Tokyo churches came to the Lord because of the witness of English teaching.[72] Many of the volunteer service personnel expressed their feeling that they had not been able directly to influence souls to become Christians. But they sowed many seeds. And the final story is not yet written.

Chapter Seven

The Emerging Church

The "back" coast of Yamaguchi Prefecture was considered "country" by all the residents of southwestern Honshu. Most of the people who lived along this part of the Japan Sea coast were involved in activities related to farming, fishing or lumber. Hagi and Nagato were the only large towns along the Yamaguchi coastline as far as Shimonoseki, the meeting point of the transportation arteries of Honshu's two sides and the gateway to Kyushu. In addition to being called "country," the area was also known as the "dark" side of the prefecture. It was distinguished from the "sunny" side by the term "*San-in*" which meant "in the shadow of the mountains." It was no doubt designated in this way because of the forested range which separated it from the eastern side where the morning sun first shone each day.

However, so far as the Japanese were concerned, the term also applied to the weather. The Hagi area was said to be more cloudy and gloomy during some parts of the year than the "*Sanyo*" side where the large industrial cities were located. Some of the missionaries were skeptical about this until they had occasion to make trips from one side of the island to the other on the same day. They discovered that, although the weather might be bright and clear in Ogori or Yamaguchi City, at the same time it was, in fact, "shady" on the side where they lived.

To the missionaries, the term "shady" took on another meaning also. It signified a spiritual darkness. They realized that the area to which God had called them was one of the most difficult in which to work. The people seemed entrenched in their traditional communities and ways of thinking. Although gracious to the foreigners, they seemed unwilling to leave behind the religious atmosphere in which they had been reared. Pete once admitted to the board that things had not happened quite as they had discussed together. He hoped that the people back home could be confident that the missionaries had nevertheless been "moving with God." He noted that God does not force himself upon anyone. He affirmed that, although God's purpose for Hagi was not being fulfilled in the hearts of the hundreds, or even the dozens, it was being fulfilled in the ones and the two's.[1]

The *San-in* coast of Yamaguchi Prefecture did indeed seem dark. Yet it was along this coast that little lights began to appear. These were the churches of the Brethren in Christ.

Hagi

We have already traced many of the early events of the Hagi church. The meetings of the church moved from the rented store on Hashimoto to the missionaries' residence on Tokaichi Street. However, following Mary Willms's hospitalization in 1957, it became evident that the church would need to find another place for its activities. The house would need to be kept quiet and free from unnecessary callers for the sake of Mary's recuperation. In October 1957 the church moved to the home of Jihichi Oba, handyman and eel fisherman, in the Imaguru-Hagi section of town. It remained there until early 1959 when the Graybills came to Hagi in order to allow the Books three months language study. It was then decided to move the meetings once again to a much larger and more conveniently located house on Watariguchi Street. Mr. and Mrs. Ichikawa moved into the rented building to serve as caretakers.

At about the same time, the church people decided to purchase a plot of ground in the same area as Oba's house. They recognized that the location was not very convenient for a church building, but they felt that having a reasonably priced site on which they could build would provide a measure of security. They purchased the lot with John Graybill's help in March of that year.[2] Two years later a far superior location became available on the main street which led south to Hagi station. A two-story structure stood on the site, and there was an open piece of land behind the building large enough for games like volleyball. The former lot was sold and the new location was purchased in June 1961. The lower floor was remodeled into a chapel, and the church formally opened the new worship center in August with a week of meetings led by Christian and Missionary Alliance evangelist Suteichi Oe. The Brethren in Christ had purchased their first church building in the land of Japan.[3]

Henry Hostetter and Carl Ulery were present for the final payment on the property in October. Hostetter was impressed with the way the transaction was carried out. The purchaser did not negotiate directly with the seller but used a middleman to carry on the dialogue. This position was supplied by church member Oba. The board members accompanied him and Pete to the bank. They were "served cups of green tea and chatted with the banker." The money which the board had sent earlier was released in yen—one million twenty thousand in cash! The bills make a stack "six or seven inches high."

At the church building once again, the church representatives seated themselves on the *tatami* in a circle with the seller and the mission members. All necessary papers had previously been signed. After tea and various bits of conversation, the middleman placed the stack of money on the table. The seller counted the money and then wrapped it in his *furoshiki*, the ever-present, all-purpose carrying cloth, which he tied by its four corners. He then departed with the bundle of cash to his destination, and the transaction was complete.[4]

Anticipating the legal implications of holding property and the likelihood of future expansion, the mission had taken steps two years earlier to incorporate as a religious juridical body. The process was accomplished by Doyle

Book and Jihichi Oba, who had served as negotiator, then with the prefectural authorities. On November 30, 1959, the incorporation of the "Japan Brethren in Christ Church" was officially registered at the Hagi Law Office. Doyle Book was listed as the chairman of the incorporation and Oba, Hajime Kaneshige, Seiichiro Aburatani and Koichiro Sugiyama were verified as officers.[5]

There was good growth in the early years of the church. At the end of 1956, there were fourteen baptized members in the fellowship. Five were added in 1957 and six the following year. The year 1959 saw fifteen take the step of baptism and fourteen more followed the Lord in 1960.[6] These memorable occasions were observed on the bank of the nearby Matsumoto River or else on the beach near Shizuki Park.

However, they were not always without some unexpected event. Just as one service began—at the exact moment, the account states—"strong winds blew suddenly in from darkened skies and torrents of rain followed." The group consulted, finished the first part of the service under a nearby shelter and consulted again. The new Christians declared they were ready to be baptized, rain or no rain. The witnesses agreed to continuing the service. "The wind stopped but the rain fell hard. A few had umbrellas. Those in the water needed none!" The believers shared in a gracious time of communion later that morning in the mission residence.[7]

Several outreach projects of the church involved literature. In October 1959 ten church people "invaded" the Shoin Shrine festival with pockets full of tracts. Six of them moved among the hundreds of people on the shrine grounds while four went downtown "to encounter the milling crowds of visitors and sightseers." A few of those who received the tracts later sent in the cards which had been enclosed, and one man began attending the church. One month later the Christians set up literature tables for the passers-by headed to another shrine festival. This "booth" arrangement had already become a yearly affair. A few Bibles were sold and thousands of tracts were passed out. The Christians were encouraged by their involvement in such a direct witness.[8]

In 1961 the Sunday School Commission of the American church gave $2,325 for various literature projects. The missionaries were delighted with the funds, which allowed projects that had previously been impossible. They felt "like children let loose in a toy store or candy store!" They designated $600 for Bible portions to be distributed door to door. Two hundred dollars went for two thousand English-Japanese New Testaments for junior high and high schools. Five hundred dollars provided one hundred fifty sets of colorful Moody Bible Story Books for primary and junior high school libraries. Two hundred one-year subscriptions to *Gospel for the Millions* were placed in banks, barber shops, doctors' offices and hospitals for $300. The rest of the money was used for some basic material for the Hagi and Nagato churches and for miscellaneous projects.[9]

The Hagi people showed their support for the Mennonite Central Committee by participating in its work camps on two occasions. In the summer of 1960, Mr. Hajime Kaneshige accompanied John Graybill from Nagato to

Korea for two weeks. In August 1970 Mr. Kiyoshi Fujita and Miss Akiko Yamamoto traveled to Hong Kong for a similar project.[10]

The Willmses served the Hagi church during their second term from 1959 to 1964. When they went on their second furlough, the Zooks left language school and moved into the Hagi residence for one year. During these years younger leaders began to emerge in the church. One of these was a clerk of the local electric power company named Hajime Onimura. Onimura passed by the front of the Tokaichi residence/church on Sunday in the fall of 1955. He opened the *genkan* door but hesitated there. Miss Kanakubo invited him into the service. He appeared occasionally during the next few months, always expressionless and saying very little.

In April 1956 Takashi Yamada stopped in Hagi on his way to Miyazaki, Kyushu, where he was to begin pastoral work with the General Conference Mennonites. He had recently given up a high-salaried position with a company in Kobe and had entered Bible school to prepare for the ministry. He held five days of meetings in Hagi, his first evangelistic experience. The Spirit of God moved mightily in the services and life-changing decisions were made. One of those decisions was by Onimura. He had previously begun to grasp the idea of God and salvation, but the Cross was incomprehensible for him. Now he understood "that head knowledge could not bring salvation, but only the work of God's Son on the Cross." He was baptized in September 1957 and became a strong leader for the church.[11]

Onimura was married to Yaeko Kaneshige in May 1961 and took her family name. This was a perfectly acceptable arrangement in Japanese culture. Such an arrangement was usually made when the girl's parents wanted a son who would bear the family name. In the marriage proceedings the man was, in a sense, adopted into the family. In the case of the Kaneshiges there was a different reason for the young man to take the girl's name. Onimura meant "devil's village." The young people decided this would not be a suitable name for a Christian home. They also wanted their children to avoid the teasing Hajime had received as a youngster. The Kaneshige wedding was the first Christian wedding in the Hagi church.

With Kaneshige, Goro Shibata and his wife, Yaeko, also moved into a position of leadership in the Hagi church. Shibata's story is one of simple faith and a series of miracles. The story has been told in detail in *Firewood Field of Japan*.[12] Another young man who was to share leadership with the older Shibata in later years was Masaharu Okano. He had been hospitalized with tuberculosis as a high school student in 1957. After his recovery he began attending a Bible class at the Hagi church. He made a decision for Christ in one of the summer camps and was baptized in August 1959. He received a position as a clerk in a Hagi bank. He joined the little Bible school taught by Pete Willms in 1963. There he developed into leadership material. Okano was deeply moved as the group talked intimately about things they could not say in a public church service. He was impressed that, even if they were wrong on some ideas, Pete never scolded them but rather encouraged them to further prayer and Bible study. Okano was later married to Kikumi Onimura,

Hajime's younger sister, and the two formed one of Hagi's few dedicated Christian homes.[13]

Attendance held up well during Willmses' 1964 absence for furlough. Offerings increased seventeen percent. A large amount of the offerings was channeled into outreach,[14] but the debt on the church building also shrank rapidly. Under Kaneshige's leadership the church grew also in inner strength. There were thoughts of dividing the group and beginning a church in another part of the city. It was planned that Kaneshige would lead this group. But he was suddenly asked by his company to move to Yamaguchi City. The move meant a substantial promotion. The church people realized that God would undoubtedly use the Kaneshiges in that city also, but their spirits sagged at the thought of losing such a strong family.[15] The church recovered from the disappointment, and Goro Shibata was officially appointed lay minister for the group.[16]

After one year back in Hagi, the Willmses also moved to Yamaguchi in October 1966. This was a realization of Pete's longstanding hope to begin working among university students in the prefectural capital. The mission house on Tokaichi Street was sold. The Willmses' move meant another difficult adjustment for the Hagi church. However, for some time Pete returned to Hagi each Sunday to share in the worship service. Seiichiro Aburatani again assisted in the leadership of the church and Okano was recognized as another leader.

In 1967 Shibata performed a baptismal service for the first time. Pete was delighted with this sign of indigenous strength. In 1968 Pete's visits to the church decreased as his contacts in Yamaguchi grew. The church began a children's meeting in the Matsubara home in Ezaki with Miss Chisako Arita in charge. But Arita soon married a young Mennonite pastor and moved to Hokkaido. Other members of the church moved away because of marriage and jobs. Still others left in favor of the more formal, professionally pastored congregation on Tamachi Street.[17]

The Hagi church seemed to lose much of its strength. Then the Willmses, on furlough in America in 1969, decided not to return to Japan. They felt that God was leading them into another important ministry. The Hagi church was extremely disappointed, even to the point of shock. However, with the encouragement of regular visits from Marlin Zook, who was now living in Nishiichi, and with the dedication of the aging Shibata and a very busy Okano, the little group bravely carried on. Mr. Kiyoshi Fujita and Mr. Toshiharu Igeta also began to assist in the responsibilities of the church. The twentieth anniversary of the work in Japan saw more than one hundred former members of the Hagi church scattered all over Japan, many of them contributing their energies to other churches.[18]

Nagato

A two-week tent meeting in early August 1958 marked the beginning of the church in Nagato. The tent was pitched next to the train station in Senzaki, the part of town that harbored many commercial fishing boats and that led to the scenic island of Omi which lay at the tip of its peninsula. Tourism, a wholesale fish market, and *kamaboko*, a product of ground fish mixed with flour and baked over charcoal, were Senzaki's main industries.

The evangelist for the campaign was Tatsumi Hashimoto of Kobe. Pete Willms and Doyle Book pitched the tent with the help of Mr. Susumu Goto of Senzaki and some of the Hagi believers. Children's meetings were held in the afternoons. These were led by Noriko Matsuura and Yaeko Kaneshige of Hagi. Attendance at the evening services varied from thirty-five to sixty-five.

The campaign was beset with various difficulties. A typhoon threatened to sweep the tent off its moorings. Pete, Doyle and Goto spent several nights on beds made by pushing together several of the ten-inch-wide wooden benches which had been brought from Hagi. They were prepared to jump up and grab the tent ropes should the tent begin to fall. Water covered the ground underneath the benches. Toward the end of the meetings, Hashimoto preached a message on the cross of Jesus. At the climax of the message, a tremendous racket outside made hearing impossible. Several dogs fought each other with loud barks and growls. The commotion continued for some time. Later Hashimoto commented that there was almost always some kind of disturbance when he preached on the cross and the blood of Jesus.

In this setting a church was born. Twenty-seven people expressed an interest in the Christian faith.[19] Two of the seekers, Takashi and Shizue Takamura, opened their little house for follow-up meetings. The Willmses left on furlough, and Doyle Book began weekly Saturday visits to Senzaki from Hagi, thirty miles up the coast. The first meeting following the campaign was August 23, 1958. Forty people jammed the tiny room for the service. The Takamuras made a sign which they set outside the house each Saturday. The sign boldly proclaimed: "Senzaki Christian Church." The first baptisms were held exactly one year later. On August 30, 1959, four young people, Mr. Keijun Oka, Miss Shizuko Sugiyama and sisters Sachiyo and Kazuyo Nagata testified to faith in Christ in the blue waters near Omi Island. On September 6, Takashi Takamura and Miss Kiyo Yoshizu were also baptized.[20]

John and Lucille Graybill took responsibility for the Senzaki believers in the spring of 1960 when the Books went on furlough. The Graybills moved into the newly purchased residence in the Fukagawa section of the city. Two more baptismal services followed soon with the Misses Yoko Ishii, Miyako Onaka and Seiko Sugiyama testifying to their faith on August 18, and Mrs. Shizue Takamura and Mr. Susumu Goto on October 2.

The city of Nagato soon became aware of the Christian presence. The tent was pitched once more near the main Nagato station for a series of meetings which went from August 19 to 28. John placed news releases and advertisements in the local newspapers. Six thousand five hundred handbills were also inserted in the newspapers at delivery time. Posters were placed around town, and the Chevy Carryall was once more pressed into service with its loudspeaking system. Attendance averaged 82 adults each evening with a high of 115. Children overflowed the tent for their meetings which preceded that of the adults. They averaged 153 with a peak of 228. Evangelist Kogo's messages drew 66 people to express some kind of interest in the Christian faith.[21]

The presence of the Christians was also felt through the first public Christmas celebrated in Nagato. The town hall was secured for the occasion and announcements were spread all over town. One hundred ninety-four children flocked to the afternoon meeting. After the evening service, 80 adults and young people, both saved and unsaved, formed a procession and went caroling through the streets of the city.[22]

The Graybills returned to America for their first furlough in the summer of 1962. The Books replaced them in Nagato and remained there until they moved to Shimonoseki in 1969, with the exception of one year, 1966, when they were on furlough and the Zooks came to take their place. Growth was exceedingly slow during this time, chiefly because of the loss of many faithful members to the larger cities. John had warned of this unhappy trend while he was still in Nagato. The Books once reported an "unforgettable farewell party" for six of their eight faithful high school young people who went off to college.[23]

In spite of slow progress in numbers of Christians, the believers exhibited strength in leadership. Takashi Takamura assisted the missionaries despite conflicting schedules in his work as railroad engineer. Misses Toshiko Funaki, Miyako Onaka and Seiko Sugiyama were steady supporters and served as teachers. Mrs. Masako Ishii prayed, testified, and encouraged everyone. Miss Takeko Iwamoto developed in teaching and other leadership skills. She exhibited a marked degree of self-sacrifice as she went away to Bible school at her own expense and then returned to give herself to the church without pay for a period of three years. Asao Nishimura came to the Nagato church from Hagi, when he married one of the Nagato members, Kimiko Ueda, in May 1965. Nishimura, a schoolteacher, shared in leadership duties until Iwamoto was tragically drawn away by a pseudo-Christian cult, Swedenborgianism. He became the official lay minister of the church in 1971.

The church showed strength in other ways. Several members went away for short terms of Bible school training. Toshiko Funaki was one of these. The church in America, hearing of her venture of faith and that of Noriko Matsuura of Hagi, supplied some of the funds for their Bible school training.[24] In the summer of 1965, the church members conducted a children's vacation Bible school by themselves. The effort marked the first totally indigenous evangelistic effort of the Nagato church. It was carried out primarily through the encouragement and talents of Kenji and Kazuko Okuaki. This couple had been transferred from Tokyo to the fisheries co-operative in Senzaki for a period of two years. Their vibrant testimonies and concern for witness added much strength to the Nagato group.

The church also assumed full responsibility for the youth camp in August 1966. Earlier that same year, on March 19 and 20, they hosted the first deeper-life conference for the Yamaguchi churches in a nearby resort hotel. Sixty-seven adults registered for a time of heart searching and inspiration under the preaching of Suteichi Oe of the Christian and Missionary Alliance

Church. They sponsored a second similar conference two years later, when they invited evangelist Tsuneo Mandai to share on the work of the Holy Spirit in the life of the Christian.[25]

With the Books' move to Shimonoseki on April 1, 1969, the Nagato church purchased the mission residence.[26] Iwamoto lived in the new church facility until 1971, when she left the fellowship. The Nishimura family took up residence in the building in August of that year. The tiny church quickly recovered from the disappointment of Iwamoto's defection, and Nishimura and his wife served the church nobly even though the only other faithful male member, Takamura, eventually moved to the metropolis of Tokyo. Doyle Book continued serving the church from Shimonoseki on one Sunday each month, and in 1969 Marlin Zook began to assist the group from the new mission residence in Nishiichi.[27]

Takibe

Of all the Yamaguchi churches, Takibe began on what seemed to be the best footing. From the beginning there were several mature couples who formed the nucleus of the group, and several men well respected in the community volunteered to take over the leadership.

The Takibe witness began as an outreach from Nagato. In 1959 Akira Ehara was visiting his sister in Senzaki and was invited to the Saturday night meeting. There he met Doyle Book and became interested in his message. His work required him to move to Takibe, an hour down the coast by train. After Graybills arrived in Nagato, he asked John to come to Takibe and "teach Christianity." This request was followed with a visit by Ehara and Taro Akidomi to the 1960 Nagato Christmas program in the city hall. Another acquaintance of Ehara, Hiroto Okazaki, a teacher at Otsu High School in Nagato, met John in April of 1961. Monthly meetings were started in Takibe in July. They were held in the public Youth Hall near the center of town. Okazaki began attending the meetings in Nagato and Takibe with his wife Hideko.[28]

The group at Takibe was unique. It had strong indigenous church leaders before they had even become Christians! Ehara took it upon himself to invite his fellow townspeople to the meetings. Twelve to fifteen usually attended. Three of the men decided that they would be the "officials" of the group. They sold Bibles at the meetings and took up offerings. A fourth "deacon" was soon added. Mr. and Mrs. Okazaki approached John one day and expressed interest in baptism even though, they admitted, they knew nothing about it. John responded with a special series of meetings on that subject.[29]

The Graybills left the Takibe group in the care of the Books as they went on furlough in 1962. After each meeting was over, Doyle waited for the midnight train, as John had done, in the nearby home of the Eharas. The Graybills returned to Japan the following year to take up residence in Tokyo, but visited Takibe on the occasion of its first evangelistic meeting in August. Evangelist Oe spoke on the claims of the gospel for three nights. About sixty people assembled each night in the town hall auditorium. Among those who made decisions was Okazaki's twelve-year-old daughter.[30]

Takibe boasted no industry other than farming and some lumbering. The town was situated in the hills about fifteen miles from the coast and about midway between Nagato and Shimonoseki. The rural community's rice fields were irrigated by many small streams. There was no lake and no river suitable for swimming. Thus, when four candidates asked Doyle for baptism, the church group traveled to Agawa for a service beside the clear waters of its gently sloping beach. The service was held on December 1, 1963, with Mr. and Mrs. Okazaki, Mr. Tsutomu Kuboe and Miss Teruyo Yasumura declaring their faith in Jesus. Visitors from Nagato and Hagi joined in the celebration and the fellowship which followed. This was held in the home of Seiichiro Aburatani's mother which was located beside the beach. Marlin and Ruth Zook also were present for the occasion, having come to the country for their first visit from language school in Tokyo.[31]

In August 1964 another evangelistic meeting was held in the Agricultural Building auditorium. This time a seventy-three-year-old lady evangelist, Mrs. Matsuyama, shared the gospel with forty to fifty people on each of the three nights. A few made decisions for Christ and replaced those who had already moved away. Later Ehara and Akidomi dropped away from the fellowship. However, Tsutomu Kuboe began to exercise leadership along with the Okazakis. Mrs. Yoshiko Hatano was a constant help as were Mrs. Makiko Akidomi and Mrs. Yoshiko Masaoka. Another couple, Toshiaki and Emiko Arita, added steady support. In 1965 the group decided to meet on the first and third Saturday nights of each month in the rather old and drafty Youth Hall. In 1967 they began meeting every Saturday night in Kuboe's home. Doyle came regularly from Nagato to assist in the services.

In 1968 Akidomi became very ill. Through Doyle's witness and Billy Graham's book, *Peace With God*, he opened his heart to Christ. He died soon after in May. Even though he had not been attending the church with his wife for some time, his death was very hard on the church people.[32]

In November 1968, Kuboe married Setsuko Matoba. The couple provided good leadership for the group along with the Okazakis. On Easter Sunday, April 6, 1969, the church instituted a weekly Sunday morning service. The Books had just moved to Shimonoseki and attended the service from there. Doyle continued his visits to Takibe during the next year until the Shimonoseki work developed further. Marlin Zook also began serving the Takibe group from Nishiichi. One Sunday in May 1970, two of the Zooks' children, Elaine and Stephen, were dedicated to the Lord along with Kuboe's baby boy, Keichi.[33]

During the next four years attendance began to dwindle. The Kuboes moved to Kita Kyushu City. Mrs. Hatano moved with her husband to Tokyo. The meetings became sporadic and finally convened only on occasions when a special call went out.

Agawa

Through the efforts of Hagi's Aburatani, meetings were begun at his mother's home in Agawa on February 28, 1965. Doyle Book gave his help, coming from Nagato for the initial service and then attending on the fourth Sunday of every month. On each visit he presented the worship message and taught an English class in the afternoon. Mr. Aburatani made the train trip of one and a half hours every Sunday from Hagi. The Hagi church people gave their support, and Pete Willms traveled from Yamaguchi once a month to share in the service. Marlin Zook assisted the cell meeting from 1966, first from Nagato and then from Nishiichi. Except for Grandmother Aburatani, there were seldom local adults among the ten or more who attended the services. Then one day, Grandmother Aburatani was injured in a street accident and was hospitalized in Hagi for a long period of time. The Agawa meetings were finally suspended in May 1970.[34]

Yamaguchi

There were three main reasons for placing a missionary family in Yamaguchi City. First, Pete felt strongly that such a move would encourage the Hagi church toward the next step in its growth—it would learn to rely more on its own lay leadership than on the resident missionary. Second, there was a desire to evangelize university students, especially young men. One obvious result of winning young men to Christ would be the availability of Christian marriage partners for the young women of the country churches. There was a growing conviction also that winning college men was one of the keys to infiltrating the entire Japanese society with the gospel.[35] Third, Pete wanted to "practice what we preach" by earning money toward his support. He suggested that it was inconsistent for the mission to insist on self-supported lay ministers in the church when the "professional" missionaries were supported totally by the home church.[36]

The Willmses moved to Yamaguchi on October 21, 1966. Pete visited Hagi twice each month and assisted at Agawa occasionally. He also kept up the contacts at Susa and Ezaki on the Hagi coast. Many other contacts opened in the mountain areas and on the Sanyo side of the mountains, both for Bible studies and English classes. Pete was delighted to see that Hagi church leaders, as he had hoped, took more responsibility, especially in performing a baptism ceremony.[37] Pete and Mary rented a house on the outskirts of the city. The children, for the most part, made a good adjustment into the neighborhood school.

Pete and Mary accepted teaching positions in several high schools and on the new campus of Yamaguchi University. With these appointments they were able to contribute about $200 each quarter to their support. Pete taught an English class in a large chemical plant in Hofu. He also rented an office space in downtown Yamaguchi and made himself available for discussions with students and teachers. He provided literature and Bibles for those who were interested. There were numerous witness opportunities both in the office and on campus among students who were "untouched by church-building-centered evangelism."[38]

The Kaneshiges began Christian meetings in their home after they moved from Hagi in 1964. In 1969 they invited Thelma Book from Shimonoseki to teach one of these meetings, a ladies' Bible class. As time went on, however, the family became more and more involved in a nearby church. At last, the Kaneshige family became members of the church and contributed much strength to it.

The Willmses left on what was to be a short furlough in 1969. But they decided not to return to Japan after a call came to serve as pastor among the students at Messiah College. The decision was an extremely difficult one. It was made only after much soul searching. In the absence of the Willmses, the mission had no personnel who could pick up the new work in Yamaguchi. As a result the residence there was closed in 1970.

Nishiichi

Since the Willmses had moved away from Hagi in 1966 and the Books were planning to turn over the Nagato work and residence to its leaders in 1969, the mission felt that it should provide someone who would be available to all the country churches. The churches themselves desired such a resource person, especially in the area of Bible and leadership training. The mission felt that Marlin Zook, with his seminary degree, was the best qualified for this kind of ministry. They thus decided to try to find a location for the Zooks that would serve Hagi, Nagato, Agawa and Takibe, that would not be in any town where a church already existed, and that would allow the possibility of planting a new church.[39]

The Zooks returned from furlough to more language study in Tokyo in 1968. In January 1969 they took up temporary residence in Yamaguchi City with the purpose of trying to find a suitable location for the new mission station. Oda and Shuho were considered. A Takibe member, however, found a place to rent in Nishiichi. A study showed that Nishiichi was closer to more of the coastal locations than either Oda or Shuho. Furthermore, nothing had opened up in either of the two latter locations.[40] The Zooks moved into the rented house in April 1969 and began to make plans for buying land and building a residence. This project was completed in the fall through funds supplied by Andy Stoner's English earnings and by the Women's Missionary Prayer Circle in America.[41] The new Nichiichi house was dedicated in February of 1970.

Nishiichi was an agricultural center nestled midway between the two coastlines of the prefecture. It was a strongly Buddhist area, and there was a strong homogeneous unit mentality among its own inhabitants. The people on one side of its river considered themselves the "Hagi Group" and those on the other side were proud to be the "Chofu Group." The townspeople were friendly but did not accept strangers into the inner circle of the society. Watchmaker Haruyama, who was later baptized, said that it took him ten years to be accepted, even as a Japanese. The population of Nishiichi had decreased ten percent in nine years as the people moved toward Shimonoseki and other cities which offered more conveniences.[42]

The Zooks were busy making contacts with the existing churches and conducting English classes, a Sunday night Bible study in their home and a cooking class. Marlin served as visiting lecturer in English at the Shimonoseki City College.[43] Ruth offered cooking classes in Hagi and Nagato and later in Shimonoseki and Takibe. Although her class in Nishiichi was well-attended, little interest was shown by the ladies in the gospel message. The Sunday night Bible study averaged ten to fifteen in attendance, but most of these were students. Haruyama was baptized on April 22, 1973. He was the only one to take that step during the ten years of the mission station. However, he also dropped away from the fellowship later, and a student meeting was all that remained. The coastal churches, however, were much encouraged by the Zooks' ministry. The Hagi leaders, in particular, discouraged over the Willmses' decision not to return, enjoyed close fellowship with Marlin and were encouraged to press on with the work of the church by his help.[44]

Marlin was appointed by the mission to be the *madoguchi*—"open window" or liaison person—between the churches and the mission and board.[45]

The Zooks went on furlough in 1979 and returned to Tokyo the following year in order to place the children in the Christian Academy in Japan and to open a new work in Fuchu. The mission sold the Nishiichi property.

Shimonoseki

The Books bade farewell to Nagato after their seven-year stay and moved to Shimonoseki on April 1, 1969. The work there, however, had begun long before that time. Shimonoseki was one of the larger cities that received part of the exodus from the country areas. It also produced some of the responses to the radio broadcast. While Nagato was a planned, evangelistic thrust into a new and unknown area, Shimonoseki began from an attempt to conserve believers from the country and to follow up radio responses. Several young ladies who once were a part of the Hagi fellowship had married and moved to Shimonoseki. Among these were Yukiko Yamamoto, Mitsuko Kato and Michiko Kaneko.[46] Yoshiko Matsuo, later to become Kimoto, was commuting from Takibe to work in a large Shimonoseki department store. After marrying, she took up residence in the city.

Pete maintained contact with the Hagi people. Several times Doyle accompanied Pete in calling on them. On February 25, 1963, a meeting was held in the Kato home. Doyle was then asked to take responsibility for the contacts. He continued the meetings from Nagato.[47] A room was rented in the Labor Hall, and invitations to the meetings were sent to the radio responses in the area. In order to appeal to the radio listeners, the gathering was called "Good News Meeting," after the radio program.

Miss Matsuo invited Mr. Mariya Nagai to the meeting. Nagai worked with her in the department store. Although Nagai was already a member of a nearby church, he attended the meetings faithfully and invited Mrs. Setsuko Abe, a fashion designer who also worked in the store. The cell meeting averaged only six to ten in attendance, but its influence reached many more who came occasionally. Part of its influence was to "lonely and tired Christians." In 1965, the meeting was moved from the Labor Hall to Setsuko Abe's home. Abe posted a sign outside her front door which announced, "Good News Meeting." Doyle reported to the mission that there was "a great potential in Shimonoseki, but it is almost impossible to do the visitation and follow-up from Nagato." He recommended that the mission consider placing a resident missionary in Shimonoseki.[48]

Mrs. Abe was deeply impressed with the Christian teaching, but could not understand the conversion experience. She "followed" the Books of California on their furlough in 1966 and there "opened her heart's door to the One who had been standing outside, knocking."[49] She returned to Japan a totally changed person and, with Nagai, gave strong leadership to the cell meeting.

After moving to Shimonoseki, the Books lived for three months in a small house hidden in the crowded Sakurayama neighborhood. On July 1st they moved into a house which had been found for them by Kyosuke Yoshioka, Mrs. Abe's uncle, a medical doctor. The house was located in Yamanota, a bustling commercial and residential area on the northern outskirts of the city. Through Yamanota passed the highway and the rail line that led up the back coast toward Takibe and Nagato.

During his first year in the city, Doyle taught English classes at a girls' high school and college, continued the weekly meeting in Abe's home and began a men's Bible class composed mainly of English teachers.[50] He also visited former country people in Kita Kyushu City, across the bay from Shimonoseki, responded to invitations to speak in local churches and visited Nagato and Takibe once a month. Thelma began a ladies' meeting in the Yamanota house. The two together held Sunday evening meetings in English and in Japanese. Their assurance of the Lord's call to Shimonoseki grew as the people responded to the various ministries.[51]

One day a young man appeared at the door of the Yamanota house. He was a teacher in Shimonoseki City College, a few blocks away. A committed Christian, he had asked about a church in the area and was told about the Books. His name was Takanobu Tojo. Tojo responded to the idea of a pioneer work in Yamanota and joined forces with the Books.

Weekly services were initiated on Easter Sunday, April 5, 1970. The first baptism took place on December 20 when Mr. Noriaki Odani, a college student brought to the church by Tojo, confessed his faith. In July of the following year Mr. Toshio Morioka, Miss Keiko Yamada and Mrs. Masako Akimoto were baptized. On the Sundays when the Books went up the coast to the other churches, five different Christians were ready to take responsibility for the Yamanota meetings. Doyle once suggested that they might establish an official group of leaders. Tojo responded that they should leave it open so that anyone could be made to feel that he or she was available for a need when it came.

By mid-1971 worship service attendance was eighteen to twenty. Others were expressing an interest in baptism. Thelma's ladies' class flourished as the members invited their friends. A mature Christian couple, Eiji and Eiko Uchida, transferred to Shimonoseki for Uchida's work and found their way to the Yamanota fellowship. They brought years of leadership ability and Bible teaching experience to the group. The believers declared themselves to be the "Yamanota Christian Church." Dwight and Carol Thomas arrived and began an English teaching program. They also added their music skills to the fellowship.[52]

In early 1970 a piece of land in a newly developing section of Yamanota became available. In a far-reaching step, the mission and board accepted Doyle's suggestion that it be purchased and quickly advanced the money. In a few months the land tripled in value. In the spring of 1974, the mission sold part of the land to the Shimonoseki church. An inexpensive prefab building was soon erected. The dedication of the new church facility was held on September 22, 1974. Visitors from Hagi, Nagato and Takibe swelled the Shimonoseki crowd to 120 for the grand occasion. The festivities continued into the afternoon with a buffet meal prepared by the Yamanota ladies.[53]

The Books decided to conclude their service in Japan with their furlough in 1972. Tojo and Uchida took full responsibility for the Shimonoseki group, which commissioned them by the laying on of hands. The ladies Yamamoto, Kaneko, Kato and Tomie Hori led the ladies' group, which continued to grow. Marlin Zook assisted the church from Nishiichi and Ruth contributed several cooking classes. In March 1973, the Uchidas were transferred to Hokkaido and young Odani was moved to Fukuoka by his company. Others also moved away. But Hiroyuki and Yasue Susuki came into the church and began to assist Tojo. Yoshito and Reiko Abe returned to Shimonoseki after several years of residence in other cities. Other new members were also added gradually to the fellowship.[54]

The contribution of Takanobu Tojo's leadership to the Shimonoseki group must be acknowledged at this point. Again and again Tojo refused attractive offers from large universities in Tokyo and Osaka. He considered the Yamanota church first of all his God-given ministry. He also chose to continue his witness, as a Christian teacher of economics, among the Marxist-leaning young men of Shimonoseki City College. His dedication contributed as much to the strength and growth of the Yamanota fellowship as any missionary effort.

Tokyo

The Graybills returned to Japan from furlough in late 1963 with the purpose of opening Brethren in Christ work in Tokyo. There were four reasons for the mission's choice of Tokyo: follow-up of the Yamaguchi people, evangelizing the more receptive urban population, cooperating with the Mennonites in follow-up and evangelism, and education for their children in an English speaking school.

The first of these four reasons had been a longstanding one. There was a tremendous drain on the strength and numbers of the country churches caused by the exodus to the cities. The exodus was felt by craftsmen also, who were hard pressed to find apprentices to carry on their trades. It was determined at one point that one-third of the churches' converts moved into the large cities of Japan.[55]

The mission had been looking toward Tokyo long before the Graybills actually went there. In 1961 it recorded its interest: "Our immediate goal is the conservation of our Yamaguchi-ken converts but an ultimate goal is evangelism."[56]

In the fall of 1963 the mission bought a house in Fuchu, one of Tokyo's suburbs. The Graybills moved in, and John soon began going from door to door, trying to find those who were interested in Christian meetings. John and Lucille offered English classes and a cooking class in their home. On April 24, 1964, the first "formal" Christian meeting was held. Eight people attended, and the meeting later grew to fourteen. The house, however, was much too small for a family of seven, and the front room could hold no more for the meetings. Rather than enter into an extensive remodeling project on a plot of ground that was only 1,100 square feet, the mission decided to purchase a plot in neighboring Koganei City and build a new residence. The entire project cost about $25,000, a very reasonable price for the city which boasted the world's most expensive land. The Graybills moved into the house on September 30, 1964. The cell meeting in the Fuchu house was moved into the home of one of the seekers.[57]

At Koganei the Graybills once again offered English and cooking classes. One of the first to respond to an English class was Mrs. Mitsuko Kaneda. She proceeded to tell Mr. Morio Seno that a missionary had moved into the community. Mrs. Teriko Ito then met the Graybills. She worked at a kindergarten which Debra began to attend. One day she sang a song, "Come to Jesus," in English for the children. Debra reported to her parents that there was a Christian teacher at the kindergarten, and John and Lucille went to see her. Mrs. Chie Matoba saw a poster advertising a meeting in the missionaries' house. She had just moved into the area and gladly joined the little group that was forming.

Meetings began in the Graybill house. The unique thing about these meetings was that all of those who came were Christians! This phenomenon continued for some time. As Seno said, "It was a strange church—from so many different backgrounds!" Several believers from Yamaguchi joined the group—Miss Matsuura from Hagi and the Misses Funaki and Yoshizu from Nagato.[58]

John began organizing cell meetings in community homes as quickly as they became available. The number of cells rose to four and then to eight. The Koganei group grew considerably during one year of these cell meetings, and they rented the spacious second floor room of a music school just across the street from the Graybills' house. The first worship service was held in the building on September 26, 1965. This facility served the church for eight years as the group grew to about seventy members. The emphasis on cell evangelism continued during this time. In 1966 thirteen different homes were involved in cell meetings. Seven of these homes belonged to believers and six of them were those of non-Christians.[59]

Part of John's assignment in Tokyo was to work with the General Conference and Old Mennonite missions in a cooperative effort of follow-up evangelism. Literature projects and other joint efforts were already being carried on. The Mennonite church located in Honan-cho was designated as the local church for believers from all three districts—Hokkaido, Miyazaki and Yamaguchi. Buildng policies for possible new churches were agreed on by the three missions.

The Brethren in Christ both contributed to a church started by the General Conference Mission in Misato and also received financial aid from the other missions for the building project which later developed in Koganei. A committee for evangelism was organized with representatives from the three missions and the national churches. The committee proposed an Anabaptist Center in Tokyo and began moving toward that goal.

Gradually, however, the Brethren in Christ detached themselves from involvement in the various cooperative projects. There were several reasons for this. First, there was an increasing demand upon the small mission for finances and time. At one point, the Brethren were asked to furnish full-time personnel for the cooperative work. The mission felt that it could not commit itself to that extent. Second, the Koganei church decided that it wanted to be an independent community church unaffiliated with the other Mennonite groups. And third, the work in the Koganei area began to grow and produce many additional openings for evangelism. John was more than busy with these crucial projects, and it was felt that the mission should reap to the fullest extent of its limited resources first of all in the Koganei area. At last the Brethren withdrew from special involvement with the other missions in November 1979. It did, however, continue in informal fellowship with them.

As the Koganei church grew, the emphasis on lay leaders and cell groups continued along with the regular worship services which were held in the music school. Mrs. Matoba, an evangelist in her own right, gave herself tirelessly in "visiting, working behind the scenes and in keeping things moving smoothly."[60] Mr. Masanori Tange was converted and became a faithful leader along with his wife, Yachiyo. Tange was the "victim" of a cell meeting held in his own house. He noted that Graybill was very clever—he made Tange promise to have a meeting in his home from which he could not escape! Gradually the atmosphere of love in the meeting and the inspiring testimonies won his heart. Then he no longer wanted to escape! Tange was joined in leadership roles by Chiyoko Horiuchi and David Nagashima, both of whom frequently served as interpreters for guests from the church in America.[61]

As late as 1970, the church affirmed its desire for a self-supported, lay-pastor type of leader rather than a paid professional pastor. It decided, however, to buy or build its own place of worship. The opportunity for such a facility came when a building next to the Graybill residence came up for sale.

The church people, with John's supervision, remodeled the building into a chapel and pastor's residence. On July 25, 1973, the first meeting in the unfinished chapel was held. Kenneth Hoover and J. Earl Musser represented the Board for Missions at the celebration.

Soon after this event, the church called one of its own members to become its salaried pastor. Mr. Hirotoshi Hashimoto was installed on March 27, 1977, as the first pastor both seminary trained and appointed full-time in the Japan Brethren in Christ Church. The reasons for the departure from the earlier affirmation of the lay-pastor concept seem to be, first, that several of the original members who had come from other fellowships wanted the traditional type of pastor and, second, that Hashimoto felt that his health would not permit holding a secular job and trying to pastor the church at the same time.[62]

Several years prior to this occasion, however, John and Lucille Graybill made a strategic move. The Koganei church was well-established in the music school building. Thinking of further outreach, the Graybills sold the Koganei mission residence in 1969 and built in the next city to the north, Kodaira. They still cared for the Koganei church from the new location. Lucille began cooking classes for the Yayoidai neighborhood ladies. English classes taught first by Andy Stoner and later by Tim and Nancy Botts attracted many people to the new location.

In May 1975 a "daughter" to the Koganei church was born when eight members from the mother church officially began worship services at Yayoidai. The group met in a newly built room under the VS apartment. In three years weekly attendance grew to twenty-six. Miss Sachie Hashimoto became the lay leader. Soon, however, the group began to provide partial support for her.

In 1977, a "granddaughter" church was also born when Eiji and Hiromi Suzuki left the Yayoidai group to begin a cell in their own home in Tachikawa. The Suzukis conducted Bible studies, VS personnel provided English classes, and Lucille Graybill contributed a cooking class. A second floor was added to the Suzuki house with subsidies from the mission and from the Koganei church. On April 20, 1980, the conference of the Tokyo churches recognized the Yayoidai group as a self-supported church. The same conference also officially separated the names of Yayoidai and Tachikawa members from the Koganei church rolls.[63]

In June 1980, Marlin and Ruth Zook took up residence in the Yayoidai house following their furlough. The Graybills returned to the United States for one year. The Zooks, working with the Koganei church, which assumed the financial responsibility, secured a building in Fuchu for a new evangelistic outreach and English center. Three new VSers, Mary Brubaker, Connie Lofthouse and Dora Myers, joined the Zooks to begin classes at the center. On Sunday, October 12, 1980, a ceremony marked the opening of the Fuchu location.[64]

A New Denomination

As churches began to form in various localities of Yamaguchi, a long-discussed question took on a note of urgency. The question was: What is to be the relationship of these churches to one another and to the church in America? Behind the question was another one: Does the Brethren in Christ Mission of Japan propose to create its own denominational organization, or should the result of its work be independent, local churches?

The issue had been raised from the very beginning of the Japan mission. Pete Willms was convinced that denominations were foreign to the New Testament and that they created an obstruction to witness in Japan. In a 1954 letter to Henry Hostetter, Pete indicated that there was a growing feeling among Japan missionaries that "we need to keep from starting a lot of denominations here." He noted that the Wesleyan Methodists had decided to work with several other groups under one common name, willingly giving up their own individual identification. He suggested that the same group might welcome the Brethren also. Then he raised the pointed question: "Is the board determined to organize and develop a Brethren in Christ denomination in Japan?" If not, he continued, what principles would the board offer as guides in determining which group the mission might work with?

The board raised the issue in its own midyear meeting. They suggested that the home church would not go along with the idea of merely lending the Willmses to another society since the Brethren had already designated Japan as a mission field under its own board. The board offered no further answer at that point, but the way was opened for dialogue that was to continue for eighteen years.[65]

The board tried to be open to the idea of not pressing a denominational organization upon the new converts. It declared that it wanted to move with the needs of the Japanese Christians within their particular culture. In one letter representing the board, Samuel Wolgemuth assured Pete that the board was "intent with you upon the setting up of a course of procedure that would place the least amount of restrictions upon you and open the way just as fully as possible for a fruitful and productive ministry." Wolgemuth suggested that the Lord had worked with them to this point and would help them not to bring injury to the work from here on. He expressed his feeling that "there is a very real sense in which church membership that makes some demands and thus has the sense of cohesion and unity in fellowship and advance is completely wholesome and within the plan of God." Nevertheless, he stated, the board was willing to go along for the time being with Pete's feeling that "setting up a conference which would bring the congregations together organizationally would be detrimental."[66]

The missionaries who joined the Willmses quickly began to share the same concern. They saw that the Church in Japan was hopelessly enmeshed in a maze of denominational names and that attitudes of exclusiveness and superiority often accompanied these diverse organizations. Christians had polarized along denominational lines and the church was divided. The expression of Christianity in Japan was little more than a duplicate of western culture and, as a result, had little indigenous vitality. The missionaries also quickly realized that non-believers were totally perplexed by the proliferation of Christian denominations. The explanation that these were something like the various sects in Buddhism was not sufficient. The Japanese saw that the Christian churches were extremely possessive, competed with one another and even denounced one another.

Other Japan observers shared the concern that the mission felt. Paul Peachey observed that the church in Japan had made very little progress "in expressing her faith in the idiom of Japanese thought and experience." Theology in Japan seemed merely to be a fad of keeping up with the latest theological fads in the West. The same problem existed on the level of church organizations and polity. The entire institutional apparatus of the Japanese churches was seen to be largely an organizational transplanting from the West. The copied system of professional clergy and denominational training institutions weakened the churches and led to a sense of dependence. Peachey recognized the distinctives that urge some denominations to retain their own special identity. But, he declared, the idea that "denominations stimulate each other, or complement one another like members in the body is a shocking example of *eisegesis.*" The notion of denominations, he argued, is contrary to the Word of God and to Jesus Christ as Head of the Church. He raised two questions: "How shall the pagan soul, confronted with Christianity so variously packaged, make his decision? How shall I speak of Christian peace witness when we cannot unite ourselves as followers of Christ?" He declared, "These two are among the most serious obstacles I have encountered . . . here."[67]

On various occasions the Japan mission referred to its denominational ties and seemed to indicate that it was thinking of an organization of its churches. Pete early had proudly announced the formation of a group that "we now call the Hagi Brethren in Christ Church." At another time he indicated that the mission was working in Japan "toward the establishment of the Brethren in Christ Church." At one point it was suggested that a goal for the second decade of the work was a "formal conference of churches."[68]

It is clear, however, that in the minds of the Japan missionaries such a "conference" would consist merely of an informal fellowship of churches. The fellowship would naturally provide mutual encouragement and an exchange of ideas. It seems evident also that, in his early communication with the home church, Pete was responding to their expressions for a church of their own kind—he was trying to encourage them with the fact that fruit was being born from their gifts and prayers. In regard to the use of the name "Brethren in Christ," Pete indicated that this term related to the mission rather than to an emerging group of churches.[69]

Pete tried to make it clear that he was "not anti-church or church membership." He was merely anti-denomination. He felt that denominations were not God's best for the church and that in Japan they represented a major obstacle to witness—a man-made offense to the gospel. He recognized that one cannot rid the world of denominations any more than one can rid it of other offenses like sin and unbelief. But, he declared, we are to do what we can. At least, he suggested, we can avoid *adding* another denomination to the many that already exist.[70]

The Japan missionaries agreed in general that they did not want to promote an organization of churches that would bring about a new denomination. The board concurred in principle with their feeling. This consensus was shared with the national leaders over the years as the churches developed. It was also indicated, however, that the mission did encourage a loose fellowship of local, autonomous churches and that should the churches eventually decide for a more formal organization, the mission would cooperate with the decision. It asked only that the church consider adequately the implications of such a move. It assured the leaders that most of all it wanted the church to be a genuine expression of the Japanese believers themselves. This meant that, although the mission would give counsel, it would gladly defer to the church on decisions that particularly affected its life.

The first meeting of leaders from all the Yamaguchi churches took place on June 27, 1965. The participants were Shibata, Yamane and Aburatani from Hagi, Takamura and Nishimura from Nagato, Kaneshige from Yamaguchi, Okazaki, Akidomi and Arita from Takibe, and Nagai, Y. Abe and Yamazaki from Shimonoseki. The group also included missionaries Willms and Book. The meeting was a time of exchanging experiences and of prayer for one another. Other similar fellowships took place over the next several years. Usually these meetings coincided with visits by members of the board and served mainly to provide communication with them. During these years, the mission kept working with its own policies regarding evangelism and its relationship to the churches.[71]

Several leaders, however, felt a growing desire for clarification of some mission policies and called a meeting of leaders and missionaries on January 26, 1969. National representatives, both men and women, attended from Yamaguchi, Hagi, Nagato, Agawa, Takibe, and Shimonoseki. Kaneshige had prepared a list of questions to which he asked the mission to respond. The questions were: (1) When does the mission withdraw a missionary from a certain church, and who makes the decision? (2) Should the Yamaguchi churches work toward forming a conference or should they join efforts with some other group? (3) How does the mission propose to help the churches? (4) What is the mission's plan for evangelism in the future? (5) Is a church begun by the mission to be considered an independent church or a Brethren in Christ church? (6) What is the churches' relationship to Mennonite churches?

There is little doubt that the questions arose out of a growing sense of uneasiness in one or two of the groups in particular. This uneasiness related especially to the Willmses' withdrawal from Hagi in order to go to Yamaguchi. It may have related to the planned move of the Books to Shimonoseki. The mission presented its views on the various questions which had been raised, and the meeting ended with a sense of mutual appreciation and plans for further dialogue.[72]

Two events occurred shortly, however, which dramatically hastened the call for an organization of the Yamaguchi churches and which made the organization tighter than it might have been. The first of these events was the sudden decision of the Willmses not to return to Japan. The Hagi church was shocked by the decision. The Willmses had assured them that they would return in six months. Naturally, in time the church recovered from the emotional blow and tried to recognize the leading of the Lord in the decision. But an uneasiness began to grow within the various churches about the mission's decision-making processes. Furthermore, the leaders were feeling somewhat dissatisfied with the process of having to go through the mission in order to communicate with the board. They were not sure that their feelings were being expressed adequately or that they were, in turn, receiving the feelings of the board clearly enough. Even the earlier appointment of the mission liaison person was not fully satisfactory.[73]

The second event was, in some ways, more shocking than the first. It was certainly more tragic because of its spiritual implications. Miss Takeko Iwamoto was serving the Nagato church as lay pastor. She was assisted in the responsibilities of the church by Asao Nishimura and others, but she was giving herself in a special, sacrificial way to teaching, visiting, tract distribution and many other aspects of leadership. She had gone to an Osaka Bible college and had offered herself to the Nagato church with no consideration of remuneration. Her Bible ministry was a blessing in many ways. However, some changes began to occur in her attitude. The Books later recalled that they had noticed these changes while they were in Nagato, but they were unable to identify what they felt at the time.

In early 1971, the matter became clear. Iwamoto often devoted herself to prayer and fasting. One day she borrowed a vacant room from a Shimonoseki believer and began an extended time of fasting. Another person living in the same house expressed concern because she heard no movment of any kind from Iwamoto's room. Wondering, the Books called on her. They found her deep in study of the writings of Emanual Swedenborg, a mystic and intellectual of the eighteenth century. Iwamoto told the Books that she had discovered the "true church" in the writings and that Swedenborg had helped her to understand some doctrines of the Bible that were previously incomprehensible to her. Alarmed, the Books pointed out the heresy of Swedenborg and the historical position of the church on his doctrines. But she could not see the danger.

The Books immediately reported the encounter to the other leaders of the Nagato church. They also shared their concern with the Shimonoseki leaders Tojo and Uchida, both of whom were accomplished students of the Bible and church history. The Books also informed mission superintendent, John Graybill, of the danger. The Nagato church, with Tojo, Uchida and the Books, counseled Iwamoto and asked her to give up her interest in Swedenborg. She was unresponsive to their pleas. An experienced pastor from Yamaguchi was asked to join them in another session of counseling. Iwamoto flatly rejected their appeals for reconsideration of her views. She left the fellowship and began her own group under the name "Church of the New

Jerusalem."[74] Only one person, however, a young lady who was quite close to Iwamoto, went with her from the Nagato group. The others quickly regrouped under the leadership of Asao and Kimiko Nishimura. They thanked the Lord for his protection, and the fellowship continued with a renewed sense of oneness and joy.

Some of the other Yamaguchi leaders, however, did not react so positively. A meeting of all the churches was hastily called by several leaders on July 11, 1971, and a call for an immediate organization of churches was issued. It was stated that a channel of communication was needed for the churches to discuss matters of importance. The concerned leaders declared that a matter like the Iwamoto incident was not a local problem but one that must be dealt with by all the churches. This was so because the person involved was considered to be a pastor. It soon became evident, however, that other factors were involved in the sudden call for formal lines of communication. Some of the leaders had been offended because they had not been notified early of the incident and had not been included in the initial discussions.

The missionaries had once again overlooked an important cultural perspective. To the Japanese, an older person or the group with the longer existence was to be acknowledged as having seniority and was to be approached first in matters of importance. In this case, because Iwamoto had been appointed by the local church, not by the combined churches, it had not occurred to the missionaries to bring the other leaders into the counseling sessions.

One leader was commissioned to draw up a list of bylaws for the proposed organization. These were presented to the group in another meeting on July 25. Time had allowed emotions to settle, however, and most of the leaders felt that the suggestions were too rigid. The articles were revised in a meeting of August 8 and were formally adopted on September 15. The items officially inaugurated the "Yamaguchi Brethren in Christ Conference." Council meetings of representatives from the various churches were instituted on a monthly basis. Asao Nishimura of the Nagato church was elected chairman of the new conference.[75]

Another consequence of the Iwamoto tragedy began to emerge. Iwamoto had earlier become deeply interested in the work of the Holy Spirit and had herself experienced an infilling of the Spirit. The Books also had been deeply moved by the new evidences of the Spirit's working in the church during the 1960s. They had always believed in the doctrine of the infilling of the Holy Spirit as taught in their youth by the Brethren in Christ. Now they experienced a renewal of that work in their lives. The few leaders who had reacted in anger to the Iwamoto situation apparently associated her interest in the Holy Spirit with her aberrations and assumed that this interest had opened her up to false spirits. There was some suspicion toward the Books also. This suspicion lingered and became one of the reasons that the Books chose not to return to Japan for a fourth term in 1973.

There was no misunderstanding, however, on the part of those who were close to the incident. The Nagato people easily distinguished between Iwamoto's deviations and her experience in the Holy Spirit. They recognized that much of her ministry had been genuine and true. Several of them testified that they had sensed something strange earlier but had kept quiet. One said that she discerned a wrong spirit and was afraid to be in the same service with Iwamoto. A mature observer from outside the group indicated that he earlier had noticed something wrong in Iwamoto's manner. A teacher of the Bible school where Iwamoto had attended stated later that she had expressed some strange ideas even while she was there. The Nagato believers rejoiced that God had allowed the problem to be discovered before others could be deluded. And they testified unitedly that God had brought good for the church out the situation.[76]

The effect of the new conference on the Yamaguchi churches will be evaluated in the next chapter. But it should be noted here that there has been a general, positive response to the organization and its monthly *Kyogikai* (council meeting). As the Hagi leaders later indicated, the meetings of the conference are, in fact, quite informal and loosely structured. Since the forming of the conference, they admitted, they have hardly looked again at the bylaws.[77]

The Tokyo churches did not become a part of the Yamaguchi organization. Their decision not to unite was understandable, perhaps, because the two districts were five hundred miles apart. Furthermore there was a "markedly different style of life" between the two areas. It would seem also that no special effort was made to have the two groups come together organizationally. The Koganei church incorporated separately on April 2, 1973. The Yayoidai and Tachikawa groups were listed as branches of this incorporation.[78]

Chapter Eight

The Challenge of Growth

The process of birth and nurture involves much effort and, at times, great difficulty. This is true for the human family. It is also true for the church. The goal for an organism is maturity. In the church, maturity is effected by the work of God through his Holy Spirit. But he always builds his church with the cooperation of human beings. And because human beings are involved, so are their frailties and failures. For the Brethren in Christ churches in Japan, there were many ups and downs in the growth process. There were obstructions and there were successes as the believers began to walk with the Lord.

The year 1963, the end of the first decade of the mission effort, saw a combined membership in the Yamaguchi churches of 83.[1] Gradually, however, the pattern of the country churches became one of merely "holding on" rather than of making numerical progress. The beginning of the Tokyo work brought a new upsurge in membership statistics. By the end of 1965, their second full year, the Koganei group had seen thirteen baptisms. The country churches had lost some members, but the combined figure for the two districts was 98. During the next fourteen years there were 124 baptisms, most of them coming from Tokyo and Shimonoseki. The graph in Figure 1 gives an idea of the growth during these years.

The sharp drop in the graph in 1973 occurred when Hagi, and possibly other churches, purged from their rolls inactive members—those who had moved away or who no longer participated in the fellowship for other reasons. The membership list included an average of twenty "associate members" each year—those who fellowshipped in the Brethren in Christ churches but retained their membership elsewhere. Worship attendance records were not kept until 1970. From that time the number in worship on Sunday morning increased from 74 to 113. The offerings, however, increased at a much more rapid rate. From $1,350 in 1965, combined giving grew gradually until 1974, then shot up from $12,900 to $19,900 in 1975, $27,500 in 1977 and $39,500 in 1979.[2]

Tokyo

The beginning of the Tokyo work was boosted by a hardworking missionary and a group of already mature Christian leaders. For the first several years, worship attendance was higher than the actual membership, which reached twenty-seven in 1969. The increase in membership to 104 during the next ten years came mostly through conversions. New converts accounted for

69 percent of the growth, while 22 percent came from those who transferred into the churches, and 9 percent resulted from the children of church families. The growth rate for this ten-year period was 285 percent, a very high rate of growth for Japan. The chart of growth for the Tokyo churches appears in Figure 2.[3]

From the above figures we see that the combined worship attendance for the three groups reached 68 in 1979. Several other significant factors appear. Although the Koganei church purchased its own building in 1973, this did not contribute significantly to its growth. Neither did the acquisition of a full-time, salaried pastor in 1976. Quite to the contrary, attendance at the Koganei church decreased over the next several years. On the other hand, the new work at Kodaira, which was led by the missionary, grew in four years from eight to twenty-six.

Several reasons were suggested for the decline at Koganei. First, eight members suddenly left the mother church to begin the new work at Kodaira. Some suggested that the Koganei church was not yet prepared for this kind of reproduction. Second, two of the eight members who left were the missionaries, John and Lucille Graybill. This meant that, at a time of already significant change, the leadership of the church also changed drastically from missionary to national pastor. Third, within the next year, several members who lived on the border between the two cities found the Kodaira location more convenient

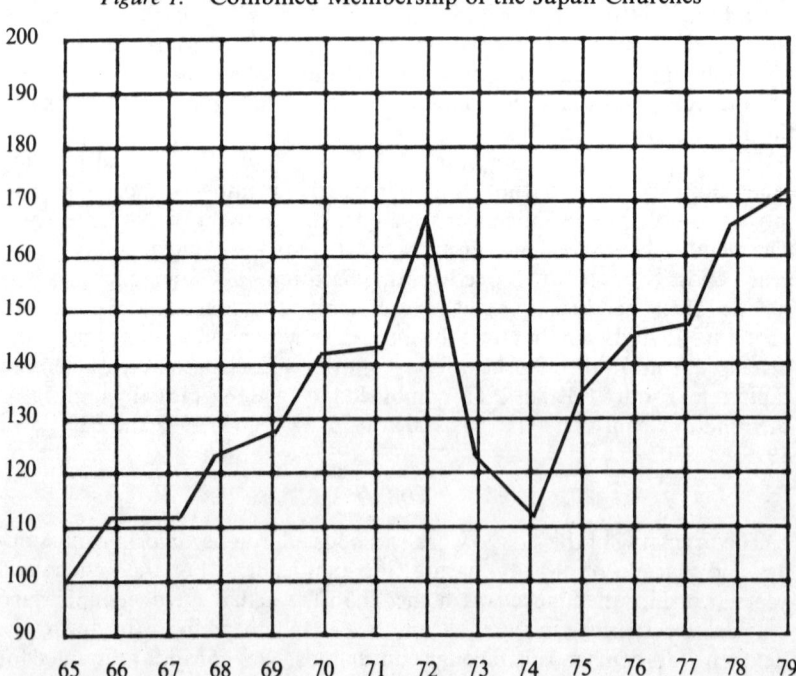

Figure 1. Combined Membership of the Japan Churches

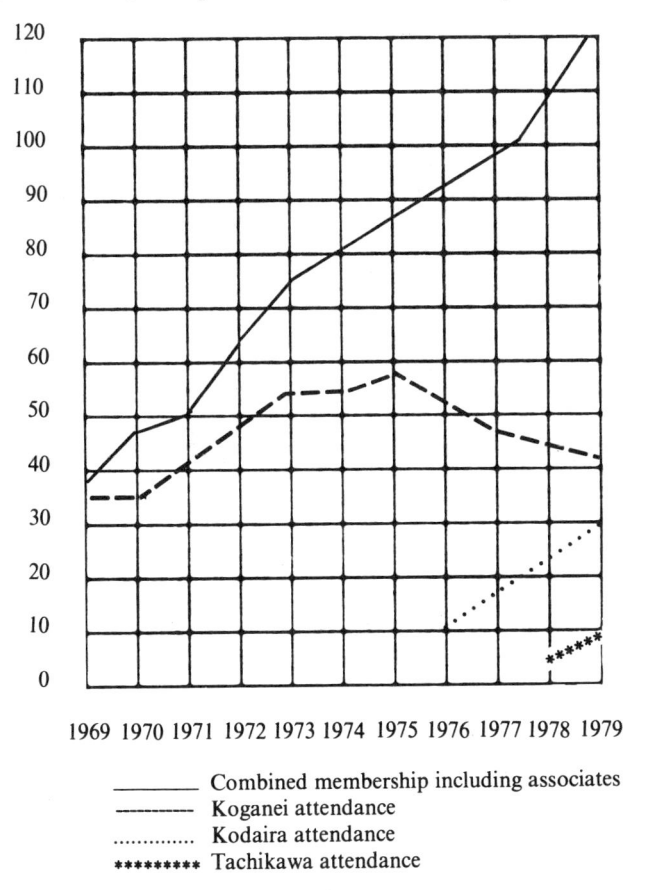

Figure 2. Membership and Attendance of the Tokyo Churches

1969 1970 1971 1972 1973 1974 1975 1976 1977 1978 1979

———— Combined membership including associates
---------- Koganei attendance
.... Kodaira attendance
✱✱✱✱✱✱✱✱ Tachikawa attendance

and changed to the daughter church. This caused more empty seats at Koganei.[4]

In addition to these factors, it must also be realized that the new pastor was at a decided disadvantage for several reasons. First, he was just out of seminary with little intern training and no experience in pastoring. Second, the pastor was young and without a family. In Japanese culture it is not easy for a young person to gain the confidence of the people. Third, the church members had an emotional attachment to the missionary. This was due, in part, to his earnestness and his aggressive pursuit of his evangelistic goals. It was no doubt due also to the attraction that an English-speaking foreigner offered. The differences in personality and in nationality of the new pastor demanded considerable adjustment on the part of the members.[5] By the end of 1979 the Koganei pastor had gained much experience, had his own family, and there were signs that the decline was leveling out.

Yamaguchi

During the period of time that the Tokyo work was developing, membership of three of the four Yamaguchi churches declined. The exception of the trend was in Shimonoseki where attendance reached eighteen to twenty in its first two years and where membership was approximately thirty-five at the end of 1979. In addition Shimonoseki, only Hagi and Nagato recorded regular worship services. An average of forty-six gathered on the Lord's Day at the three locations. Hagi had declined from an average of twenty in 1966 to fourteen in 1979. Nagato's average was somewhat less, with only two men found on its rolls. No new extension churches had been started by the national church and very few cells were to be seen.[6]

While the above facts were disappointing, the full picture was by no means a gloomy one. The country churches continued in vibrant, though small, weekly fellowships where the Word of God was faithfully taught and the love of Christ often moved the believers to tears of joy, testimonies of victory and concerned prayers for one another and for loved ones. In Hagi, leaders Shibata and Okano, with no missionary remaining in the prefecture, were training others to assume more responsibility.[7]

The influence of the Hagi church reached far beyond the borders of its own city. As early as 1967, strong Christians from its ranks were serving churches in Fukuoka, Okayama, Kobe, Osaka, Wakayama, Kyoto, Nagoya, Fujisawa, Tokyo and Sapporo in addition to others within Yamaguchi Prefecture. Some of them served as leaders of churches. Others were witnessing actively in places of employment.[8] In 1979 the Hagi people around whom the Shimonoseki work had begun fifteen years earlier were still putting their energies into the leadership of that church.

In Nagato, the presence of the Holy Spirit was very real in the services. Asao and Kimiko Nishimura were well known and respected around the city by merchants, educators and other townspeople. The members of the fellowship were always ready with a helping hand and a clear testimony for someone who was hurting or spiritually hungry. A quadraplegic on Mishima, an island two hours off the coast, called the Nagato church and expressed a hunger for the Christian message. Nishimura began to lead him to Jesus over the phone. Calls were exchanged during the following year. Finally, at the man's request, seven Nagato members plus the three Nishimura children journeyed to Mishima by boat, stayed overnight, and administered baptism to the new convert. The father of the man was moved to tears at the display of Christian love. Other dramatic events took place in and through the lives of those who had left Nagato for other places.[9]

As to the reasons for the lack of numerical growth in these churches, let us consider some of the issues involved in the dynamics of growth within the Brethren in Christ work and venture a few observations.

City Versus Country

The steady movement of the people from country areas to the city is a worldwide phenomenon. Nowhere was this phenomenon earlier visible, nor was it of greater proportions, than in Japan. For the Japanese, the large city areas have always had a strange fascination. Tokyo, of course, has been the most appealing of all. One obvious reason for this continuing fascination with the large cities is that the largest and most famous universities are located there. Thus Japanese tend to feel that most worthwhile ideas originate in Tokyo and its companion metropolises of Osaka and Nagoya. This feeling is usually accompanied by an aura of prestige for the people who live there.

A second obvious reason for the fascination about the large cities is that more jobs, and better ones, have always been available there. Japan's industrial revolution has created factories with insatiable appetites for workers. As heavy industries grew, many new supporting jobs were also created. To a lesser degree than Tokyo, Osaka and Nagoya and other cities as well—in proportion to their size—draw people from the country and from smaller cities.

As people respond to the "pull" of the city, a mental metamorphosis also takes place. In most cases they leave behind traditional patterns of thinking. They see new and exciting things in the city and come to feel that the country is "backward." They leave their former homes not only physically but also emotionally, and create new homes for themselves in crowded apartments and on small, personally-owned plots of ground. They become mentally prepared for change and for a variety of new concepts. The obstructions to change are fewer in the city because people have been removed from the group that exerted upon them the greatest pressure for conformity. They are uprooted from their past. Thus city people in Japan have consistently been more responsive to the message of the gospel than people still living in the country areas.

With a change in mental attitudes, there is often a change in social status. People of the salaried class tend to group themselves in certain areas of the suburbs. A survey of the Koganei church membership once revealed that the church's witness was chiefly to the "above middle" class of people. It reported that approximately 92 percent of the men in the Koganei church were university graduates and that 78 percent of the ladies had more than a high school education. Furthermore, it found that 68 percent of the church members were homeowners and thus were quite stable, but that there were no laborers or semi-skilled workers in the congregation.[10]

The story of churches in the country is one of constant loss to the cities. It must be recognized that this factor of loss to the cities most likely became the greatest single obstruction to growth in the Yamaguchi churches. The more the country churches grew, the more they also lost to the cities. The missionaries' reports contained numerous examples that were typical of the loss sustained by the country groups. The Hagi church alone gained sixty members in the first ten years of its existence. However, fully half of these had already gone to other cities by the beginning of its second decade. It was also found that one-third of the converts in the country churches moved to Tokyo alone.

In the case of Nagato, it was noted that God had worked graciously in the five years since the church had begun. A good number of people had responded to God's call. Most of these were in their late teens and early twenties. Some of them matured rapidly in their Christian experience and could have formed the nucleus for church nurture and evangelism. However, because they were searching for education and better jobs, one by one they went elsewhere. It was reported that out of twenty-five who had been baptized in the Nagato church, only nine remained in the vicinity and two more were preparing to leave in the near future.[11]

There are an increasing number of testimonies to the effect that good church growth can be achieved in Japan. A missionary-led Bible Baptist group has evidenced a remarkable rate of growth in western Tokyo not too far from the Brethren in Christ churches. Some of the possible reasons suggested for this success are these: a missionary wife who is a specialist in Sunday school work and who methodically trains national workers, who now number thirty-five; facilities which were always comfortable and large enough for continued expansion; and an emphasis on "faith-promise" giving which resulted in a yearly doubling and redoubling of offerings until the church of 110 members reached the extraordinary peak of $171,600 in 1977.[12]

In 1979 a study was made of eight growing churches scattered throughout Japan. The churches represented both independent and denominational approaches. Methods which were reported as successful in some of the churches included an emphasis on tithing, a special focus on men, Sunday schools in the homes, a "family system" of home fellowships, and note-taking during services for the purpose of "preaching" the message to others during the week. The report also noted some characteristics which were common to most of the churches. These included the involvement of every Christian in the witness and work of the church, a training program for these lay workers, establishing priorities for the ministry of the church, setting goals, and strong leadership. The eight churches were described as experiencing rapid and solid growth amid great enthusiasm on the part of their members.

One thing was clear in the report—nothing was achieved without hard work on the part of both the leaders and the members. However, another significant factor stood out clearly—all of the churches researched were located in or near bustling urban centers with large populations. No attempt was made to include country churches in the study. A similar type of study should be made of rural churches, focusing on their attempts to cope with the conservative mentality found in the country and with the tendency of the members to move to the cities. In spite of this lack in the report, however, it presents an exciting story of God at work in churches in Japan.[13]

A study of this type is welcome and can be helpful to many other churches. The awareness that God is at work and that churches in Japan also are growing can give impetus for other churches to reach out both to God and to studies of methods which might enable them to achieve a similar kind of growth.

Mission Deficiencies

The question presents itself: Was the Brethren in Christ mission wrong in going to the country areas first? The question needs to be considered, not for the purpose of resurrecting and criticizing what already lies in the past and has, in fact, been beautifully blessed by God, but for the purpose of discovering insights for the future concerning the ways in which God might do an even greater work. The board had an inner assurance that God had led them to open the Japan work in the country. Pete Willms at first was uneasy about the choice. Later, as he saw lives changed by the gospel and the church begin to grow, he acknowledged the leading of God to Hagi.[14] The conviction of God's leading is a foundational principle for mission. The board's assurance that God had led need not now be challenged.

However, it is true also that the Holy Spirit works with people in terms of their mental orientation. He does this even though he is able to see that their perspectives are molded by their immediate concerns. Thus it is possible that the Holy Spirit allowed the board leaders a sense of his leading because they were not able to assimilate certain insights which were just appearing on the horizon of mission strategy.

One of these insights was the principle of receptivity. Later research revealed that the greatest harvest is reaped where the fields are heaviest with fruit. It was recognized, to use another analogy, that the best fishing is where the fish are many and are already prepared for the bait. These analogies suggest that the Holy Spirit might have desired to direct the mission more quickly to the urban areas. Thus it is possible that, in seeming to direct to the country, the Holy Spirit accepted the lack of awareness in the leadership concerning the principle of receptivity that he had been wanting them to see.

It is possible also that the Holy Spirit allowed a sense of his leading to the country because of the cultural orientation of the board members. The Brethren were basically a rurally oriented people. Most of their churches were located in the country. In the 1950s they had already been influenced by the pull to the cities, but most of them still looked on the country and small town life with appreciation and nostalgia. Many of the brethren were still involved in occupations related to the farm. This rural orientation possibly influenced the mission board to bypass the bustling cities in favor of the more peaceful rural setting.

It is likely, furthermore, that the prevailing concern of the time for comity influenced the decision of the board. This concern declared that one should not go near the work of another mission lest interference be felt or competition result. It is true that the brethren were sincerely concerned about the places where there was no witness at all. There was an innate sense of responsibility to go where no one had yet gone. It is possible, however, that the decision in favor of the country resulted largely from a concern for not transgressing on other mission territories.[15]

It is not our purpose to cast a reflection upon decisions that were made at an earlier time. These decisions were of a spiritual nature. We must, however, for the sake of the mission of the future, be willing to evaluate past methods and recognize the lacks which existed in some cases.

The fact remains that the Japan mission proceeded in its early years without developing a strategy for mission that recognized already existing studies of population trends and receptivity factors. Such a strategy would have considered going first to the larger population areas where people have been uprooted from their past and are thus more open to change, more responsive to the Christian message. It would have suggested that one should "go where the fish are already biting" and that, after discipling those who are more ready to receive the message, the mission could then train the national converts for an approach to their own people. Such training should include proper methods for an approach to the country mentality and the homogeneous groupings found there. Thus prepared, national evangelists would be able to penetrate the more resistant cultures far more effectively than the foreigner ever could. A policy of this type would also enable the foreigner to avoid some of the frustrations that tend to cause a needless waste of emotional and physical energies and time and money resources.

A strategy of missions suggests that one should concentrate on the more strategic places first with the greater amount of one's resources. As people respond in these places, they can then be equipped for ministry to the less responsive areas.

It is true that Hagi and Nagato were, to a small degree, strategic. Hagi played a significant part in Japan's cultural past, and Nagato was a transportation center. Nevertheless, they were still "rural" towns. Their people were constantly looking to the larger cities for their education and careers. The later choice of Nishiichi for a new work showed that the mission had not yet learned about the principles of receptivity. If a survey had been made, the factors which the Zooks later discovered concerning adverse population trends and the division of the town into two competing homogeneous units would have shown that the planting of a new church there would be a difficult process at best. Nagato already afforded a satisfactory location for nurturing the existing churches up and down the coast. The thought of planting a new church in Nishiichi, and the purchase of a mission property there, should have been backed by further research.[16]

The call for a strategy in church planting is not an attempt to supersede the eternal absolutes of the sovereignty of God and the dynamic of the Holy Spirit. But the Holy Spirit works through people. And he expects his people to use the insights that he has already made available to them. Of course the Holy Spirit can raise up a church in any place he desires. But he asks his servants to work with him by considering certain key factors which he has placed within various cultures and which, if discovered and used, will aid in the growth of the church.

God's people in mission need more than an inner witness. They also need a calculated strategy for missions. Such a strategy need not be void of an inner assurance of the Holy Spirit's leading. On the contrary, it can be planned with the awareness that it is fully Spirit-inspired and directed. The Holy Spirit has insights in regard to evangelism. He sees the factors which can be used in penetrating various cultures. He expects his people to discover and use these factors, not only through prayer but also through diligent research and careful strategy.

The question which faces us is not, "Was the mission wrong in opening work in the country?" God does, indeed, have a concern for the country people also. Furthermore, none of the missionaries could bear to think of never having known the precious fellowship and love of the believers there. Participating in the radiance and victory of the Aburatanis, Okamotos, Shibatas, Nishimuras and Ishiis, to use a few representative names, was a foretaste of heaven itself. The issue is not one of right or wrong. But we need to recognize that some of the mission leaders were enlightened as to the ways in which the Holy Spirit desires to work and as to insights concerning the places where the greater part of the mission's energies should have been focused. The lack of attempts to research appropriate places where maximum growth might have resulted is the first deficiency in mission methods that needs to be acknowledged.

The second deficiency is the lack of adequate training for the lay leaders. Without question the most significant single venture in the efforts of the Japan mission was the little Bible training school that Pete Willms initiated. The people who received training are today committed Christians and church leaders. The mission, however, did not follow through on the matter of providing training at the local level. Perhaps the missionaries assumed that encouraging the believers toward taking responsibility and discussing with them the principles involved in the leadership of the church would be adequate. Perhaps also their energies were sufficiently drained with other duties that seemed to press in upon them. But as one church leader pointed out, it is not enough to say "go out and witness" or "here is the church—care for it and develop it." Thorough training must be given to those who are to care for the church. It was indicated by other leaders that "the missionaries sometimes said, 'lead the church' but they didn't tell us how to do it."[17]

At one point the mission, sensing the growing need for adequate instruction in Bible and methods of church administration and evangelism, decided to inaugurate a theological education by extension approach within each local church. Personnel were assigned to carry out such a program.[18] However, for various reasons—some, no doubt, related to the organization of the individual churches into a conference just at that time—the program never materialized.

Lay leadership demands the involvement of much of the resources and energies of a person. For the church to grow, individual members also must put themselves vigorously to the work of the church. For this kind of involvement, an understanding of the Word and a vision of the need is necessary. These qualities can be developed only by a systematic and adequate program of training. The mission did not place such a program high enough on its priority list. As a result the leaders of the churches were left ill-equipped and, in some cases, uninspired for the work of the church.

There is yet a third deficiency in the mission approach that needs to be recognized. The mission failed to provide a transition from its lay leadership policy to supported and professionally trained national personnel. This criticism is not to suggest that the policy of self-supported, locally trained pastors was not correct. On the contrary, there are many reasons why the lay leadership concept is still a viable and even necessary approach for the evangelization of Japan. The criticism is to acknowledge, however, that the mission did not recognize the time for making certain adjustments. Nor did it understand the extent of the adjustments that needed to be made.

In modern Japan, it is very unlikely that laymen, by themselves, can provide all that is necessary for the growth of the church. They can possibly care adequately for an established small church, provided that demands for visitation of the sick, commemorative services for members' families and other duties do not overwhelm them. In some cases they might also be able to start a cell group and assist in its nurture if the traveling distance involved is not too great. But it is unreasonable to expect laymen to take the responsibility for the kinds of church planting efforts that the missionaries engaged in. As one leader expressed it, "we are merely maintaining the church—it takes all our energy just to do this." Others pointed out that the age of thirty-five to forty-five is the time of peak productivity for salaried workers. It is also the time for key promotions. In Japan jobs often require commitment far beyond the forty-hour working week common in the West. Little time remains for the work of the church. This lack of time is the Japanese lay leader's biggest problem.[19]

Several questions were once raised in a discussion between missionaries: Why have no new congregations been started in Yamaguchi since Shimonoseki was begun in 1970? Why is there no appreciable Sunday school work in Nagato and Hagi? Why has not the church started one extension point? The answer would seem to be that the national church leaders simply do not have the time or energy which such activities demand. The most crucial factor in the growth of the church is strong—even aggressive—pastoral leadership. But such strength comes from sufficient time and energy to do the necessary tasks at the time they are required.

In Pete Willms's early development of the lay leadership concept, he declared that an outside person is necessary to provide help for lay leaders.[20] This person may or may not be considered an "authority" or a specialist. The missionaries filled this position for the church leaders for many years. But as they drew back, hoping to encourage the leaders to assume more responsibility, they failed to see adequately the limits of the lay leaders. They did not realize that the lay leaders by themselves could not do everything the missionary hoped to see accomplished and which had previously been achieved with the help of the missionary. A transition was necessary at this point to national, professionally trained workers who could provide some of the guidance and assist in outreach as the missionary had formerly done. The mission failed to provide that transition at the proper time.

In order for a church to grow, the provisions for growth must be adequate.

This fact relates to location, facilities, or, in the United States, even to the size of the parking lot![21] It applies also to adequately trained, sufficiently strong pastoral leadership. Hopefully this leadership would be of the self-supported, "non-professional" type. But adequate leadership must be provided, even if it is professionally trained and partially or fully supported. The mission was late in adjusting to this pastoral concept.

Challenge for the Churches

In a discussion of growth in the church in Japan, several factors stand out as crucial for the consideration of the churches themselves. The first of these is the matter of a deep spiritual commitment. This commitment is primarily to the Word of God and, more particularly, to the command of Jesus to make disciples of all people. It is clear that a concern for evangelism must be central in the life of the church if it is to grow. As one person commented, "God works as people pray and commit themselves to the great task of gathering in the harvest."[22]

The apparent lack of aggressive personal witnessing caused the missionaries concern over the years.[23] Some of the leaders felt the same concern. One of the Yamaguchi leaders maintained that an understanding of the lordship of Christ is imperative among the believers. Another commented that her fellow Japanese lack a sense of discipleship. They want to remain observers in the church and are unwilling to accept responsibility. Perhaps the Japanese Christians have been lulled into ignoring how desperately their own people need Jesus Christ.[24] In order for the church to grow, God's people must see that God wants it to grow. They must also desire that growth with God and expect it to take place.

The leaders were challenged to renewed commitment in evangelism and church growth by Bishop Don Shafer in the fall of 1979. Shafer outlined five practical steps that must be given careful attention in the process of evangelism. (1) always remember the goal—make disciples, (2) have a definite plan for evangelism, (3) be flexible in methods, (4) be aware of needs in the body and help one another, and (5) keep in mind that the church ought to grow. Some of the leaders were deeply moved by Shafer's challenge. They wondered why they had not been informed of these things before. Others, however, hesitated to believe that such steps could actually bring about the growth of the church.[25]

The first challenge for the Japanese churches is for a renewed commitment to the Great Commission. There must be the realization that the unfinished task begins with family members and neighbors. The end of the 1970s revealed that such a concern is growing among the Japanese leaders. In 1976, the Koganei church, while attempting to pay off their building debt, gave an offering of 150,000 yen to the Board for Missions in America for its work around the world.[26] As we have already seen, the same church assumed the financial responsibility for the new outreach in next-door Fuchu, asking the mission only for the personnel for the project. Plans were being inaugurated among the Yamaguchi churches also for church planting ventures early in the 1980s.

The second challenge for the national churches is to develop strong leadership. This leadership may be of the "professional" type or it may be from the ranks of the laity. Japanese people respond to firm, enthusiastic leadership. Conversely, they do not carry responsibility where this kind of leadership is lacking. Japanese social structure is built upon hierarchical concepts. People are paid respect according to their age or their social status. The *sensei* (teacher) in Japan is one of those given high respect. The church needs to take advantage of this natural social attitude. Church leaders should assume their right as *sensei*, whether ordained or not, and lead the church firmly. For church growth, the laity must be mobilized. Successful churches involve every member in the ministry of the church and teach each member to be a soul winner.[27]

Leaders must be aggressive. Good biblical teaching is not enough. They must provide bold plans for outreach and organize the members into evangelistic units. Church growth does not happen by itself even in cities which are said to be more responsive. Evangelism involves hard, sacrificial work. Community surveys must be made, doors must be knocked on, literature must be passed out, earnest prayers must be offered, and sacrificial offerings must be given. At Koganei the missionary provided this kind of leadership, and the people followed him into that pathway of growth.

To develop strong leaders the right kind of person is needed. In the Orient this means men. John Graybill suggested that a typical Japanese church may be composed of eighty percent women and twenty percent men. At one time, he reported, the Koganei church had approximately eighteen ladies whose husbands never attended church.[28] However, it cannot be left up to the wives to win their husbands. In Japan men must win men. In most non-western countries the church will not grow so long as it is seen to be a gathering for women. This is true of the Orient in general. It is also true of Japan where men are still looked to for leadership in most affairs. The winning of men must be one of the top priorities for the church in Japan. Recognizing this priority has contributed greatly to the growth of the church in Shimonoseki. It is out of the winning of men that strong leadership can be developed for the church.

The third challenge for the churches is the creation of goals. The primary goal, as Shafer declared, is making disciples (Matt. 28:19). This primary goal can be reached, however, only by setting specific goals and then making every effort to reach them. Goal setting includes faith projections. It decides how much growth the church will work for in a given year, or during the next five years. It includes bold, specific plans for implementing the faith projection. It tries any method that seems reasonable. Goal setting also includes frequent evaluation of the methods used and, when necessary, a change of methods.

One researcher asserted that goal setting is a characteristic common to all growing churches in Japan. He acknowledged that Japanese Christians all too easily fall prey to discouragement and pessimism. The growing churches, he pointed out, "have chosen to walk through the wide open doors of opportunity rather than to be discouraged." He declared further that these growing churches "intended to grow" and, furthermore, "they intend to continue growing."[29] Church growth is, in part, a choice. Growth is first of all a decision. It is a decision implemented by goal setting. The setting of specific goals is one of the challenges that confront the Brethren in Christ churches in Japan.

The Yamaguchi Conference

It was the hope of the Japan mission that the churches to which it gave birth would not become encumbered by an organizational structure or present to the nation one more denomination in the list that was already so perplexing. This particular desire on the part of the mission was not realized. Furthermore, the organization of the Yamaguchi churches began upon a precarious foundation. It was born out of a reaction and a moment of high emotion on the part of a few leaders. However, all the leaders were men committed to the Holy Spirit, who guided them into an arrangement both workable and helpful to the churches.

The creating of the conference met several needs that the Christians had been feeling. One of these was, no doubt, the desire for a sense of relationship with one another. The desire to relate closely to each other is a natural part of Japanese society. This desire is present on the individual level and also on the group level. The formation of the conference helped to give the assurance that the churches belong to something bigger and more stable than themselves.[30]

A second need which the conference met was for a structure through which the national churches could communicate with the board. They felt that mission policies were, in some area, unclear. The Japanese leaders wanted a direct line to the American *hombu* (home office). Earlier visits to the United States by Asao Nishimura in 1972, and by Masaharu Okano and Takanobu Tojo of Yamaguchi and Hirotoshi Hashimoto of Tokyo in 1978, had helped the churches to feel that new lines of communication were being formed and that they were being accepted by the North American church. The formation of the conference added to this sense of direct communication and acceptance.

Third, the Japanese leaders had long been desiring more of an identity with their Brethren in Christ roots. There was a growing request for information about the background and doctrines of the church. The organization of churches helped provide a sense of identity with an older, more mature body of Christians.[31]

The original desire of the missionaries to move away from a denomination was valid. However, the new conference, although with an imposing set of bylaws, is nevertheless functioning in an informal manner and with a spirit of mutual cooperation. The *kyogikai* (council meeting) convenes once a month to discuss matters of mutual concern and to offer encouragement to individual churches. Some of its members stated that it is not the purpose of the conference to rule the churches. Rather it recognizes the individuality of the groups and encourages it. Often non-official members of the various congregations also attend the monthly meetings. They sometimes bring up too many problems for discussion, but this also contributes to the strength of the larger group as they listen to the concern of the individual members. The leaders declared that the *kyogikai* has contributed greatly to the feeling of unity among the churches. The leaders help to balance each other with their different personalities. The meeting times become occasions of praise to God and encouragement for one another. God, the leaders affirmed, has made good come out of the struggle.

By the middle of 1980, the Yamaguchi conference had showed its strength in a variety of ways. Most significantly, perhaps, it assumed part of the support for two young men who entered a Tokyo seminary from the Shimonoseki church. Plans were made for Kazayuki Hirokawa to return to the Shimonoseki church in a leadership role and for Masashi Furuta to be involved later in church planting, perhaps together with personnel supplied by the mission. In 1978 the conference sent Hagi's Okano and Shimonoseki's Tojo to the General Conference which convened at Messiah College. They were accompanied by Koganei's pastor Hashimoto.

The strength of the Yamaguchi church organization was further shown when it organized and held the twentieth-anniversary celebration of the Brethren in Christ work in Japan on October 10, 1973. The all-day celebration was held in a rented hall in Hagi with all the churches well represented. The morning program consisted of a combined worship service, a presentation of the vision of the various churches for the future, and a brief message and presentation by mission superintendent John Graybill. After a relaxed time of feasting and fellowship, representatives from the various churches spent the rest of the afternoon in a discussion based on the topic, "Believers' Witness and Evangelism Which Bears Fruit."[32]

On two occasions, September 1975 and May 1978, the churches combined in a camping weekend at Kiyo, a seaside spot north of Hagi. Seventy-eight people registered for the first meeting and one hundred for the second. On the second occasion, the emphasis was on children, who made up sixty of the one hundred who attended. Hajime Kaneshige, formerly of the Hagi church, inspired children and adults with his message. It was reported that "the Holy Spirit ruled the service and Jesus' love flowed through each mind." The time together was climaxed by a baptismal service for three people.[33]

Asao Nishimura of the Nagato church no doubt expressed the feelings of many of the Japanese Christians on the occasion of the twentieth anniversary of the church:

> I am very thankful that the missionaries worked hard to spread the light of the Lord and have led many people to Christ. We owe these missionaries that we can live abundant lives now praising God with thanksgiving. . . . I realize with regret that I have not been sincere enough to do my best for Him. . . . But when I believe that anything can be done by the power of the Almighty God that works through me, I can get ready

to do my best. Without this Spirit, no work can bear abundant fruit. . . . I believe that if we continue to do our best, relaxing in His peace and joy, we can surely bear good fruit, because people will see the brightness of His abundant life through us.[34]

And in that confidence, the Yamaguchi churches continued their "Walk of Twenty Years" with the Lord into the 1980s.

A leaders' meeting in Nagato in 1969. (Left to right, standing): Arita (Takibe), Nagai (Shimonoseki), Nishimura (Nagato), Yamamoto (Nagato), Shibata (Hagi), John Graybill, Marlin Zook, Mrs. Kuboe (Takibe), Peter Willms, Okano (Hagi), Doyle Book. (Seated): Onaka (Senzaki-Nagato), Iwamoto (Nagato), Yoshioka (Shimonoseki), Kaneshige (Yamaguchi), Kuboe (Takibe), Okazaki (Takibe), Abe (Shimonoseki), and Okazaki (Takibe).

Mrs. Matoba and a "seeker" at the Koganei (Tokyo) church, in 1979.

Mr. and Mrs. Takanobu Tojo and family in 1986. The first chairman of the Yamaguchi Brethren in Christ Conference, he pastors the Yamanota church.

Hirotoshi Hashimoto, the first pastor to be seminary trained and appointed full-time by the Brethren in Christ in Japan, here being ordained by John Graybill.

Worshippers at the Shimonoseki church in 1984. Ray and Winnie Hock are visible in the back row.

A worship service in Nagato around 1975. Marlin Zook and Asao Nishimura are at the head table.

Ruth and Marlin Zook and Jean Maedke (front row, from left to right), with a Hino City English class for a Christmas part in 1984.

John Moody, Jean Maedke, and Kathy Kennedy—three of more than twenty Voluntary Service persons who have taught English as a second language for the Brethren in Christ in Japan. (1984 photo)

The Nagato church building in Yamaguchi, around 1982.

The Yamanota church building in Shimonoseki, around 1982.

The Hagi church building in Yamaguchi, around 1982.

The Nukui (Koganei) church building at the time of its dedication in 1973.

Chapter Nine

The Future Mission

The four basic principles which guided the missionaries in their approach to the work in Japan were important not only in the beginning stages of the mission but also throughout its development and in its continued attempts to nurture the churches. The four principles can be summarized as follows: (1) groups of worshippers—or cells—in many communities rather than one centralized place of worship, (2) autonomous, community-type churches rather than a denominational organization, (3) local organization, and control of the group by the believers themselves rather than control by the mission, and (4) self-supported, lay leaders rather than professional, paid pastors.

The mission's concern for the development of locally autonomous, independent churches has been dealt with in chapters 7 and 8. The concept of lay leadership has been discussed at length, but further evaluation and comment is needed at this point. Likewise, the remaining two emphases of cell groups and self-government need to be considered briefly.

Cell Groups

The mission was not amiss in its emphasis on cell group evangelism. The gospel is not something to be secured only by going to a centrally located dispensing point. It should rather be present as a group of believers in every neighborhood and social grouping. The church should "belong" to a community. It should be readily available to the circle of acquaintances of the Christians who are the only light in a particular neighborhood.

The cell concept is a principle which should be used to an even greater extent by the mission of the future. Japanese people respond to the informal nature of the small, house meeting. On the other hand, it is difficult for them to cross the threshold of a formal assembly where they will have to meet many strangers and possibly be singled out in a public introduction. The cell is a valuable tool for the nurture of believers. In the intimacy of the small group setting, all the participants can share equally in response to the Bible study, personal needs can be expressed, and prayers can be freely offered.

More importantly, however, the cell meeting is a valuable tool in evangelism. Again its value is seen in the intimacy it offers. This intimacy provides the open door for the establishment of relationships which are more easily formed in the atmosphere of open discussion and the inevitable tea time. After an initial response to the gospel has been expressed in such times of close sharing, a bridge for the seeker to the larger church can more easily be built.

The advantages of the use of cell groups in evangelistic outreach can be summarized in the following manner. First, such groups are natural. It is much easier for a person to enter the house of a neighbor than to go to a strange church. Second, they are convenient. An unsaved neighbor is much more likely to respond to an invitation to walk across the street than to board a bus or train for a distant place. Third, cell meetings are economical. It usually costs the mission or church nothing to make use of homes. Fourth, they are biblical. The early church met in believers' homes (1 Cor. 16:19, Col. 4:15 and Acts 2:46). Fifth, they encourage the participation of members of the group in discussion and in leadership. And, sixth, they are well adapted to the culture where people respond more readily to group discussion than to monologue preaching.[1]

Concerning cultural adaptation, the Non-Church Movement (*Mukyokai*) has flourished with its emphasis on neighborhood, informal meetings. At one point in the early years of the mission, it was estimated that the Christian group which kept no membership figures numbered approximately 50,000 adherents. Furthermore, the post-war, indigenous Japanese religions have capitalized on the small group concept with great success. Memberships of religious groups like Soka Gakkai, Seicho No Ie and PL Kyodan have soared into the millions through vast networks of cell groups.

A study of the methods of these modern religions confirmed the fact that the small house meeting is congenial to the Japanese today. The study declared that millions of people gathered in the homes of their neighbors all over Japan for religious meetings. The ever-increasing urban and industrial structuring of society leads to the mechanization and depersonalization of life. The resulting emptiness is further aggravated by the breakdown of the communal and family patterns of the past. "The swift growth of these religions is in large measure due to their ability to fill the void left by these modern phenomena . . . . The warm fellowship of . . the small group provides relief from loneliness and a sense of social support."[2]

The topic of "house churches" has received a great deal of attention in recent years. This is primarily because of their use by several "super-churches" in South America and Korea. But the cell group concept is not concerned chiefly with large churches which cannot accommodate all the worshippers in their sanctuaries. It is concerned rather with small churches which can make effective use of house meetings in order to envelop more and more nonbelievers. It has been pointed out that rapidly growing churches in Japan emphasize the decentralization of meeting places.[3]

The success of the Japan mission in the use of cell groups varied considerably. But the principle is sound. Small, informal meetings are well understood, and even preferred, by most Japanese. In view of this fact the mission should "shape its evangelistic efforts to this aspect of Japanese culture." It should develop skill "in the use of the small house meeting as a means of enlarging established churches and of rapidly multiplying new ones."[4]

Indigeneity

The Japan mission also emphasized that, as quickly as possible, the local church should be encouraged toward self-government. This included the selection of church officers, support for the financial needs of the church and an exercising of responsibility in outreach. The internal strength of the churches today testifies to the validity of this emphasis.

The approach of most missions at this time was to provide money for buildings, to train and support pastors, and to exercise control over the churches in other ways. The result of this approach was dependence upon the mission and little or no evangelistic concern on the part of the church. Most church members settled into the rut of merely attending church and "being warmed and fed." They felt that outreach was the mission's concern. In the case of the Brethren in Christ mission, it was felt by some that the mission urged self-management upon the little churches too quickly. But the mission was concerned that the believers learn that being a Christian involves evangelistic responsibility. It was moved by the question: How in the shortest possible time can the mission establish a completely self-supporting church that will bear the burden of the Great Commission, reach out to convert their own brethren, and then go out to cover the globe with the gospel?[5]

The mission policy of refusing to provide church buildings for the believers and encouraging the use of homes and rented halls is compatible with the concept of cell groups. However, it also pertains to the question of indigeneity. The churches themselves made the decision as to when they should move toward ownership of their own buildings. They showed wisdom and gained courage as they wrestled with the problem of incredibly high land costs. And they had the satisfaction of knowing that they had set their own goals and had met them.

Economic conditions of modern Japan suggest that the mission was wise in its church building policy and that it should be continued. Land values continue to increase at more than thirty percent annually from levels already ten times higher than comparable space in America. Because of this fact, the mission should stress the multiplication of churches in homes and rented halls. As an existing church grows to its capacity, it should be encouraged to begin daughter churches. This practice would avoid the cost of building larger or moving to another location. In this way even smaller groups of Christians can maintain full control over their own affairs, including the matter of paying their own expenses.

Lay Ministry

We return once more to the discussion of the leadership of the church. The mission was right in its concern for a ministry more flexible and mobile than the traditional "one-paid-pastor-per-church" system. The winning of Japan "will be accomplished only by the planting of thousands of new churches in communities all over the land."[6] But if the planting of those churches has to wait for trained professionals to provide the leadership, it is unlikely that they will be planted. It is still true today that "if Japan's villages are ever going to be evangelized and have their own witness, that witness will have to be supplied by self-supported lay leaders."[7]

The Church of Jesus Christ belongs to every community, every village, every ethnic group of the world. The Japanese culture, however, is one that depends on professionals for every part of its life. In that dependence on them, it excuses the layman from any responsibility in carrying out the duties which it attributes to the professional. In relation to the church, such an attitude will stifle growth. If Japan is to be won, every Christian will have to see his place in the task of evangelism. Each believer will have to be mobilized in direct witness and in ministry within the church body.

The lay ministry concept is still a valid principle in the growth of the Japan church today. The mission should promote this principle in all its outreach. However, the mission must be ready to adapt the principle to various situations. As we have already noted, it must be ready to supply outside assistance to lay leaders where that is needed and it must do so at the right time. It must provide a "consultant" to encourage the leaders and give professional guidance. This consultant can be a missionary. If this is impractical, the mission should then be prepared to encourage a national to fill this need. And it should help him to secure the proper training which will enable him to serve as a *sensei* to the church leaders.

One thing is needed, above all, to preserve the potential of the self-supported lay ministry today. That crucial element is adequate training at the local level. Training must be provided where the layman resides and while he carries on his normal activities in society. It must enable him to continue functioning efficiently in his regular environment and at the same time improve his skills in church leadership. In fact, proper training at the local level operates on the principle that better learning takes place when one can immediately apply to the local situation what he has learned. In this way, theory is immediately tested through application and is thus reinforced. Thus, the local church and its evangelistic efforts immediately receive the benefits of the insights learned. Such benefits cost nothing because the lay ministers can support themselves at their jobs while they learn.

This approach by no means rules out the value, or even the need, for formal seminary or Bible school training for a few professional leaders and teachers. But obviously, "if lay training is the objective then the school must be taken to the laity, not the laity torn out of their jobs and sent to one central school." Those who are removed from their natural situation may never again be the laity, for how will they once again get secular jobs upon returning from such schools?[8]

Local training should be made available not only to those members of the church who are considered leaders but to other members as well. The Shimonoseki women who were in the original, missionary-led Bible class indicated their gratitude for the Bible teaching received. They suggested that part of the strength of the present Yamanota church and their own leadership abilities stem from those times of learning the Word together. A rapidly growing church in another part of Japan was mentioned earlier. In this church all the members were urged to take extensive notes during the worship service and then go out and "preach the message" to others. This is an excellent example of "in-service training." This kind of activity not only causes the believers to learn their lessons well, it also aids in the evangelistic outreach of the church.[9]

Proper local training can also help avoid dependence on the professional pastor. As one leader suggested, the believers should first be given thorough training in the faith and in principles of evangelism. They should then be taught not to depend on the pastor but to "do the work of the ministry" under his leadership (Eph. 4:12). If training of this kind can be provided, the presence of a professional pastor might accomplish more for the church than leadership comprised only of laymen.[10] The challenge for both the mission and the church of the future is to provide adequate training for both lay leaders and members in or near the local church itself.

Ministering in Culture

Evangelism always takes place in a cultural setting. The most successful outreach is one which first studies the culture carefully in order to discover its perspectives and response patterns and then adapts its communication to those patterns. The task which faces the Japan mission is to focus on those elements of the culture which can be used to create a response to the gospel message. Several important cultural elements evident in Japan are suggested below. These must be considered carefully by the national church as well as by the mission and must be included in any strategy of evangelism.

First, every attempt must be made to win whole family units. Japanese society generally operates on the concept of the consensus of the group. The individual decision is not considered as important as the feeling of the group. Family units possess a strong sense of group consciousness. It is true that the father will sometimes make a decision to which family members are expected to agree. Usually, however, if a radical decision is made by one member without consideration for the rest of the family, the sense of family unity is weakened. This may create a negative response, or resistance, to the cause or idea espoused by the individual. In such a case the opportunity for further witness to the family may be closed.

Outreach attempts should appeal to this sense of family unity. It is recognized that salvation is not procured by a group on behalf of its members. Conversion can take place only through the individual response to the claims of Jesus Christ. However, incorporation of the convert into the local church should always be made with the thought in mind of winning the entire family unit. This may mean denying a young person baptism for a time until family consent for the baptism can be gained or until the rest of the family can be given the opportunity to consider Jesus Christ. It may mean that parents will want to postpone their own baptism until the children can also be encouraged into a conversion experience.

There is no more powerful witness to a community than that of family members being baptized together. The one-by-one approach taught by western missionaries for so long must be replaced with the awareness of group dynamics. Non-believers must be shown that the Christian faith is for family units and not merely for children or certain peripheral individuals. They must be made to see that Christianity allows social groups to retain their social identity and express the Christian faith in the context of their cultural perspectives.

In order to win family units, a primary focus of both mission and church must be on men. The wives of non-Christian men should not be expected to win their husbands by themselves. The responsibility for the conversion of men in Japan rests upon the entire church. Christian men must carry a clear witness to unsaved men at their places of work. They must lunch with them, play with them and offer help where that is needed. They must make an effort to include their colleagues in activities involving Christian men.

The Christian home, whether missionary or national, should be seen as a tool in evangelism. Several of the Yamaguchi leaders testified to the profound impression made upon them by the warm welcome into the Christian homes of the missionaries. The openness of the homes—the willingness to include them as one of the family—was most impressive. Invitations to meals and hospitality extended in other ways allowed them to sense the atmosphere of love and see the parent/child relationship. Such experiences were influential in their conversions, in their decisions to seek a Christian partner and in their establishing a Christian home of their own.[11] Christian families should open their homes for special activities with non-Christian families. Whenever possible, the invitation should be issued through the man of the house. This will help to acknowledge his place in the gradual involvement of the family in Christian fellowship. Where special efforts have been inaugurated in Japanese churches to win men, men have been won.[12]

Second, all church members and seekers should be incorporated into a fellowship network. The congregation should be organized into districts or blocks. The church members within a given area form a group for the purposes of fellowship, relaying information, responding to prayer needs and lending a helping hand at times of emergency or special need. Their goal is to form a "web" of love to envelop the home of every believer and seeker. The center of this web is the church. A strong Christian is made responsible for up to ten homes in his area, depending on the size of the church. Each of those ten can then be made responsible for ten others as growth occurs. Special announcements, prayer needs, and news of a death are relayed from the primary contact person throughout the network. The believers then respond with prayers, aid, food, house-sitting or sympathy.

As soon as a seeker expresses an interest in the message of the gospel, his home is to be included in the network. At that time the personal, neighborhood ministry of the believers to the home begins. Such a network would also help to retain those who have once entered the fellowship of the church but who are about to leave "by the back door." It would enable the web of caring to be drawn more closely around them. Whether for seekers or for weak believers, the purpose of the fellowship network is the same—evangelism.

Japanese social structure has similar networks. These networks are called *buraku*. In the rural areas they become closeknit, rather rigid communities of families. Even in the larger cities where people think they will be lost in the sea of impersonality, such networks function throughout communities from the city hall down to the individual household. They are organized chiefly for the purpose of disseminating information and collecting various contributions. The popular, rapidly expanding modern religions referred to earlier hold and encourage their believers with similar types of networks. The mission and church should realize that here is a structure already understood by Japanese and make use of it in the context of Christ's love and the fellowship of believers.

Third, the mission must be prepared to meet felt needs. These are the special concerns held by the people themselves. Although they are usually culturally or socially derived, they frequently involve deep emotional attachment. In many cases the people need to know how Christianity relates to these areas of awareness before they are able to consider the spiritual needs which the missionary is most concerned about. This means that the missionary may have to postpone the preaching of Christian doctrines for a time and communicate the church's willingness to identify with these cultural needs.

The most crucial area of concern for most Japanese is that relating to death. This area includes the care of the tablets on which the name of the deceased is inscribed and a place to keep the ashes of the family member. It also includes the many ceremonies which are required in order to commemorate properly the memory of their loved ones. Buddhism requires that such ceremonies be held on the first, seventh, thirteenth, thirtieth and fiftieth anniversaries of the death of the family member. The Christian church, or the mission that plants it, must show the seeker and his family that it is prepared to supply whatever is desired for the memorials of former family members. Such an expression is crucial in the initial stages of communicating the gospel. To ignore such concerns or to dismiss them as inconsequential may close the door to further witness.

Many felt needs are connected with happier occasions. One of these is the formal engagement ceremony. Another is the festival for children who reach the ages of three, five or seven during a given year. Yet another is the dedication of a new house. At the latter, hundreds of pink and white rice cakes are thrown from the roofless rafters to delighted children and adults who scramble for them on the ground below. In some cases the religious connotation of such activities is clear. In others the event is considered only a custom. In either case, it is an important event in the minds of the people. Such events present one of the greatest challenges to the Christian church. They also present one of its greatest opportunities for evangelism. Where certain aspects of these ceremonies are found to be irredeemably pagan, something Christian must be substituted for them. Where the ceremonies are acknowledged as purely cultural expressions, the church must adopt them and provide attractive and appealing expressions of them.

The point is that the church can at no time afford to dismiss or ignore such activities. They are inseparably intertwined with the emotional make-up of the Japanese people. The church must provide for these occasions with activities which are more satisfying and meaningful than were the ceremonies previously provided by the shrine or the community. When non-believers see that Christianity relates to their indigenous customs and makes them more enjoyable than before, the doors for further witness are opened. The gospel is no longer dismissed as a foreign religion, and the church is seen to be a church of the Japanese people themselves.

Felt needs are emotional in nature and are lodged very deeply in the consciousness of the people. The church, or the mission which plants it, must respond to these needs. It must further make use of them as a means of drawing people into the fellowship of believers.

Fourth, the mission should continue to respond to the intense interest of the Japanese in English conversation. There is no doubt that teaching English provides many contacts that the missionary would otherwise not encounter. Some of these contacts continue on a social level only. But many of them turn into fruit for the Kingdom. One missionary estimated that fifty percent of his English contacts become Christians.[13] A Japanese believer said that one of the most important reasons for missionaries to teach English is that it enables people to see a Christian home.[14]

The Hagi leaders maintained that English is the most effective way at present to reach high school students with the gospel. They pointed out that it is now impossible to conduct camps for high schoolers. The reason is that school officials have become alarmed about proliferating religious groups which are vying for students' loyalties. In some cases these groups are enticing the students away from their schools and families. Because of this the schools have refused permission for their students to participate in any organized religious activity. Thus the opportunity for evangelism through camps is closed. However, students can still be attracted to the church through English classes. It is true, of course, that most of these students will later go away to college or to jobs. Thus any influence the church exerts will be for only one or two years. However, as the leaders pointed out, "If we don't get them for that much, we won't get them at all!"[15]

It is obvious from expressions like these that teaching English conversation is still an important evangelistic tool. The mission should take advantage of this fact and form part of its strategy around it. The door should be opened for an increasing number of voluntary service personnel. However, several things are necessary for the evangelistic potential of this method to be fully realized. First, a bridge must be created between the classes of the VSers and the missionary himself. The missionary should be brought into the classes at strategic points. He should make attempts to get acquainted with the students. He should open his house to them on occasion or plan excursions with them. Second, the English classes must always be seen to have a connection with the local church. The best way to give this impression is to hold the classes in the church building. It may be desirable to include a brief Bible message by a church member as a part of the session. In such a case, however, the plan to do so must be included in the publicity about the classes. Whatever means are used, the student should be helped to become familiar with the church and be made to feel that it is "his church." The future mission will do well to increase efforts in trying to reap the potential contained in this evangelistic tool.

Missionary Qualities

God always uses people in carrying out his work—usually very ordinary ones. But in God's hands they become instruments of usefulness and beauty. Proper preparation and proper attitudes in the missionary enable God to use him or her in the most effective way. Let us consider some of the qualities that are needed in the missionary of the future. These qualities are: sensitivity to culture, flexibility in attitudes and methods, ability to get along with others, and openness to the Holy Spirit.

First, the missionary must be sensitive to culture, which includes having a respect for different customs and a willingness to adjust to different perspectives. No culture is either intrinsically good or bad. Each culture has both good and bad elements in it. The good elements found in one culture do not make that culture in itself superior to any other, or more sacred. Thus God does not approve of American culture as a whole more than any other. He is, no doubt, pleased that so many Americans have responded to his Son and that some changes which are in conformity with his Word have occurred in society. But he is surely grieved that some aspects of that society are as degrading, in comparison with the standards of his Word, as practices of so-called "pagan" societies, and in some cases more so.

The missionary must understand that the American culture is not superior to any other. It may have many technological achievements to its credit, but it does not meet the needs of its people any better than other cultures meet the needs of their people. Each culture is valid in its own right. Therefore the customs of one culture are "strange" only to the observer from another culture.

Most importantly, God chooses to work with cultures just as they are. He does not demand that they change certain practices before he begins to express his love to them. He does not require that they conform to certain ethical standards before they can know him, any more than he requires this of individuals. God comes to both individuals and cultures just as they are. He acknowledges them as ready to receive his love. A missionary must look at cultures as God looks at them—and as he once looked at the missionary—as objects of his grace. Such a view frees the missionary to appreciate different customs. It helps him to try to understand the thinking behind those customs. It frees him from a judgmental attitude that may block effective communication. And it helps him to trust God to bring about the change that God sees is necessary.

Second, the missionary must be flexible in his attitudes and his methods. He must be one who can change his own ideas and adapt to other ideas. It is true that he must hold to scriptural principles and affirm the absolutes of God's character and plan of redemption. But he must also be able to recognize the differences between those absolutes and human interpretations of Scripture which have been termed "sacred." He must discern between biblical principles and a cultural, although sincere, application of those principles.

In relation to methods, the missionary must be prepared to work with others in a variety of situations. The day of the missionary functioning alone as leader or decision maker is past. The mission of the future will be one of partnership with national Christians. The Japan church leaders expressed a desire for the continued help of the missionaries. They acknowledged their lack of certain strengths which the missionaries possess. One of these strengths is training and experience in methods of evangelism. Another is the many biblical insights that missionaries have been gaining over the years. The leaders indicated that it is easier to receive admonition from foreigners than from their own people. They acknowledged that Japanese tend to waver on some issues. They declared that missionaries can hold them steady by their earnestness and the strength of their convictions. On the other hand, it was pointed out that cross-cultural evangelism is difficult. Neither the missionary nor the national alone can fully answer the question "What is the gospel and what is culture?" Partnership provides the opportunity for missionary and national to search for the answer together. The Japanese Christian can help the missionary understand the relationship of the gospel to culture.[16]

Flexibility in missionaries means also that they must include the nationals in many of their decisions. It means that the mission must keep the church informed about its plans and ask it for advice. One leader suggested that methods will not be the crucial issue in the partnership of the future. Instead, "Common goals and a common spirit will provide the strength for outreach together."[17] The missionary of the future must be flexible enough to pioneer or to assist, but always to serve.

Third, the missionary must be able to get along with others. It is usually much easier to get along with God than with people. When other people enter the picture, adjustments need to be made. Give and take becomes necessary. New ideas which come from different perspectives must be considered. This often creates tension. The missionary is not less susceptible to incorrect motives or self-assertion than are other Christians.

It would often be easier to minister by oneself. But the Kingdom of God is not brought into being by loners. It is built by Christians working in harmony toward a common goal. God's work is not carried out primarily by individuals. It is done by the Body together. Mission is a function of the total Body of Christ. And the Body is made up of different parts which complement one another in the work. In complementing one another, the parts often rub against each other.

The question of how to solve situations which contain possible conflict was addressed very well by Robert Hempy. He suggested that such situations are described in Chapters 4, 5, and 6 of Ephesians. But he pointed out that in each of the relationships mentioned there, a Third Party is indicated. Conflict among Christians occurs when there is no recognition of the Third Party. If there are only two people in relationship and disagreement occurs, someone must win and someone must lose. Only two sides demand a winner and a loser. Someone must back down, give up. Naturally each party wants to be the winner. This is the seed for conflict. However, if a Third Party is present, and both Christians are genuinely concerned about what he wants, then he wins and neither Christian loses. We must learn to "be subject to one another out of reverence for Christ" (Eph. 4:21).[18]

We are reminded at this point of Henry Hostetter's conviction that Brethren in Christ Missions have been characterized by two things: a deep commitment to God and a genuine concern for others. He insisted that, if these two things are present, then God can work in any situation.[19] Commitment to God and a concern for others—these two things are necessary also for the missionary of the future.

Fourth, the missionary must be open to the Holy Spirit. The Holy Spirit is a missionary Spirit. As he moves throughout the world he desires to manifest Jesus Christ in both his character—the fruits of the spirit—and his power—the gifts of the Spirit. The manifestation of the character of Jesus Christ is not enough to minister to a lost world. The world also needs a demonstration of his power.

Jesus performed God's mission. And he manifested the power of God in miracles, signs and wonders. Jesus commanded his Church to carry on God's mission. And he said, "I send you in the same way the Father sent me . . . Greater works than these shall you do . . . Signs shall follow those who believe in me . . . " (John 20:21, 14:12, Mark 16:17). The Holy Spirit desires to manifest Jesus in the same way he was manifested 2,000 years ago. He desires a people who are open to all the ways in which he might want to work.

The church needs to be willing to jump recklessly into the stream of the Spirit as it moves around the world today. Demonic powers are at work in the cultured land of Japan as they are in America. Missions frequently involves direct confrontation with these powers. The missionary who is improperly equipped for this confrontation will fail in his mission. The church needs to ask the Holy Spirit how he would like to work in the world. Together with asking, it needs to expect him to manifest the fullness of Jesus Christ through it as it goes out in mission.

The Home Church

At this point we might ask ourselves, "What of the home church in relation to the mission of the future?" The home church is a vital part of the mission venture. Its commitment should be no less than that of the mission. It should strive to develop the same qualities as those of the missionaries—it should inform itself about cultures and learn respect for different cultural perspectives; it should be willing to be flexible, both in its attitudes and in its methods; it should commit itself to love for one another and strive to live in harmony; and it should earnestly desire both the fruit and the power of the Holy Spirit in all its activities. Such qualities will prepare the church for further, effective mission.

One further challenge presents itself to the home church. That challenge is involvement in witness. Involvement in witness includes both money and energy. Church members must be involved in giving of their money and their energy to the same degree they expect the missionaries to give. The attitude that they can pay their missionaries to be "out there" and evangelize is deadly. So also is the attitude that they have done their duty in paying the tithe and have the right to spend the rest of their income on themselves. The mission of the future must be carried out by people willing to live for the cause of missions or it will fail. The mission of the future will be no more dedicated than the people behind it. And it will be no more successful in soul winning than those who support it.

Chapter Ten

Into the 1980s

A New Look in the Mission

The year 1980 brought an event that had not occurred in almost twenty years. For the first time since the arrival of the Zooks in 1963, new full-time recruits from North America joined the team of missionaries.

Ray and Winifred Hock of Carlisle, Pennsylvania, arrived in Japan with twenty-one-month-old Jason on August 25. The Hocks were sent into service by their home church, Carlisle, Pennsylvania, and their parents, Laban and Annie Hock and Walter and Mildred Lehman. Ray had received an M.Div. degree from Eastern Baptist Theological Seminary in 1980. He and Winnie met at Messiah College and were married on August 9, 1974. Amy Michelle was born in Japan in March 1983.

The Hocks moved into the tiny apartment above the Kodaira church and immediately plunged into language study at a school in Ochanomizu near downtown Tokyo.

The mission staff was further strengthened by the arrival of Dan and Karen Dehyle and their two sons, Vaughn, 5, and Cameron, 3, on August 14, 1981. Children of Carl and Alice Dehyle and Paul and Lela Hostetler, they were members of the church in Harrisburg, Pennsylvania. The Dehyles also met while attending Messiah College and were married on August 14, 1971.

Dan and Karen had been in the upholstery business in Mechanicsburg, Pennsylvania, but felt that they should make themselves available for an assignment of at least several years. They were assigned initially for a three-year term, but the possibility of their moving into a full-time capacity was being considered by both them and the mission board. Upon arrival in Japan, they took up temporary residence at Kariuzawa for a short term of intensive language study.

The two older mission families were also in a time of transition. The Zooks moved into the mission residence next to the Kodaira church. They were preparing to open a new outreach center in the neighboring suburb of Fuchu. For this purpose, financial support had been offered from the Nukui (Koganei) church, and three new VSers were soon to arrive to provide visibility and contacts through the teaching of English.

The Graybills had returned to Pennsylvania for a time of furlough. In early 1981 they moved to Pasadena, California, for a period of study at the School of World Mission of Fuller Seminary. They returned to Japan in July of that year but did not return to Tokyo. Instead they moved into the house of one of the missionary directors of the Yodogawa Christian Hospital in Osaka. Their move had been determined largely at the request of the Japanese church leaders who felt that the possibility of opening a new work in another metropolitan area should be adequately investigated. Osaka lay about halfway between Tokyo and Yamaguchi and was seen as a possible geographical link between existing churches in the two areas. The Graybills were asked to seek out likely places for a new church planting effort. During this time, John served as assistant chaplain for the hospital and pursued further language and church-growth studies.

New Outreach Locations

Bolstered by the newly-arrived missionary personnel, three new works took form in rapid succession from 1980 to 1982. Although aided by the coming of the new missionaries, the new efforts were by no means the projects of the mission alone. A new plan of cooperative ministry was emerging whereby new churches were to be planted with a Japanese pastor and a missionary working together. This approach was given the name "partnership" and will be discussed in more detail later.

The first of these new works was in the western part of the city of Fuchu. Marlin and Ruth Zook opened the Nishihara Christian Center in October of 1980 in a section of the city that contained up to 30,000 people and no churches. A narrow building three stories high was rented. The early approach was to establish "friendship evangelism," that is, "taking time to care for people and their needs."

Assisting Marlin at the center was a group of three voluntary service teachers, Mary Brubaker, Dora Myers, and Connie Lofthouse. The three were promptly dubbed "The Three Sisters" by John Graybill. These three plunged into the task of scheduling English and Bible classes, visiting new acquaintances, and otherwise trying to learn to know people. Announcements were distributed concerning the English classes, and with some of these went tracts provided by Every Home Crusade. The first public service was a Christmas program on December 20, 1980. The first Sunday worship service took place at 3:00 p.m. on April 19, 1980.[1]

Although many friendships were formed and opportunities for personal witness among the teachers and their students were frequent, response to the Christian services was very slow. For reasons to be noted later, the Center was moved in 1982 to a tiny house in a nearby neighborhood.

In a sudden change of plans, the second church planting effort was begun in Nagoya. In a joint meeting of missionaries and Japanese leaders in November 1981, John and Lucille Graybill were asked to move from Osaka to Nagoya and the idea of starting a church in Osaka was cancelled. There were several reasons for this change. The first was that there were no national Brethren in Christ members in Osaka to give assistance in pioneering a new church. Second, Mr. and Mrs. Hidetsugu Sugata, originally from Yamaguchi, were planning to move to Nagoya from Okazaki and were eager to be a part of a church planting venture. Third, there were seen to be fewer churches in the greater Nagoya area with its population of more than six million.[2]

On June 28, 1982, the Graybills took up residence in Midori Ward, a largely new area with people moving in from various parts of Japan. Preliminary research had shown that the population of that section of the city was expected to grow to 180,000 by 1990 and that the ratio of population to churches in the area was 37,500 to 1, twice the national average.[3]

In another sudden change of plans explained below, Dan and Karen Dehyle joined the Graybills in Nagoya in August. The first worship service took place on the first Sunday of October in the Graybills' living room. Earl and Sue Musser of the Chino, California, congregation were visitors on this auspicious occasion. The Sugatas moved into the Midori area in November, and the partnership team was completed.[4]

The third new work was located in Shin Shimonoseki, a new section of Shimonoseki City in Yamaguchi and across town from the growing Yamanota Church. Ray and Winnie Hock, having completed language school, joined Kazayuki Hirokawa, recently graduated from seminary, and his wife in the fall of 1982. The Dehyles were planning to assist the team as English teachers. Before they arrived, however, they found that immigration officials had closed the door to the teaching of English for remuneration by those on a regular missionary visa. In a series of rapid consultations among missionaries, Japanese leaders, and the Board for Missions, it was decided to ask the Dehyles to join the Graybills and Sugatas in Nagoya.[5]

The newer missionaries met some of the same problems that the earlier missionaries had met. They struggled with the problem of learning the language.[6] They also encountered the problem of educating their children. The Dehyles tried to help their boys "weave their way into the Japanese school system." Adjustments were difficult and were attempted with many prayers from friends in the home churches.[7]

But these new recruits evidenced a strength of Christian commitment and a quality of discipline that made a deep impression on American visitors who came to their home. Instead of cutting morning devotions short for the sake of sightseeing, each day the missionaries led their guests in systematic study and prayer, to the great blessing of the visitors and hosts alike.[8]

Evangelism Through English

The service of short-term volunteers working with existing or new churches grew in importance in the 1980s. As Mary Brubaker, Connie Lofthouse and Dora Myers completed two years of service in 1982, others were ready to pick up the challenge of becoming support personnel for the missionaries and churches.

Peter and Laura Shaida arrived in September 1982 for a one-year term. The Shaidas filled the need for English teachers at Nukui (Koganei), Yayoidai (Kodaira) and Wakabacho (Tachikawa). Marlin Zook added to his schedule the classes left by the Three Sisters at Fuchu. The coming of the Shaidas was significant in that it marked the first participation in the English program of a person with an advanced degree in a field related to TESL. With an M.A. in speech, Pete added technical expertise and credibility to the program. Laura made her contribution from the background of a B.S. degree in education.

The effort of evangelism through English gained a valuable ally in Mrs. Augusta Reid, an acquaintance of the Graybills in the Tokyo area and the widow of a man in the U.S. military forces. Mrs. Reid conducted classes not associated with the mission program, but she gave the profits from these classes to the mission. These profits amounted to several thousand dollars. She also attended services at Fuchu and Kodaira and was responsible for introducing to these fellowships several people who later were baptized and became active members.[9]

Other youthful and capable volunteers added their talents and encouragement. Steve Holland served from August 1981 to June 1982. Kathy Kennedy came in 1983 and remained for two years. John Moody arrived in 1983 for a three-year term. Jean Maedke also served from 1983 to 1986. Alice Welch assisted the program for eight months from 1984 to 1985. And Alice Dourte became the newest volunteer upon her arrival in September of 1985.

This youthful corps showed an amazing adaptability to the surprises of the new culture as well as an enthusiasm for helping people in their language needs. They boarded bicycles, busses, electric trains and subways by the hour in keeping their appointments. Connections with these various modes of transportation were made by "foot power." Their schedules sometimes required leaving home at 6:30 a.m. and standing for an hour or more at a time in the breathtaking crush of rush-hour passengers. On one occasion, Connie Lofthouse was swept out the door of a train by scores of people determined to exit and was just barely able to board again before the doors closed.[10]

The teachers met fourteen or more classes each week with pupils from children to housewives. Subject matter ranged from the mechanics of forming sounds to discussions on life-changing topics. Evidences of the search for answers to the meaning of life were frequent, and witness for Christ was given, often in time-consuming, personal encounters. Mary Brubaker testified to an awareness that her time was not her own and that there was a reason for long hours spent with her students.[11]

As a result of friendships established by the teachers, students asked for help in understanding the Bible. The gospel was shared with them with clarity over extended times of study and prayer. Dora Myers led a Bible study group that grew from three to eight as students invited non-student friends. The awesome weight of the task of sharing the Good News pressed heavily upon Dora.[12]

Dora not only fell in love with the culture but also with a particular young man. After returning to America, she accepted the invitation of Toru Kawate to become his wife and returned to Japan, where she and her husband became supporters in the small church at Miyoshi Cho (Fuchu).[13]

The teachers helped form a bridge from the English classes to the church services, which often seemed too difficult for the uninitiated students to understand. Jean Maedke found such a bridge crucial in her assignment to the new work at Fuchu. During Jean's term, policies relating to teaching English at Fuchu were changed to include thirty minutes of English Bible reading and study and sixty minutes of the study of conversation and other materials. Bible study worksheets were provided for the first period. These brought students face to face with the question, "What do *you* say about Jesus?" With growing interest in the Christian faith, one student was referred to Pastor Furuta. He was soon baptized and became a member of the Fuchu church. John Moody and Kathy Kennedy each saw one of their students accept Christ at the International Dinner organized by the teachers. Some of the seed sown had borne fruit beautifully.[14]

The bridge between the classes and the church was further developed by having the Japanese pastor conduct a short Bible study in the Japanese language after the English lesson with the foreign teacher. In this way, the English students were able to know the leader of the church on a more personal basis. In order to strengthen the bridge, much extra time was frequently given by the teacher. In one of Marlin Zook's classes, after an hour of English conversation and one of Bible study in the Japanese language, the students and teacher went out to eat together and converse for another two hours. This extended contact seemed to provide the necessary encouragement for several people to begin attending church.[15]

Peter and Laura Shaida, upon their return to the United States in June of 1983, provided an experience exciting to both their students and some American families. They organized a Home Stay Tour for students with whom they had formed friendships during their year of teaching in Japan. The applicants for this unique plan grew quickly to twenty-three. John Graybill in Japan took care of travel details for the group while Laura Shaida enlisted host families in Lancaster County, Pennsylvania.

The Shaidas' former students, along with more recent members of classes in Tokyo, Nagoya and Shimonoseki, arrived at Philadelphia on July 25. The schedule was full of sightseeing activities, but the Christian homes of the hosts formed the deepest impression on the visitors. Some of the group clearly felt "drawn to God" through the home and church activities. American hosts reported their own happy experiences as "beauty, courtesy and laughter entered our home." The experience underscored the tremendous potential for involvement in missions "on our own doorstep" through Christians opening their homes to international students and shorter term visitors from foreign lands.[16]

A New Relationship

The 1980s brought about a marked change in the role of leadership in the growing national church. Not unlike the experience of John the Baptist who declared, "He must increase but I must decrease" (John 3:30), the missionaries realized that the time had come for them to relinquish the reins of policy and methodology to young and capable Japanese brethren, also called of God and increasingly seminary trained. The transition was effected largely through the encouragement and guidance of Roy Sider, who became the Secretary of Overseas Ministries for the Board for Missions in 1978. The concept, inaugurated through consultations from 1980 to 1983, was expressed in the term "partnership."

The missionaries now found themselves designated as co-workers with their Japanese brethren. They found that they were now subject to the requests and decisions of the Japanese leaders. The adjustments necessary in learning to work in this new relationship brought some perplexities and frustrations. Some felt that the mission had now been "dismantled." In fact this was the case and was part of a plan which "called for the phase-out of administrative organizations of missions in each country."[17] Mission leaders recognized that "no longer can we in North America hold and dispense 'the master plan.' " Furthermore, they noted, believers in at least seven countries lay claim to the name Brethren in Christ. Because of this, future strategies can be used of God only if a sense of true partnership is maintained.[18]

The board now consulted directly with the national leaders. Missionaries no longer met alone as a policy-forming body. Their occasional meetings as foreign emissaries were for "professional enrichment and to consider intermissionary matters."[19] They now participated in decision-making meetings with the national leaders at the invitation of their hosts.

Likewise, the English classes came largely under the direction of the local Japanese churches in whose area the teachers served. Organization of the classes and registration in them were supervised by the local pastors, and income from the classes was handled by the pastors and disbursed according to agreements between the mission and the national church. Thus the teaching of English became a conscious and planned joining of hands with Japanese believers in the planting and nurture of churches under national leadership, and teachers were placed at the request of national pastors.[20]

A New Church Structure

With the missionary assuming the role of partner instead of director, the Japanese church refined its organization under the leadership of Takanobu Tojo, college professor at Shimonoseki City College and pastor of the Yamanota church. He was assisted by newly seminary-trained Masashi Furuta serving at Fuchu and Kazayuki Hirokawa at Shin-Shimonoseki, along with earlier lay pastors Asao Nishimura of Nagato and Masaharu Okano of Hagi.

A planning committee for bringing the Yamaguchi and Tokyo churches into one official conference was inaugurated in 1981. In November of 1983 this conference was officially established. One notable exclusion from the conference was the Nukui church in Koganei, which had helped to encourage several of the newer works in the Tokyo area. The Nukui church had earlier established its own formal registration with the government as a property-holding religious incorporation and chose to keep that independent identity.

At the same time, Pastor Hirotoshi Hashimoto and his group continued their interest in and cooperative efforts with both the Tokyo and Yamaguchi churches, attending denominational discussions and occasionally contributing funds in evangelistic efforts.

In November of the following year, at the Second Annual General Conference, an executive committee for organization was chosen. Tojo, already the appointed chairman of the conference, became the chairman of the committee. Four areas of function under the committee were established: Administrative, Financial, Education, and Pioneer Evangelism. The chairpersons appointed for these various functions were Nishimura, Okano, Tojo (on an interim basis), and Futura, respectively. Discussions began in 1983 for the forming of a confession of faith for the youthful denomination. At the third General Conference held in November 1984, the articles were approved. A decision to continue refining them over the next ten years was also affirmed.[21]

As in traditional creeds, the basic tenets of the Christian faith concerning the Bible, God, man, salvation, the Church and the end times are clearly affirmed in the Confession of Faith. Unique to the creed of this new church, however, is the freshness and force with which the age-old truths are expressed in the Japanese language. A church in a land formerly strange to the gospel had been born from missionary efforts, and that church was now declaring itself in conformance with orthodox Christianity, yet with a perspective distinct from western culture and with a style of articulation special to its own understanding of the faith.[22]

Plans to discuss in more detail the matters of church leadership, ordination, and the walk of the believer were also initiated at the 1984 Conference. An over-arching theme for the first three conferences emerged clearly. It was summarized as follows: What is the uniqueness or identity of the Brethren in Christ? How can the spirit of "Piety and Obedience" be realized in the present Japanese society? It was agreed that the two most crucial needs in the Japan church were (1) leaders who express the true Brethren in Christ spirit and (2) adequate seminary training for its leaders.[23]

The forming church was likewise becoming more aware of its roots in the vision and prayers of its North American brethren and of its connection with the worldwide fellowship of believers. With missionary John Graybill, conference chairman Takanobu Tojo, Shiroyuki Suzuki of Shimonoseki, Eiji Suzuki of Tachikawa, Masashi Furuta of Fuchu and Mamoki Kuroda of Kodaira attended the World Brethren in Christ Conference held July 19-20, 1984, in France, and participated in the World Mennonite Conference which followed it.

Spiritual vitality in the young denomination was shown in the deeper life retreats held each year from 1980 to 1985. Guest speakers at these retreats included missionaries Marlin Zook of the Brethren in Christ and Farris Huggins of World Mission Fellowship, pastor Rinya Komiyama of the Christian and Missionary Alliance, and professor Toshiyuki Kuodera of Orio Women's College. Themes for the retreats over four of the five years were: "Prayer and Witness," "Everyday Life Evangelism," "Prayer and Witness in

Daily Living," and "The Gospel and the Shape of the Church." The last theme was repeated in 1984 with the added subtitle, "Healing for Hurting People."[24]

Perhaps the clearest signs of vitality were seen in the formation of the Pioneer Evangelism Committee. The committee was brought into being at the General Conference of November 22-23, 1982. Both national leaders involved in church planting and foreign missionaries were declared members of the committee. Pastor Hirokawa was appointed as the interim coordinator. The group held its first official meeting March 11-12, 1983, in Nagoya, where a new church group had just formed in October of the previous year. The committee—soon to join in the celebration of the thirty-year anniversary of the work in Japan—spent most of its time seeking possible lessons from those thirty years of witness. The second meeting of the group was in July of 1983. It was held at Shin-Shimonoseki, where another pioneer work had just begun. Here the focus was on the concept and outworkings of partnership. At the General Conference in November, the working articles for the committee were approved and Masashi Furuta was elected the official committee chairman. Succeeding meetings took place in March, June and November of 1984 and July of 1985.[25]

The General Conference of 1984 was a time of great significance and celebration in the life of the church and the mission. It marked the thirtieth anniversary of the beginning of the Brethren in Christ presence in Japan. The conference met in Shimonoseki, Yamaguchi, the part of Japan that drew the first missionaries from the American church. The celebrants joyfully recognized the fulfillment of God's Word which declares, "those who wept as they went out carrying the seed will come back singing for joy as they bring in the harvest" (Psalm 126:6).

The report of the auspicious occasion recalled the difficulty of sowing the seed in feudalistic rural Japan with its entrenched Shinto and Buddhist traditions. It acknowledged the exceedingly slow growth of the church in a pyramid-like social structure which knits the community tightly together against any non-traditional intrusions. It declared that the proclamation of the Truth must go beyond a confrontation with the mind of the individual and must identify with the hearer's emotional realities. The proclamation must, indeed, repeat the fact of the Word becoming flesh.[26]

With this backdrop, participants in the conference noted the special significance of the simultaneous convening of the Pioneer Evangelism Committee. Realizing that abundant harvest depends on abundant sowing, they declared that "the Spirit which led us to celebrate the past is also leading us to pray and plan for the future." Japanese and North American brethren in the Lord Jesus lifted up their united prayer, "May the anticipation of joy in the harvest once again sustain us as we sow in tears."[27]

The Fruit of Sowing

As the Pioneer Evangelism Committee itself was taking tenuous form, it was at the same time supervising the birth of some fledgling churches. As was mentioned, worship services began in the Tokyo suburb of Fuchu in April 1981 through the efforts of Marlin Zook and the contacts made by the volunteer English teachers. Masashi Furuta, a product of the Yamanota church, came as pastor after finishing seminary in 1982, thus forming the partnership team with Marlin. Furuta was in charge of the worship services, preaching three times a month, leading the Japanese Bible study and dealing with individual needs. Marlin preached once a month and taught ten English classes and two Bible classes. Ruth Zook contributed through a popular cooking class.[28]

In February 1982 the Fuchu group moved its meeting place from the original store front in Nishihara to Miyoshi-cho and the newly-acquired residence of the Furutas. The pressure of high rental costs at the former location was one factor in making the decision to move at this time. More importantly, however, it was felt that the program needed to be seen as "a church-centered program which offered help in English rather than an English program with accompanying evangelistic activities." It was hoped that the move of the English program into "the church"—the residence of the Japanese pastor—would make the pastor the contact person for the community in the eyes of those seeking studies in English.[29]

The tiny assembly now found itself squeezed into a nine-by-twelve room with a path hardly wide enough to walk among the neighboring houses. The street which ran through the neighborhood seemed almost inaccessible. At the end of the street was a huge Shinto shrine. The press of the surroundings threatened to stifle the tiny group which met regularly each Sunday. But, as one observer noted, the believers formed a family of God in a society which "worships the gods at the end of the street." Into the open Futura living room came the Zooks, the Kawates, new English teacher Jean Maedke and a few others who appeared on foot and by bicycle. The time of teaching, praising, singing and praying brought great encouragement to each member of the believing family.[30]

In Shin-Shimonoseki, Ray and Winnie Hock joined Pastor Kazayuki Hirokawa in 1982. The Hirokawas had secured an apartment which was to serve as a meeting place in the church planting attempt. The Hocks plunged into a schedule of teaching English and Bible classes. Contacts were sought in several neighboring communities for the purpose of building relationships. The partnership team looked for ways to begin home Bible studies, and a Sunday morning worship service was begun in the Hirokawa apartment. Pastor Hirokawa took a step of faith by quitting his job to devote full time to the ministry. The year 1984 saw sixteen "seekers" meeting regularly. Several special evangelistic events were attempted. One of these brought a well-known Japanese evangelist to a rented public hall for a series of messages. A total of sixty-nine people attended the meetings, and nine gave written indication of their desire to receive Christ. The patient workers prayed that their seed sowing might yet bear fruit in the hearts of the others who had also heard.[31]

In Nagoya, the 1982 partnership team became complete with the arrival of the Dehyles in August and the Sugatas in November, joining the Graybills who had rented a small house in June. The form of the worship services which began in October and the outreach attempts changed considerably over the next three years. A somewhat rigid, traditional service with hymns, offering and extended preaching gave way to one with more sharing of personal praise experiences and prayer requests. As the need for a Sunday school was felt, a program for the children was provided on alternating Sundays, replacing the worship service for that week. Church members took turns as game leader, Bible story teller, workbook teacher, and song leader. Missionary and neighborhood children alike expressed their delight. A new family became part of the church because of the Sunday school. Later, the Sunday school began to meet each week along with weekly worship services.[32]

Ladies' meetings evidenced particular enthusiasm. Led at first by partnership team personnel, soon many of the ladies began alternating in planning and teaching the lessons. The former cooking class with a one-hour Bible lesson gave way to a varied program of crafts, charity projects, outings and extended times of personal testimony, discussions on Christian books, and messages by guest speakers. The group named their meeting time, "Happy Room." Ladies shared their faith with friends and returned to the group to related results and state prayer requests.[33]

Seeking some effective means of reaching men who seldom appeared in the services, Dan Dehyle joined a local softball team. With the encouragement of the church members, Dan absented himself from the worship service two times a month in order to take a Christian presence into the daily activities of the men of the community.[34]

June 11, 1984, marked the first baptism celebration in the Nagoya church as Mrs. Masako Sato made public confession of her faith.[35]

The Older Churches

Meanwhile, the churches of earlier birth continued faithful in fellowship and the teaching of the Word. With one exception, however—the Yamanota church in Shimonoseki—the Yamaguchi churches showed no numerical growth. It seemed that the continuing loss of members to the larger cities and the entrenched Buddhist society of the rural areas were difficult to overcome. The churches' witness broke through the shell of that society at times, however, even causing a Buddhist priest to try to conduct a Christian funeral on behalf of a deceased believer in Jesus.[36]

The commitment of the lay pastors to nurture and the encouragement of the believers continued unabated. It seemed, however, that there was little time left to expand church activities or promote outreach after finishing each day's job requirements. With the aging Goro Shibata now in the background, banker Masaharu Okano continued to lead the Hagi fellowship. Toshiharu Igeta and Kiyoshi Fujita gave partial support. School principal Asao Nishimura remained the primary leader at Nagato. Occasionally, new faces appeared at the services there and in Hagi. Believers seemed encouraged.[37]

Little remained of the Takibe fellowship but an occasional meeting of retired teacher Hiroto Okazaki with his wife and one or two other villagers.

Okazaki continued to meet regularly with the leaders of the other Yamaguchi churches. These times of informal fellowship and discussion provided encouragement and a sense of mutual support.[38]

The work at Yamanota was the most encouraging of those in Yamaguchi. Under the leadership of economics professor Takanobu Tojo, thirty members met regularly for worship in 1985. The members were divided into areas of responsibility—"service ministries"—which were functioning with enthusiasm. Small groups called "families" met in the homes of lay leaders for encouragement and Bible study.

The Yamanota church had touched the lives of hundreds more over the years and had supplied church-planting partners Furuta, Hirokawa and Mrs. Sugata to the three new works mentioned above. Plans were in process to build new facilities in 1986. The estimated cost of the facilities was $120,000. The biggest potential source of discouragement was the impressive Mormon church building erected right across the street. With huge amounts of money supplied readily from Mormons in America, the two-story edifice seemed to shout haughtily down at the modest pre-fab of the Yamanota Christian Church.[39]

In Tokyo, the Nukui church in Koganei remained strong under the leadership of Pastor Hirotoshi Hashimoto. Although separate from the combined Tokyo-Yamaguchi Conference, representatives attended some of the denominational meetings and remained open to opportunities for interchange.

Because of the lack of strong leadership, the Yayoidai group next to the mission residence in Kodaira dwindled. The believers who remained, however, matured spiritually and developed a stronger sense of unity and love. Seminary student Ryuzo Matsuya came to provide the weekly Sunday messages. Dentist Mamoki Kuroda served as a board member and congregational representative, and gave much encouragement through his words and his deeds of service. Noriko Matsuura of early Hagi days returned from studies in the United States to become a spiritual leader and a counsellor in the group. She shared the room above the church meeting hall with Alice Dourte, who joined the VS team in August 1985.[40]

The Wakaba church in Tachikawa was meeting in the second-floor room of the home of pastor Eiji Suzuki where it had started. Suzuki supported himself by driving a truck. Still in its infancy, the church counted only ten adults in its membership. But it made the most of witness opportunities through the thirty-five children who attended. The pastor formed a nineteen member Sunday school baseball team which played almost every Saturday and Sunday afternoon. Trumpets, clarinets and drums in the hands of their supporters added to the cheers and the excitement. But most uniquely, all the attending parents and friends of both teams were asked to sit on the grass before each game while the believers preached from the Bible and sang hymns. With the addition of summer and spring baseball camps sponsored by the church, Wakaba was attempting to build a foundation for the future.[41]

The Challenge That Remains

As the year 1985 moved toward its close, cause for great rejoicing was evident in the Brethren in Christ Church in Japan. The dedication of the leaders, both professional and lay, was reason for admiration and also thanks to God. New life was clearly evident in the recently planted churches, and plans for further outreach were being made. With the rejoicing, however, there were matters which called for further reflection. Some of these matters were cause for concern to the observer.

With the mission having relinquished its independence to the national church and having offered its personnel to the directives of the conference leadership, the challenges for the future were no longer chiefly those of the mission. The principles for outreach suggested in the previous chapter, "The Future Mission," no longer carried the same meaning as when written in 1980 for the missionaries were no longer free to set their own policies apart from their national brethren.* The church was now faced with the urgency of evaluating these principles and discerning how they could be most effective in witness within their own cultural milieu. The church now had to wrestle with the shape that it would take in the future and the impact that shape would make on its world.

The challenges that awaited were summarized in a general way by John Graybill in an address in June 1983 to the Formation Committee of the General Conference and the Pioneer Evangelism Committee. On the eve of the thirtieth anniversary celebration, he raised some very pointed questions both to current church leaders and to missionaries who had preceded them in leadership. He inquired, Why is it that we don't have several thousand members on our rolls instead of our present 185 members? And why don't we have scores of house churches along with our church buildings instead of the present nine to ten little groups? Pointing to Acts 2:41-47, he asked, where is the *vitality* possessed by the New Testament church? While lifting up the spiritual truths of the Acts passage, Graybill noted the dangers of not welcoming warmly enough the stranger or neighbor who ventures into the church service, of focusing on the form of the service rather than on "worship in spirit and in truth," and of substituting the worship service for the prayer meeting.[42]

But there were also more specific challenges awaiting the developing church. The first of these was the challenge of working out the concept of partnership in a way comfortable for all. The mission recognized that the church it bore was no longer an infant, that the church must be set free to relate the gospel to its culture in its own way, and that the mission must be ready to be the servant of the church. It therefore supported the desire of the national church to assume its own leadership. The principle of partnership and its applications were discussed with the Japanese brethren in meetings

---

*The preceding chapters and the sections to follow were completed in 1980-81, and partially fulfilled requirements of a doctoral program. This chapter was written later to update the account to 1985.

from 1978 with Overseas Secretary Roy Sider. Finally, in a lengthy session in November of 1982, it was agreed by the church and the missionaries that "the church and the Board for Missions are established in direct partnership roles. The missionaries will serve the church with assignments and job descriptions agreed upon by the church, the mission and the particular missionary."[43]

In December 1982, the Board for Missions affirmed the concept of partnership in church planting. Its minutes recorded the principle that "the national will be the leader and the missionary a resource partner in church planting ministries." It likewise affirmed the plan that each church planting project "shall be under the general administration of the Pioneer Evangelism Committee of the churches in Japan."[44]

At this time the board also strongly encouraged the goal of having a missionary present in one church planting project no more than six years and preferably only three. The intent was clearly that the church would meet the challenge of developing and supplying permanent pastors to take over such new projects and allow the missionaries to become a part of a church planting team in a new area. Such a schedule would promote a much more rapid rate of establishing new churches.

One should not be surprised if, in the implementation of such a bold plan, some tensions were felt. And so it was as the missionaries were relegated to the unaccustomed role of following and the Japanese attempted to adjust to the new responsibilities thrust upon them and to learn the art of utilizing smoothly the talents of those working with them. Differences in cultural patterns surfaced again as the partners worked and learned together. The missionaries' background interpreted "partnership" to be a sharing of equals in a task of mutual concern. Being partners suggested being in constant communication and making decisions together. It seemed, however, that the national leaders approached the idea of partnership somewhat like the marriage relationship within their own society. In this understanding, the husband exercises the decision-making authority, and the wife supports him and carries out his wishes. Likewise the company structure may have exerted its influence on their thinking. In Japan, company relationships are hierarchical in nature. The employer is clearly the "boss" and the employee the subordinate.

It was certainly natural that the national leaders would be influenced by the patterns of thought, although subconscious, which form the core of their culture. These patterns came from the only life experiences they knew. On the other hand, for the missionary to be placed in the role of "wife" or "employee" could result only in perplexity and frustration.

There emerged a danger that the missionaries' energies might be wasted in the process of conforming to traditional national structures. The call of the missionaries was to do direct evangelism and to train national leaders. There was now a danger that these concerns might be overlooked in favor of their obvious skills in making contacts through the teaching of English and the general curiosity felt toward foreigners.

There is little doubt that the intent of the 1982 board minute on partnership was to recognize and affirm the autonomy of the Japanese church. The concept of partnership clearly was designed to renounce any paternalistic, possessive attitude and at the same time to lift up the biblical model of brotherhood. It was intended to allow both national leaders and missionaries the opportunity to function in their God-given roles and callings.

The first challenge, then, that confronted the church in the mid-1980s was to discover the biblical implications of leadership and mutually comfortable ways of carrying out the principle of partnership. Their challenge was to capture the servanthood aspect of leadership and discover how to make the most effective use of the missionaries' "heart for evangelism" and their gifts in the training of leaders.

The second challenge concerned what form the church would take in presenting itself to its own society. The form of an organization depends largely upon the attitudes of its leaders. Several possible dangers were seen which might prevent the church from realizing its full potential for growth.

The first danger was that the concern for a proper organizational structure might detract from a concern for an aggressive strategy for evangelism. As committees were appointed for defining policies and forming doctrinal statements, the challenge to establish clear goals for church planting seemed to be postponed. There seemed to be a reluctance to meet the goal of three years for a missionary in one church planting venture and to make top priority the development of new pastors for these places.

Along with a concern for structure, the traditional worship service seemed to be the focus of church life for some of the leaders. Adequate time was given to planning for the services and discussing the nature of the church, but time for strategies for outreach seemed to be lacking. Gladness was expressed when new faces appeared at the services, but little effort was made to "bring them in" through warm expressions of welcome and through friendly, carefully planned follow-up.

Perhaps the cultural pattern of non-involvement in the affairs of others was exerting a subtle but strong influence upon the leaders. Pastors seemed willing to let the missionaries make contacts and draw the net of relationship, but it seemed difficult for them to follow up those contacts and extend caring and warmth outside the setting of the church building. Perhaps a "smallness" mentality also made some reluctant to reach out with a more deliberate and aggressive plan. Occasionally a feeling that "we are too weak," or "Japanese society is too tight," or "we can't expect large churches in Japan" was evident.

The second danger was that an emphasis on correct teaching might detract from a concern for warm, personal relationship with the Lord in the life of the individual believer. The importance of correct doctrine seemed at times to replace the call to personal encounter with the living Lord. The reasonableness of the faith was ably expounded, but, although the mind of the hearer was amply informed, the heart seemed untouched.

Perhaps John Graybill was alluding to this danger when he asked, "Where is the *vitality* of the early church?" It is true that excitement in the Christian life was one of the marks of the New Testament believers. Someone has referred to this sense of excitement as the experience of the "burning heart" (Luke 24:32).

Likewise, and possibly in direct relation to this, a lack of openness to the Holy Spirit in the life of the believer was evident. Pastors seemed uncertain about the role of the Holy Spirit in the church and even fearful of exposing their people to the New Testament picture of the Holy Spirit. It is not too much to suggest that hesitation about the validity of teaching on the person and work of the Holy Spirit would contribute to a lack of spontaneity and warmth in the individual's experience and a sense of excitement in the church.

Perhaps a fear of where an openness to the Holy Spirit might lead caused some leaders to hold back. Comments had been heard occasionally to the effect that "the cults emphasize healings and other miracles, and we don't want to be identified with them."

The second challenge, then, that confronts the Japan church in the mid-1980s is the matter of how it will express itself to its society. It will need to reckon with traditional forms of worship and teaching as opposed to more flexible, open styles and methods. While upholding the importance of the body of believers in corporate worship, it will need to consider aggressive plans for reaching outside its walls and identifying with its neighbors. It will need to face the biblical principle of bringing the Kingdom of God on earth instead of waiting for it to appear. It will need to weigh the importance of the order of service and forms of worship against that of the felt needs of individual people. The church must see that it must go to the people—it cannot wait for them to come to it.

Many Japanese leaders seem suspicious of strategies for evangelism or principles of church growth. It is true that setting goals and planning strategies is very intimidating. These force one out of the comfort of traditional approaches and demand great commitment of faith and energy. It is hoped that the church will decide to make that commitment.

It is hoped also that the national leaders can be open to a personal experience of excitement in the Christian life along with a proper emphasis on sound teaching. Correct doctrine is crucial, but warm, personal relationship with the Lord brings edification. Not only is sound teaching imperative for piety and obedience, but a sense of intimacy with God is likewise crucial for their development. The church needs to consider the role of the Holy Spirit in the life of the church and the individual believer and to recognize how new power and joy can be experienced in both the believer and in the corporate Body, even while maintaining the biblical boundaries of balance and order.

And with these observations and prayers, the recording of the history of the Brethren in Christ in Japan is suspended for a time.

Chapter Eleven

Fellowship in the Gospel

The following stories concern some of those who have responded to the call of Jesus. There has been no attempt to make the stories complete. They are only glimpses into the lives and thoughts of some of the members of the church in Japan. The people whose stories have been chosen are no more special than many others. They are only representatives of the many changed lives that have brought much joy to the Japan missionaries. They are examples of the many ways in which God works and manifests his grace.

Yukiko Yamagata Yamamoto

The first Christian that came into Yukiko Yamagata's life was one of her junior high school teachers. The teacher, Mrs. Kaneda, was a member of the Hagi Catholic Church. Yukiko noticed that she seemed always serene. Occasionally she would say to the pupils, "Jesus is our peace."

Yukiko's father was a physical education teacher at Hagi High School. He had close contact with Yasuo Miyamoto, an English teacher in the school who had been baptized earlier in life. When Peter and Mary Willms began their work in Hagi, Miyamoto became a part of the group of believers which formed. Miyamoto had Pete appear in his classes at the high school and introduced him to Mr. Yamagata. The Yamagatas invited the Willmses with Mr. Miyamoto into their home one day. There Yukiko met the missionary for the first time.

On Easter Sunday Yukiko visited the little Hagi church at Miyamoto's invitation. She had felt that someday she would like to become like her junior high teacher, Mrs. Kaneda. Since Mrs. Kaneda was a Christian, it seemed reasonable to attend a Christian church. When Doyle and Thelma Book arrived in Hagi in 1955, Yukiko began attending Thelma's Bible class. She also practiced English with Doyle at the high school.

After graduation from high school, Yukiko went to Kita Kyushu City for junior college. One day she attended a meeting in a Baptist church. Following the message, the minister asked those who would like to be baptized to raise their hands. Even though Yukiko understood nothing about the meaning of baptism, she raised her hand. She was baptized and continued attending the church.

She married Mitsuo Yamamoto and went to live in Shimonoseki, where

171

she began attending the Baptist church. Gradually, however, her attendance at the church decreased. After about two years it came to a halt.

Yukiko placed her first daughter in a Christian kindergarten. Her contact with the school made her want to renew fellowship with Christians. At that point, the Books moved to Shimonoseki and began meetings in Yamanota. Yukiko began attending their English classes, then some of the beginning church services. She did not yet know what true Christian faith was. But she observed the Book family and felt her own lack of a vital faith. She saw a Christian family "living in the presence of God." After a time, she transferred her membership from the Baptist church to Yamanota.

She became an active participant in the ladies' Bible class taught by Thelma. Through this fellowship and through the church services, she came into a vital, personal relationship with Jesus Christ. After the Books left Shimonoseki, Yukiko continued to grow in her understanding of the faith under the teaching of Takanobu Tojo and through the visits of Marlin and Ruth Zook.

With her conversion she became personally aware that Jesus was working in her life. This awareness was heightened during the time of her mother's illness and death. Her mother's condition had worsened until communication with her was impossible. Thelma suggested that Yukiko read Bible passages to her mother. On the second day of Bible reading, a smile appeared on the face of her mother and she answered when Yukiko spoke her name. Yukiko knew that God had done a special work by the power of the Holy Spirit.

Her mother became better for a time, then lapsed again. The illness affected her vocal chords, and she was unable to speak. She became unconscious and lay near death's door. Yukiko stayed all night with her in the hospital room on one occasion. She started to leave the room in order to prepare more tea, when she heard her mother call. Yukiko quickly went to her bed and asked if she wanted something. She heard a faint, "No, nothing." Yukiko was amazed for she knew her mother's voice was gone. She felt inwardly that the Holy Spirit had relayed the feeling of her mother's heart so she could hear it. To Yukiko this, too, was a miracle of God's love. She realized that God's power can work when man is unable to do anything.

Yukiko often felt conflict because of her sense of duty to her father and her husband, both of whom are not Christians. But she learned to pray, and the Lord taught her to forgive. Her two daughters became Christians and members of the Yamanota church. Yukiko continues as a leader in the church which, she declares, came along at just the right time to keep her going "along the pathway toward Jesus."[1]

Izumi Hasegawa Awaya

Izumi Hasegawa began attending the English conversation and Bible class at Nagato when she was in high school. Her two older brothers had participated before her, and eventually the three of them were baptized. Their father was a medical doctor in the nearby village of Furuichi. He had come under YMCA influence during his school years and had been baptized, but that was as far as his outward profession of faith had gone. Since college days he had cultivated no Christian association, but he was very friendly toward the missionaries and open to his children coming under the influence of Christianity.

One day Izumi said, "I am afraid to be baptized. What if my faith is not genuine and will drop away as did my father's?" But her friend, Kimiko Ueda, urged her into open confession through baptism. As things turned out, all three of the Hasegawa children, once they took jobs and got married, did drift away from the Lord and the church. But the story does not end there.

After Izumi was graduated from high school she went to Tokyo to study textile designing. She did well and took employment in a department store where she designed cloth and then sold her own creations in the store.

Several years passed until a marriage was arranged for her to a young man from her area of Yamaguchi Prefecture. He also was employed in a good job in Tokyo. A year or so later they had their first child, Kiyoko, a little girl. When the baby was given her six-month check-up the doctor discovered that her heart was backwards. He also found that the vein running from the heart was too small. "She can live only a few years," he told them.

As the months passed and the little girl became more active, the meaning of the doctor's words became more and more obvious. Breathing became difficult when she moved around. Her cheeks and lips took on a brownish tinge and her flesh became pale.

The young parents were distraught. Izumi's mother and father advised them, "Bring the child to the country so that for the few years she may have left to live she can at least breathe clean air away from the noise and pollution of the city." And so Mr. Awaya, Izumi's husband, left a very good job in Tokyo and moved his family back to Yamaguchi. He found adequate, but lesser, employment in Shimonoseki, an hour and a half from Furuichi by train.

The invalid baby was alert intellectually. She was interested in all things connected with life and tried to do everything any eager, curious youngster would try. But her exploits left her weak, hardly able to breathe or crawl. The young mother could do nothing but watch the child's struggles. The ache in her own heart grew until she could hardly bear it.

Kiyoko was three when her condition became so acute that her parents took her to the university hospital in Kita Kyushu, just across the strait from Shimonoseki. Izumi sat beside the bed of her suffering little girl. She wanted to run away. But she was the mother and could not run away. "What is life doing to me?" she thought in anguish.

Meanwhile each day the doctors were doing examinations and making tests. They told Izumi that there was an operation they could perform, but because of the backwards position of the baby's heart, they could not insert the camera to learn what they needed to know. A certain vein or artery seemed to be missing. If they operated and it was not there, there would be nothing more to do. She would surely die within three months. But if they operated and found it was there, there was about a twenty-five percent chance that she would live. What should they do, they asked?

For three days and two nights Izumi sat in that hospital room feeling that she could not endure watching her baby suffer any more. The doctors gave her sleeping pills each night, but she could not sleep. On the third sleepless day she became alarmed. "I will go out of my mind if I cannot sleep," she thought. Because she had not been following the Lord, she felt that God would not hear her even if she prayed. But she became more desperate. Finally, she called her high school Christian friend, Kimiko, now Mrs. Nishimura. She shared her sorrow and need and asked Kimiko to pray that she might be able to get a good night's sleep.

Kimiko immediately alerted the Nagato believers, Marlin Zook at Nishiichi, and Yukiko Yamamoto, leader of the women's fellowship at Shimonoseki. Marlin and Mrs. Yamamoto went to the Kyushu hospital that very day and prayed for Izumi, laying on hands. That night Izumi slept long and awoke refreshed. She knew it was a miracle. "God really does answer prayer," she marvelled.

Even with this evidence of God's reaching out to her in response to her cry, Izumi still felt that because of her years of ignoring God and his church it would do no good for her to pray. "But my baby is going to die," she thought. "She is innocent. Perhaps God will hear her. I must teach her to pray."

So in that hospital room Izumi told Kiyoko about Jesus and taught her to ask him to make her able to run and play like other children. Even as Izumi talked to her, her own mind was filled with hopelessness and despair. But the little girl believed, and every day in childlike simplicity she asked Jesus to make her well.

A decision about an operation needed to be made. The doctors were waiting. Izumi's husband, Mr. Awaya, and the grandparents said, "Let her die in peace. She is too tiny and weak to be put through all that suffering for only a twenty-five percent chance of recovery." But Izumi sensed the urge to live in her little girl, and something within her own heart would not let her give up. "Let's try the operation," she said. Her husband and parents, seeing how much it meant to her, acquiesced.

The doctors, however, now pointed out that the little girl was losing weight. "We dare not operate," they declared, "until that trend reverses and she shows some gain."

By this time Izumi began to understand that God had not cast her aside just because she had brushed him aside. For the first time in her three-year ordeal, she lifted up her face toward heaven and prayed, "Dear Father, if this operation is your will, please let Kiyoko gain enough weight to have it, in Jesus' name."

God heard her prayer. Kiyoko began to gain. Faith and hope began to blossom in Izumi's heart.

Heart surgery could be done only on certain days. Specialists were few and requests were many. On the day for the operation, Marlin and Kimiko Nishimura went to the hopsital to be with Izumi. Kimiko later said that her own heart was thumping wildly as she entered the waiting room. She noticed that Mr. Awaya was white as a sheet. But Izumi smiled at her in confidence.

Fellowship in the Gospel 175

The three Christians had prayer together, and the conviction grew in them that God had answered. The missionary had to leave, but Kimiko stayed with her friend throughout the five hours of the operation.

The operation was to be in two stages. First, Kiyoko's doctor, who knew Izumi's father, was to open the chest cavity and search for the missing vein. If the vein was there, the best specialist in the hospital would come in to finish the operation.

At that particular time a specialist unknown to Izumi was in the hospital. He was visiting in Japan from America. Many people had requested his services only to be refused because he could spend only a limited time at that hospital. When people heard that he was to operate on Kiyoko, they asked Mrs. Awaya what she had done to get his service. Izumi was amazed. She had not asked for him. She had not even known he was the one to ask for. Later she was to discover that, had Kiyoko not been ready for operation at that particular time, the specialist would not have been available to do the operation. After everything was over Izumi saw that God had been working in each happening. She turned her life back to him in gratitude and praise.

The parents had been in the waiting room three hours when Kiyoko's doctor, still in his operating gown, slipped out to tell them that the vein *was* there and that the other doctor was operating now. Two more hours passed. Finally, they were called to the closed circuit TV to see Kiyoko as she was rolled from the operating room to the sterile room where no one except her special nurse could enter.

When Kiyoko had entered the operating room, her lips were dark brown. But as the visitors viewed her leaving the room, they could see that her lips were now rosy red. Kimiko and Izumi broke down and cried. The operation was a success.

Kiyoko healed quickly, and for the first time in her short life, she was able to ride a tricycle and run and play in the waves at the seashore. She insisted on doing everything and being just like everyone else. Her parents and grandparents marvelled at this little child who before could hardly walk or even breathe.

When she was four, she began kindergarten with all the other four-year-olds. The road to the kindergarten was somewhat steep, but the doctor had said, "Let her do anything she wants to do." As winter came, however, the cold weather began to take a toll on Kiyoko. She became quite ill and was home for ten days.

One Sunday the weather became unusually warm and beautiful. Kiyoko had been cooped up inside such a long time and was eager to get out again. Izumi decided to take her along to the Yamanota church. Kiyoko was five years old now. It was communion Sunday. When the bread and grape juice came to Izumi, Kiyoko wanted some, too. Izumi felt the emblems were too sacred to give to someone who could not grasp their significance. She tried to pass them on. But, like any five-year-old, Kiyoko was not going to give up easily. Her insistence was beginning to attract attention, and Izumi was annoyed and embarrassed. But Mrs. Kaneko, also a mother, was sitting next to her. She whispered gently, "It is all right, Izumi. Let her have some since she wants it so much." And so Kiyoko ate the bread and drank from the cup of Jesus' communion.

Izuma was upset that her child had showed such bad manners in church. After service she asked Kiyoko why she had acted like that. The little girl looked up at her mother and said, "Mommy, the bread is Jesus' body and the grape juice is his blood. It will make me well."

Izumi looked at her daughter in astonishment. She could not reply. On the way home Kiyoko skipped along beside her mother. Once she looked up and said, "I feel as if I'm walking on a cloud."

The next day Kiyoko was examined by the doctor to see if it was all right to return to school. The doctor said, "There is nothing wrong with her heart. It must have been just a cold." She returned to school again and all was back to normal except that she continued to require regular check-ups from the doctor. These tests were rather painful. But from that Sunday she seldom complained about them.

The long ordeal is not completely over. The doctor reports that when she grows older there must be another operation—perhaps two. She has to be more careful than other children not to catch cold because pneumonia could kill her. But she is happy and active.

One day her kindergarten had a special field day. She came running home all excited to tell her mother that she had won first place in a race. Izumi thought the teacher must have manipulated things somehow so that the little girl could win. But when she inquired, she learned that little Kiyoko had truly won the race.

She is a miracle in her home and family. The father has seen evidence of the living God and knows that he has somehow intervened in their lives. Izumi's brothers, once baptized, are also aware of God's touch upon the little girl. Izumi tells everyone who knows her how God has done a wonderful thing. Her husband is not yet a Christian, but he knows an unseen world has touched his family.

During the first year after Kiyoko's operation her father often picked her up in the car to bring her home from kindergarten. One day she said to him, "Jesus is smiling at me from behind the clouds." He later reported the incident to Izumi and added, "This child is always saying strange things." One other time during her fifth year, Kiyoko seemed to grow weaker. The Shimonoseki church leaders, along with the Nishimuras from Nagato and the missionary, anointed her in the name of Jesus and prayed. From that time until this writing she has been perfectly well.

The doctor says that with this operation her life expectancy is twenty years. After that he does not know what to expect. But Izumi knows that Kiyoko has been the means God used to bring her back into living relationship with himself. "I do not know about the future," she says, her face glowing, "but I know God is with this child in a special way. And I know what he has done in my life because of her."[2]

Asao Nishimura

Asao Nishimura grew up in Hagi where he began attending the Catholic church as a high school student. During his second year of high school, on New Year's Day, he was baptized by the priest, Father Vera. He was urged by his teachers to enter the teaching profession. Because his high school grades were very good, he was permitted to take a special examination in order to qualify for a teaching position. He passed the exam and became an assistant teacher in the primary school on Mishima, two hours by boat off Hagi's coast.

Asao had been deeply impressed by his contact with the Catholic church and Fr. Vera. He was drawn to the life of devotion which he saw in the priest and in the sisters. After two years on Mishima, he quit his job and entered a Trappist monastery on the northern Japan island of Hokkaido. He had come to feel that prayer is the purest service one could render to God. He wanted with all his heart to please God. He determined that it was not necessary to meet people or to talk with them. He felt that, indeed, such contacts might hinder him in his desire to render worthy service to his Lord.

Monastic life was rigorous. Asao studied diligently during the morning hours of each day. The studies were in Latin. The afternoons were devoted to silence and work. Asao helped care for the fifty cows which belonged to the monastery. He also helped produce butter which the monastery sold. The clothing of the monks was made of coarse, brown cloth. The Hokkaido winters were very cold. The beds of the monks were nothing more than a straw mat and one blanket.

Asao's body finally succumbed to this demanding life. He developed a liver ailment and high blood pressure. His ill body began to swell and movement became difficult. He found it hard to remember what he studied each day. He was finally given sick leave from the monastery and was accompanied to Tokyo by another member of the community. From there he made his way home to Hagi for a time of recuperation.

As he was recovering, he began to read the writings of the Japanese Christians Uchimura and Kagawa. Gradually, he was attracted to Protestant concepts concerning the practice of the Christian faith. He realized that one cannot render the best service to God by leaving society completely. Rather, true faith is properly expressed within society and reaches out to others. Nishimura never returned to Hokkaido.

For a time he got a job in a lumber yard. The work was very heavy, and his shoulders often ached from carrying large timbers. But he thought of Christ bearing the cross and felt that he, too, should be willing to bear his difficult situations. He persevered, feeling that his lot would change in God's time. One day his former principal at Mishima invited Asao to join him at Kibe primary school. He accepted the position at the school and began his college work by correspondence. He traveled to Tokyo each summer for the required residence study. At last he was granted his official teacher's certificate.

Now seeking contact with Protestants, Asao one day visited the Willmses in their Tokaichi house. He was impressed with the relaxed atmosphere of the

Christian home. He looked through the family picture albums. He accepted an invitation to attend the Christmas service at Hagi that year. For several years he occasionally attended the Catholic church, but he also visited the Brethren in Christ group from time to time. Finally, he joined the latter fellowship after the church moved into its new building on Omotomachi Street. Pete went with him to speak to the priest and secure a transfer of his membership. Now almost thirty-five, he began to entertain thoughts of marriage. One of the Hagi church people suggested he visit the Nagato church and consider the young ladies there. There he met Kimiko Ueda for the first time.

From her childhood Kimiko Ueda had been interested in and sensitive toward religious things. She was fascinated by the white-robed maidens at the large shrines. She always bowed when she passed the small shrine which stood near her own house. Once a cushion caught on fire in her home. Others ran frantically for water, but Kimiko ran to the house altar to pray.

When the Graybills moved to Nagato, Kimiko began attending an English class. After the Books came to Nagato, Izumi Hasegawa invited Kimiko to come to the church services. In her third year of high school, Kimiko made a decision for Jesus Christ. Board representative Henry Hostetter was present that day. As he concluded his message he gave an invitation. Kimiko raised her hand, inviting Jesus Christ to enter her heart.

Her grandfather strongly opposed her going to church. He called the foreigners *keto*, a derogatory word for "brown hair." But her father had been exposed to foreign missionaries in Korea, where he served with the Japanese occupation forces, and her mother had a friend who was a pastor's child. Although neither of the parents showed an interest in the Christian faith, they did not oppose Kimiko's interest. Her father told her grandfather that everybody should be able to have "freedom of religion."

After making her decision for Christ, Kimiko plunged into the activities of the church. She attended Sunday services faithfully and midweek services in both Fukagawa and Senzaki.

One of the church members pressed her into Sunday school teaching before she was baptized. She learned the Sunday school songs from the children. She joined the little Bible school in Hagi and stayed over night each Friday, much to the dismay of her mother. She later admitted that so much participation in the activities of the church was not a very good witness to her family. But, she added, "It has certainly been good for my spiritual growth!"

After high school graduation, she worked for three years in the office of the agricultural co-operative. Her parents considered her too young for marriage, but along came Nishimura.

Asao was attracted to Kimiko. A formal engagement ceremony was arranged in the Nagato church with the missionary officiating. It was attended only by the couple, their parents and the Books. The two young people were married in a lovely outdoor ceremony on top of Kasayama, an old volcanic hill which stood on the coast north of Hagi. The ceremony took place at 6:00 o'clock in the morning on May 8, 1965.

Nishimura transferred to Kiyo primary school in order to be near Kimiko's home in Nagato. The couple became a tower of strength in the Nagato Church. In 1971, shortly after the missionary left for Shimonoseki, they moved into the Fukagawa Church building. Nishimura rose in the esteem of his school colleagues. He also became the first chairman of the new Brethren in Christ Conference of the Yamaguchi churches.[3]

Toshiko Funaki Takahashi

And we know that in all things God works for the good of those who love him, who have been called according to his purpose (Rom. 8:28).

Toshiko Funaki grew up in Senzaki, a part of the city of Nagato. She first responded to the gospel in high school and became active in the Nagato church. After several years of working in her hometown and helping in the church, she decided to go to Bible school so that she might be more useful to the Lord. At a Lutheran Bible school in Kobe she met a young man studying there for the ministry. He asked Toshiko to marry him. This sounds just like what we should expect and be happy about except for one thing—the young man was an albino. In our country, where there are thousands of tow-headed, white-skinned people, this would be a misfortune, but not insufferable. But in Japan, where everyone is black-haired and dark-eyed, an albino person is startling, to say the least.

Funaki San's family was extremely negative toward the marriage—not because the man was a Christian, but because of the hereditary nature of albinism. Toshiko herself was ambivalent in her feelings. On one hand she felt it her duty to marry him because he would need a wife in the pastorate and because she knew nobody else would consider marrying him. However, she did not feel any special affection for him.

After completing her course of study, Toshiko went to Tokyo to work for a while. During this time she attended the Koganei church. But she kept corresponding with the young pastor. A year or more passed. She decided to go back to Senzaki to be with her mother for a while. On the way she stopped in Kobe to see her friend. They became formally engaged and set the wedding date. Toshiko stayed in Senzaki for a time. While she was there, her mother, who had not been really strong for years, suddenly passed away.

Funaki San said later, "As I sat looking at the face of my dead mother, I knew suddenly that I should not marry this man."

She wrote immediately to break off the arrangement and returned to her job in Tokyo. About two years went by. The Book family was preparing to leave Japan when they heard that Funaki San was getting married—not to a Christian, but to a man whose family were members of Sokka Gakkai, a radical religious movement that puts great pressure upon family and friends to join! After arriving in the United States, the Books tried to write to her but they received no answer. They were quite concerned about what might be happening to her.

After eight years, in the summer of 1980, they were able to return to Japan for a visit. After several days in Tokyo they went to Shimonoseki, where they spent one week. The second week was spent in Nagato. From Nagato they visited Hagi and were in their last night in the Okano home. A call came from the Nishimuras in Nagato to say they were coming to Hagi and bringing a special guest. The guest was Funaki San, now Mrs. Takahashi. That night the Okanos, the Nishimuras and the Books heard the rest of Toshiko's story.

Toshiko's husband was an inventor of electric gadgets and appliances. He made them in a little shop, then took his samples to various manufacturers, trying to sell his ideas. Toshiko had told him that she was a Christian and that she would marry him only on the condition that he would not oppose her faith and church activity. He had agreed to the condition. A little girl was born to them sometime afterward.

During an economic slump many small businesses failed in Tokyo. Mr. Takahashi's business was among them. He decided to move away from the high rent of the city to one of the most isolated areas of Japan, a rural farming area in the mountains of southern Kyushu. In this small village setting up shop and hiring a few helpers was much cheaper.

And so Toshiko, who was born by the sea and had been active in the church since her high school days, found herself with a pre-schooler in an isolated area, an hour and a half by bus from a church, library, or hospital, and surrounded by people who spoke a dialect with many unfamiliar words. Her husband was often away, trying to sell his ideas, and she was alone. It was as if she were in a foreign land. There was no one who shared her faith.

She went a few times to the distant church. But buses were few and far between. In order to arrive at church on time she had to leave her town at 5:00 or 6:00 a.m. She was unable to return until 6:00 in the evening. This was not an easy schedule to keep with a little one to care for. Gradually she stopped going altogether. She had told no one in the village that she was a Christian. In her own home she gradually stopped all Christian practices except prayer before meals. No attempt was made to give her child Christian training.

She sometimes thought, "What is happening to me?" But she seemed unable to do anything about her condition. She became worried and tense, and then became ill. She went to the nearest doctor. He diagnosed her as tubercular, but Toshiko did not trust his diagnosis. She had had TB when she was in junior high school, and her present illness did not seem the same. When she got home, she looked up her symptoms in a medical book. All her symptoms suggested lung cancer.

She became obsessed with the idea that she was going to die, but she did not tell anyone about it. She thought, "I am not following Jesus. I am going to hell." These thoughts persisted and grew in intensity. Sometimes she fell asleep at night only to wake up in nightmares and screaming over and over again, "*Osoroshii, osoroshii!*" (Horrible! I'm afraid!) Soon she became unable to sleep at all. She often got up in the middle of the night and did her housework. Then she sat on the porch of the house and stared vacantly into space. This became a daily routine. The Enemy had his way in her mind. She was convinced she was lost and dying.

As is common in a country village, everyone knew everyone else's business. Even though Toshiko had told no one that she was a Christian, the neighbors knew she had been to the church in the distant town. One of the neighbors, greatly concerned about her, went to the pastor of the church. He visited Toshiko and prayed with her. It was decided to take her by train to the university mental hospital several hours away in Kagoshima. Toshiko did not remember going to the hospital. She knew only that the doctors later told her she was feverish and violent when she arrived and then slipped into a catatonic state. During this time she was sometimes aware that she was in a hospital. But she did not know why, and she was unable to communicate with anyone.

In order to understand what happened next, let us digress a bit from the narrative to report on an occurrence some years earlier. When Doyle and Thelma Book were on their second furlough, they had taken the Campus Crusade training at Arrowhead Springs. They learned there that the Four Spiritual Laws booklet and the materials that go with it were available in Japanese. It seemed to them a good idea to return to Japan and give this training to the believers in Nagato. They hoped that it would enable the believers to better bring to a point of decision people who had heard the gospel about Jesus but did not know how to receive him. They prayed and talked with the leaders about the idea and felt God was leading in this way.

Funaki San was among the believers who learned how to use the Four Spiritual Laws booklet. But even though the Books felt very positive about what they were doing and though they had been guided by the Holy Spirit, the response was not very enthusiastic. So far as they knew, none of the church people ever made use of the little booklet. For a long time they thought perhaps they had made a mistake. Years later, however, they learned that, after they had left Nagato, some of the people did begin to find it useful and are still making use of it.

Toshiko was now convinced she was going to hell. She lay in a mental hospital in a catatonic state. Then one day an image flashed into her mind. It was a page from the Four Spiritual Laws booklet with the picture of the throne in the heart of a person. She looked and she understood. "Why, Satan is sitting on the throne of my heart," she thought. "He has no right to be there. He must get off. Jesus must sit there."

That was all. But almost immediately after that she had another vision. Perhaps it was a dream—she was not sure—but it was very vivid. She had come to the gates of heaven. She heard someone beside her say, "This woman says she has believed in Jesus and is saved. Is this true?" And then she heard Jesus' voice—she did not see his face, just His robes and feet—"Yes, she has believed in me. She is one of Mine!"

Toshiko said she will remember those words as long as she lives. And from that moment she began to get well. That day her eyes began to focus, and she could understand once again what was happening. Next came her speech. Several days later she could use her arms. She was not yet able to walk, but one day a letter arrived which had been forwarded by her husband. It was from Miss Ito whom she knew from the Koganei congregation. Miss Ito, a kindergarten supervisor, had a professional meeting in Kagoshima and wondered if Mrs. Takahashi could come to that city and if they could spend some time together. She did not know that at that very time Toshiko was in the Kagoshima hospital.

Toshiko wanted desperately to talk to Miss Ito. The doctors were still forbidding visitors, but when they saw how much it meant to her, they gave their permission. A nurse called Miss Ito at her hotel and told her to come to the hospital. From Miss Ito, Toshiko learned that the Books had returned to Japan for a visit after eight years in America. From that moment she determined to see them.

The doctors later told her they had never seen a patient in such a severe condition improve so fast. When she had first arrived at the hospital in a violent state, they could tell by her ramblings that she had faith in something or someone. Now she told them she was a Christian and that Jesus had restored her mind. They were puzzled and at the same time impressed. "This is something we should look into," they agreed.

In a few days after Miss Ito's visit, Toshiko was walking around, although somewhat unsteadily. She told the doctor she must go to meet the Books. He was very reluctant to let someone as sick as she had been take a twelve-hour trip alone by train. However, he had seen a miracle in her recovery. Finally, he said, "All right, as long as you stop by here on your way back for a complete check-up." And so it was that Toshiko arrived in Hagi on the last evening before the Books once again left the country for Tokyo and America. Although she had traveled twelve hours that day, starting at 6:00 a.m., she was vibrant and glowing as she testified.

As she related the foregoing events, it became clear to those who listened that Satan meant to destroy her through the experience. But God had used it as a witness to himself and for the strengthening of her faith.

In the hospital she had already become a counselor and helper to the woman who shared her room and to the person next door. The doctors saw before their eyes the healing power of Jesus. Her husband said, "I see now how important it is for you to have Christian contact." The pastor of the church one and a half bus hours away from her village said, "I should have understood how isolated you were. Perhaps we could come once in a while and have service in your home."

Toshiko testified that she is now filled with the desire to share Jesus. She does not want ever again to hide the fact that she is a Christian.

As in the case of Joseph, Satan meant the difficulties for evil, but God meant them for good. God accepted Funaki San's earlier life choices and held her in his hand. Then he made use of the deposit of his truth in her mind and heart and, with his own divine intervention, overcame the Evil One and made *all* things work together for good. He is doing the same thing in the life of every believer who loves God. Someday we shall see it all clearly.[4]

Jesus the Same

Jesus Christ walked on this earth 2,000 years ago in a body of flesh and blood. He performed signs and wonders and drew people to God. In the Book of Acts he continued his ministry, but in a new body—the New Testament church. Jesus also walks on the earth today and continues his ministry through the twentieth-century church. Everything that Jesus was two thousand years ago he is today. And everything Jesus possessed two thousand years ago he has today. For Jesus is the same—yesterday, today and forever (Heb. 13:8).

Jesus gave his commission to the church: make disciples of all peoples. And he gave his Holy Spirit, the manifestation of all he is and possesses, to his church. Jesus wants to be all that he was in his first body to his church now. And Jesus extends to the church now everything he possessed when he was physically on the earth. The goal is the same—make disciples. And the resources are the same—the power and gifts of the Holy Spirit.

++++++++++++++

The story of the Brethren in Christ in Japan is not yet fully recorded. We have the opportunity of helping to write the story of the future. What would we like to see added to it? What will the full record of the body of Christ in Japan contain?

In the meantime Jesus walks up and down the streets and pathways of the land of Japan. He treads the cities, the hills and the fields. He is calling the people to fellowship—fellowship with him in the gospel.

Epilogue

The call came at 5:00 in the morning. The message was totally unexpected: "Daddy has gone to be with the Lord. He seemed well enough—and then suddenly he was gone." The young missionary returned to bed to report the news to his wife. The couple had sometimes wondered how it would be to have to face, in far-away Japan, the death of someone very dear to them. But suddenly they felt the living presence of the Lord. They reminisced and prayed together for Mother. They offered prayers of thanksgiving for Daddy. When their two little girls awoke, they told them about Grandpa's passing. The older girl was all excited—Grandpa was actually in heaven!

The missionaries' first sense of loss came when they thought, "Oh, we will not have his prayers for us any longer." Then they remembered that, according to Revelation, the dead in the Lord have access to the throne even though they do not yet have their resurrection bodies. Now they felt that perhaps, because of Daddy, the rest of the heavenly hosts were looking their way with love and concern. The couple pondered the words, "Blessed are those who die in the Lord . . . I go to prepare a place . . . Where I am there you will be also." The days which followed were filled with praise and the closeness of God's presence.

They shared the news with the believers at the little prayer meeting. One of the ladies said to them, "I just realized that your parents must have thought of this possibility when they sent you to Japan—that you would not be able to come to them when it came time for them to die—and yet they were willing that you should come. And had you not come, I would not be a Christian today. I wonder . . . I am not sure I would be willing for my children to go so far away."

The young couple clung sleeplessly to the sides of their bunks. The ship paused at a precarious angle after each sideways roll, as if wondering whether to return upright once again or to succumb to the monstrous waves. The wind, howling its unfriendliness, sent a chill into the hearts of the pair. During the long night they thought of those whom they had just left. They recalled the warm, farewell embraces. And they wondered about the future, so completely unknown.

What was the reason . . . Surely it was not that the young missionaries did not trust their Lord. Nor could it have been an unwillingness to obey his call. Was it some sense of dread about the unknown future? Did the possibility of never again seeing home and loved ones overwhelm them? Had the frightful storm taken a toll on their emotions? Whatever the reason, from that time on the way to Japan, the young woman's hair began to turn grey.

The missionary and her friend rounded a corner to discover a small shrine in an open place. Kneeling before it was a slender, wrinkled woman. She cried aloud in desperation as she swayed back and forth, vainly calling to an unanswering, utterly unresponsive god. The friend saw the missionary's sudden compulsion to run to the woman with the glad news that there is a Savior who hears and answers. She saw also her frustration in knowing that even the missionary heart must observe certain proprieties. Later, in her mind's eye, the friend often saw the tiny, wrinkled woman, swaying and crying.[1]

The missionaries to Japan stepped over a strange new threshold. The threshold was much higher than any of them could have known. It was high socially—the outsiders found that they were never fully accepted into the society. It was high emotionally—the conflict with what appeared on the surface and what was hidden underneath brought many frustrations. It was high personally—careers, comforts and families had to be left behind.

The missionaries stepped over the threshold into a new adventure. It was an adventure with eternal implications, for it was an adventure with God. But they saw that Jesus had walked the way before them. They stepped into his footprints. And they found that the prints were indeed glowing with warmth and life. They stepped forward in faith. And many of the people they had come to love followed them—into the path marked by the footprints of Jesus.

The young man said, "You led me to Christ—you are my spiritual father. I shall always be grateful."

The young mother declared, "You must have felt great concern for your children and their education. As my children get older, I feel a deep appreciation for the missionaries."

The young woman said, "If you had not come to Japan, I wouldn't know Jesus. I couldn't bear to be without him."

The man smiled, "See what has become of the seed you sowed! 'They that sow in tears shall reap in joy!' "

For some of the Japan missionaries, service seemed to be ended. God had led them into other paths. Their new ministries also were fulfilling and marked by a sense of his presence. But for them as well as for the missionaries who continued, one sobering thought remained: there were so many, like the little, wrinkled woman, who had not yet begun to follow Jesus. What was to be done about them?

Japan Mission Personnel

Families

1953-1969	Peter and Mary Willms Margaret (Margy) Bonnie Kenneth	
1955-1972	Doyle and Thelma Book Charity (Chari) Stephanie	
1957-	John and Lucille Graybill Michael Brenda Debra Edward Barbara	
1963-1986	Marlin and Ruth Zook Brain Elaine Stephen	
1980-1986	Ray and Winifred Hock Jason Amy	
1981-1986	Daniel and Karen Deyhle Vaughn Cameron	

Voluntary Service

1960-1962	Edna Wingerd
1967-1969	J. Andrew Stoner
1969-1972	Timothy and Nancy Botts Andrew
1971-1974	Dwight and Carol Thomas
1972-1973	Rosalind Tarnowsky
1973-1977	Michael and Holly Graybill Ethan

1975-1977	Beth Bearss
1977-1980	Miriam Bowers
1977-1979	Jay Smith
1980-1983	Mary Brubaker Connie Lofthouse Dora Myers
1982-1983	Peter and Laura Shaida
1983-1985	Kathy Kennedy
1983-1986	John Moody
1983-1986	Jean Maedke
1984-1985	Alice Welch
1985-	Alice Dourte

Mission Chronology—The First Ten Years

August 1953	Peter and Mary Willms begin the mission. Henry N. Ginder campaign.
August 1954	John Z. Martin campaign.
January 1954	Willmses leave Hagi for language training in Kobe.
August 1955	Willmses return to Hagi. Doyle and Thelma Book arrive for 1-W assignment. Hiroko Kanakubo joins Thelma for children's and adult Bible classes. Peter restricted by illness.
September 1956	Books take charge of Hagi. Willmses to Kobe for language study. Mary's illness interrupts study.
August 1957	John and Lucille Graybill arrive and begin language study in Kobe.
November 1957	Books to Kobe for language school. Willmses return to Hagi with Anna Haldeman's help.
July 1958	Books join Willmses in Hagi for youth camp and Senzaki (Nagato) campaign.
September 1958	Willmses on furlough Books take both Hagi and Senzaki (Nagato). Graybills continue study.
January 1959	Graybills to Hagi for three months. Books to language school.
April 1959	Graybills and Books exchange places again.
February 1960	Willmses return to Japan, enter language school. Graybills join Books in Hagi, renovate Nagato house.
April 1960	Graybills to Nagato, officially open Nagato Station. For the first time, two couples are in full-time field work.

August 1960	Edna Wingerd arrives (July), enters language school for one month. Willmses join Books in Hagi for summer camps. Books leave on furlough. Graybills hold campaign in Nagato. Children's school opens in Hagi (September).
August 1961	Books return to Japan, enter language school and contact Yamaguchi people in Tokyo.
August 1962	Books to Nagato. Graybills on furlough.
August 1963	Graybills return to Japan, open Tokyo work. Marlin and Ruth Zook arrive, enter language school.

Footnotes

Prologue

[1] Adapted from Doyle Book, "Each Man Felt Jesus Knocking at His Heart," *Handbook of Missions* (Nappanee, Ind.: Evangel Press), 1972, p. 8.

Chapter 1

[1] Interview with Peter and Mary Willms, June 24, 1980.
[2] He also requested ten million gospel portions in Japanese. See William Woodward, *The Allied Occupation of Japan* (Leiden: E. J. Brill, 1972), pp. 242 (Plate IV), 243, 357, 359. See also Footnote 13 in Chapter 2.
[3] Willms interview.
[4] *Ibid.*
[5] Interview with Wendell E. Harmon, October 17, 1980. Harmon was president of the Men's Fellowship in 1951. See also *Evangelical Visitor* (Nappanee, Ind.: Evangel Press) July 9, 1951, p. 9.
[6] Willms interview.
[7] Peter Willms, "Have We Lost Our Opportunity in Japan?" *Evangelical Visitor*, January 7, 1952, p. 5.
[8] Willms interview.
[9] *General Conference Minutes* (Nappanee, Ind.: Evangel Press) 1952, pp. 83, 89.
[10] Taped report by Carl J. Ulery, June 1980.
[11] Board Minutes, June 6-9, 1953.
[12] Interview with Henry N. Hostetter, June 30, 1980; Willms interview.
[13] Henry Hostetter to Peter Willms, March 1, 1953.
[14] Peter Willms to Henry Hostetter, March 11, 1953.
[15] *Conference Minutes*, 1953, p. 79.
[16] Board Minutes, June 8-15, 1953.
[17] Willms interview.
[18] Samuel Wolgemuth, "Japan to be Host of 1953 World Congress on Evangelism," *Visitor*, February 2, 1953, p. 3.
[19] Willms interview.
[20] Peter Willms, "My First Visit to Hagi," *Visitor*, August 17, 1953, p. 10.
[21] Peter Willms to families, July 27, 1953.
[22] Peter Willms letter "To Hostetter, Ulery and Martin," July 27, 1953.
[23] Interview with Henry N. Ginder, July 2, 1980; Willms interview.
[24] Ginder interview.
[25] Willms interview.

Chapter 2

[1] This is the date of the broadcast by the emperor which acknowledged Japan's defeat and announced its surrender. The signing of the surrender documents took place on September 2, 1945.

[2] Richard Drummond, *A History of Christianity in Japan* (Grand Rapids: Eerdmans, 1971), pp. 269, 270.

[3] From conversations with Hiroko Kanakubo Hataya, Thelma Book's interpreter, September 1955; Thelma Book, personal journal, May 2, 1956, p. 49.

[4] Interview with Pete and Mary Willms, June 24, 1980.

[5] John N. Hostetter, Front Lines," *Evangelical Visitor* (Nappanee, Ind.: Evangel Press), August 31, 1953, p. 4.

[6] James Broderick, *St. Frances Xavier* (New York: Wicklow Press, 1952), pp. 342, 498; Johannes Laures, *The Catholic Church in Japan* (Rutland, Vt.: C. E. Tuttle Co., 1954), p. 2. See also Doyle C. Book, "Frances Xavier's Missiological Perspectives as Related to Japan," (unpublished paper) May 9, 1977.

[7] Drummond, p. 97.

[8] See Drummond, pp. 73-125 for an excellent overview of the persecution. See also Broderick, Laures, and Charles Boxer, *The Christian Century in Japan* (Berkeley: University Press, 1951).

[9] See Laures, pp. 38 and 155 for some moving testimonies.

[10] Drummond, pp. 145, 288.

[11] *Ibid.*, pp. 172, 173.

[12] *Ibid.*, pp. 256, 261, 266.

[13] William Woodward, *The Allied Occupation of Japan* (Leiden: E. J. Brill, 1972), pp. 242 (Plate IV), 243, 357, 359; Douglas MacArthur, *Reminiscences* (New York: McGraw-Hill, 1964), p. 311. Other authorities suggest he called for 10,000 missionaries; or, ten missionaries for every one then in Japan. For further discussion of MacArthur's attitude toward Christianity and missionaries, see *Reminiscences,* pp. 219, 225, Courtney Whitney, *MacArthur* (New York: Knopf, 1956), p. 275, and William Manchester, *American Caesar* (Boston: Little, Brown and Co., 1978), p. 511.

[14] Drummond, pp. 380, 281.

[15] *Ibid.*, p. 273.

[16] Peter Willms, "Have We Lost Our Opportunity in Japan?" *Visitor,* January 7, 1952, p. 4.

[17] Samuel F. Wolgemuth, "Japan to be Host of 1953 World Congress on Evangelism, *Visitor,* February 2, 1953, p. 3.

[18] *Handbook of Missions* (Nappanee, Ind.: Evangel Press), 1955, p. 67.

[19] *General Conference Minutes* (Nappanee, Ind.: Evangel Press) 1953, p. 18.

[20] *Handbook,* 1955, p. 66.

[21] See Sumisato Arima and Hiroshi Imazu, "The Japan Communist Party," *Japan Quarterly,* 24; 2, April-June, 1977.

[22] See Drummond, pp. 264, 266.

[23] For a brief discussion on Communism in Japan see Doyle C. Book, "The Characteristics of Marxism in Japan," (unpublished paper), March 1980.

[24] Carlton O. Wittlinger, *Quest for Piety and Obedience* (Nappanee, Ind.: Evangel Press, 1978), p. 2.

[25] *Ibid.*

[26] See *Ibid*, pp. 162 ff.

[27] Various *General Conference Minutes* record this fact. In 1955 there were 80 missionaries for 7,197 members. The figures for 1958 and 1962 respectively were 87 for 7,911 and 100 for 8,555.

[28] Wittlinger, p. 178.

[29] *Ibid.*, pp. 183, 273; *Visitor,* September 1, 1898, p. 337.

[30] Wittlinger, p. 183.

[31] *Visitor,* March 15, 1898, p. 110.

[32] Wittlinger, p. 179.

[33] *Visitor,* November 1, 1901, p. 419.

[34] *Visitor,* August 1, 1901, p. 293.

[35] *Visitor,* November 15, 1896, p. 342.

[36] *Visitor,* December 1, 1896, p. 357.

[37] *Visitor,* March 15, 1898, p. 110.

[38] *Visitor,* September 1, 1898, p. 337.

[39] Interview with Henry N. Hostetter, June 30, 1980.

⁴⁰Willms interview.
⁴¹Henry Hostetter to Peter Willms, June 23, 1952; Peter Willms to Henry Hostetter, August 13, 1952.
⁴²Willms interview.
⁴³*Conference Minutes*, 1952, p. 89.
⁴⁴*Conference Minutes*, 1953, p. 79.
⁴⁵Board Minutes, January 6-9, 1953.
⁴⁶Board Minutes, June 8-15, 1953.
⁴⁷*Conference Minutes*, 1953, p. 14.
⁴⁸*Handbook*, 1955, p. 67, and 1956, pp. 97, 98.
⁴⁹Hagi was known all over Japan as the home of Shoin Yoshida, a teacher who felt that Japan must throw off feudalism and welcome foreigners and learning from the rest of the world. He was executed in 1860 for his heretical ideas, but his pupils rose to positions of prominence in the government and brought about the reforms Yoshida had urged. They helped usher in the Meiji era which changed Japan from a feudal state into a modern nation. Hagi was famous also for a unique style of pottery called *Hagi-yaki* and for the fact that it was the location of the former castle of the fedual Lord Mori.
⁵⁰Hostetter interview.
⁵¹See LaVerne Snider, *It's Happening in Japan Today* (Osaka, Japan; Free Methodist Mission, 1980). All the churches in this study are in or near urban areas.
⁵²2 Corinthians 5:18-20, 1 Thessalonians 2:4, Matthew 28:19, 20. See also Peter Wagner, *Stop the World, I Want to Get On* (Glendale: Regal, 1974), p. 21.
⁵³Taped report by Carl J. Ulery, June 1980.
⁵⁴*Ibid*.
⁵⁵See *Visitor*, February 2, 1953, pp. 3, 4 and June 22, 1953, p. 8.
⁵⁶*Conference Minutes*, 1952, p. 13 and 1953, p. 13.
⁵⁷Board Minutes, January 6-9, 1953.
⁵⁸Interview with Henry A. Ginder, July 2, 1980.
⁵⁹See *Visitor*, August 17, 1953, p. 10.
⁶⁰John N. Hostetter, "Assembled in Tokyo, Japan," *Visitor*, August 31, 1953, p. 3.
⁶¹See *Visitor*, February 2, 1953, pp. 3, 4.
⁶²See *Visitor*, August 31, 1953, p. 3.
⁶³Peter Willms, "Our Christian Witness in Hagi," *Mennonite Life*, October 1957, p. 173.
⁶⁴Willms interview.
⁶⁵*Ibid*. A feeling echoed by all the mission staff.
⁶⁶See *Visitor*, February 3, 1964, p. 7.
⁶⁷Hostetter interview.
⁶⁸*Ibid*.
⁶⁹Willms interview.
⁷⁰*Ibid*. See also Eugene Nida, *Customs and Cultures* (Pasadena: William Carey Library, 1954), p. 3.
⁷¹Ginder interview.
⁷²Hannah Foote stated that Alma B. Cassel constantly expressed her special interest in Japan and said that she supported the gospel team project of the three young men. Doyle and Thelma Book recall Miss Cassel's statements that "Japan is always close to my heart." Were these expressions an indication of an earlier call to Japan but no channel through which to express it?
⁷³Peter Willms to Henry N. Hostetter, May 7, 1953. The incident described took place in another setting and the Scripture from Isaiah has been paraphrased.

Chapter 3

¹Interview with Peter and Mary Willms, June 24, 1980.
²Interview with Henry A. Ginder, July 2, 1980.

[3] *Ibid.*
[4] Peter Willms, "My First Visit to Hagi," *Evangelical Visitor* (Nappanee, Ind.: Evangel Press), August 17, 1953, p. 10.
[5] 2 Chron. 32:8b; *General Conference Minutes* (Nappanee, Ind.: Evangel Press), 1954, p. 13.
[6] Ginder interview.
[7] *Ibid.*
[8] *Ibid.*
[9] Willms interview.
[10] *Hagi Residential News*, September 13, 1953. Adapted from a translation by Koichiro Sugiyama.
[11] *Handbook of Missions* (Nappanee, Ind.: Evangel Press), 1954, p. 102.
[12] Peter Willms, "Report to Foreign Mission Board," December 18, 1953.
[13] Peter Willms, notes, September 15, 1953, "Hagi" file.
[14] Peter Willms diary, September to November, 1953.
[15] Interview with Uno Ichikawa, July 19, 1980.
[16] Willms interview.
[17] 1980 found Mrs. Ichikawa, at age 90, living in Tokyo with her 95-year-old husband. The author and his wife had the delight of visiting the elderly couple on July 19. Both were mentally alert and reasonably well physically. At the time of this writing, all the original members of the Japan church were still living.
[18] Interview with Ritsu Iwakura, August 6, 1980.
[19] Peter Willms, "Our Christian Witness in Hagi," *Mennonite Life*, October 1957, p. 173.
[20] Interview with Koichiro Sugiyama, July 20, 1980.
[21] See *Handbook*, 1959, p. 45.
[22] From the personal journal of Seiichiro Aburatani, in 12 volumes (unnumbered) and written in English.
[23] *Ibid.* Mr. Aburatani records this experience as follows: The missionary made his earnest and fervent prayer for the Aburatanis, especially for Mr. Aburatani, lying in a sick bed. This second encounter between all the members of Mr. Aburatani and Rev. Peter A. Willms gave the unusual strong impression, in a very good sense, upon Mr. Seiichiro Aburatani and his whole family about his personality and, especially about the teaching of Christianity through his behavior and conduct based on the love teaching of Jesus Christ upon all our human beings on this earth. This second encounter also opened the eyes of Mr. Aburatani's towards the existence of a true church and its evangelical works and activities for all the ungodly people in the city of Hagi and its vicinity to the greatest extent that he had ever thought of through his whole life up to that time.
[24] Peter Willms, "Buying a House in a Strange Land," *Evangelical Visitor*, November 23, 1953.
[25] Peter Willms letter "To Hostetter, Ulery and Wolgemuth," July 27, 1953; Peter Willms "Report to Foreign Mission Board," December 18, 1953. One *tsubo* is approximately six feet by six feet or thirty-six square feet. Thus a 250 *tsubo* plot is about nine thousand square feet, or the equivalent of a 60- x 150-foot lot.
[26] See *Visitor*, September 9, 1953.
[27] See *Visitor*, November 23, 1953 and Willms Report, December 18, 1953.
[28] Willms Report, December 18, 1953.
[29] *Ibid.*
[30] See *Visitor*, May 24, 1954, p. 7 and *Handbook*, 1954, p. 103.
[31] Board Minutes, January 6-9, 1953, and June 8-15, 1953.
[32] John Z. Martin "General Report to the Foreign Mission Board," August 1954, pp. 3, 4.
[33] Peter Willms "Report to the Foreign Mission Board," circa July 1954.
[34] Iwakura, Ichikawa and Willms interviews.
[35] Martin Report, p. 6.
[36] *Ibid.*, p. 7.
[37] *Ibid.*, pp. 7, 8.
[38] Peter Willms notes, July 31, 1954, "Hagi" file.
[39] *Ibid.*
[40] Willms Report, December 18, 1953.
[41] Peter Willms to Henry Hostetter, March 9, 1954.

[42] Peter Willms "General Report to Foreign Mission Board," April 6, 1954, p. 2.
[43] See *Visitor*, November 23, 1953, May 24, 1954, and Willms Report, circa July 1954.
[44] Interview with John and Lucille Graybill, June 28, 1980.
[45] See *Visitor*, July 29, 1957, p. 7.
[46] Interview with Marlin and Ruth Zook, July 19, 1980.

Chapter 4

[1] Mary Willms, "Views and Reviews," *Evangelical Visitor* (Nappanee, Ind.: Evangel Press), November 26, 1962, p. 8.
[2] Interview with John and Lucille Graybill, June 28, 1980.
[3] Peter Willms, "Report to the Foreign Mission Board," circa, July 1954.
[4] Norman A. Wingert, "Soaring, Running, Walking," *Visitor*, March 24, 1958, pp. 6, 7.
[5] Mary Willms, "Gift Giving—a la Japanese," *Visitor*, May 23, 1966, p. 7.
[6] Ichiro Kawasaki, *The Japanese Are Like That* (Tokyo: Charles Tuttle, 1955), p. 193.
[7] Thelma Book, "To Marry or Not to Marry," *Visitor*, February 15, 1965, p. 6.
[8] Bonnie Willms to Peter and Mary Willms, March 1980.
[9] Thelma Book, personal journal, September 1, 1955, p. 12.
[10] *Ibid.*, September 7, 1955, p. 14.
[11] John Graybill, "For the First Time . . . ," *Visitor*, September 5, 1960, p. 8.
[12] Doyle Book to Henry N. Hostetter, March 22, 1966. See also *Handbook of Missions* (Nappanee, Ind.: Evangel Press), 1960, p. 66.
[13] See Mary Willms, "Views and Reviews," *Visitor*, November 26, 1962, p. 8. Doyle Book remembers many days sitting at his desk in Nagato wearing a sweater, long underwear and a jacket in addition to his regular clothing. Tape had been placed around the edges of the windows. A small kerosene heater was on its highest setting. Nevertheless the temperature would not rise above sixty degrees, and the curtains swayed as the wind blew against the house.
[14] Doyle Book to Henry N. Hostetter, January 1, 1960; Henry Hostetter to Doyle Book, January 8, 1960.
[15] Interview with Henry N. Hostetter, June 30, 1980.
[16] Interview with Pete and Mary Willms, June 24, 1980.
[17] Graybill interview.
[18] Mary Willms, "Two Enjoyable Hours in Ooya, Japan," *Visitor,* November 9, 1953, p. 10.
[19] Thelma Book, personal journal, September 8, 1955, p. 15.
[20] Interview with Hiroko Kanakubo Hataya, July 26, 1980.
[21] Names withheld. Thelma Book, personal journal, October 2, 1955, p. 20; Peter Willms to Koichiro Sugujama, September 25, 1956.
[22] Willms interview. See also Norman Wingert, "Soaring, Running, Walking," *Visitor*, March 24, 1958, pp. 6, 7.
[23] Graybill interview. See also *Visitor*, July 24, 1961, p. 8.
[24] Willms interview; Thelma Book, personal journal, October 26, 1955, p. 22.
[25] Graybill interview.
[26] Peter Willms, "Northeast of Hagi, Open Hearts," *Visitor*, January 4, 1954, p. 8; Mary Willms, "Your Prayers and Japan," *Visitor*, May 24, 1954, p. 7.
[27] Graybill interview.
[28] Willms interview.
[29] Thelma Book, personal journal, September 8, 1955, p. 15.
[30] Norman A. Wingert, "Soaring, Running, Walking," *Visitor*, March 24, 1958, pp. 6, 7.

Chapter 5

[1] Peter Willms, "Northeast of Hagi—Open Hearts," *Evangelical Visitor* (Nappanee, Ind.: Evangel Press), January 18, 1954, p. 9.

[2] John Graybill, "For the First Time . . . ," *Visitor*, September 5, 1960, p. 8.
[3] Interview with Peter and Mary Willms, June 24, 1980.
[4] Interview with Marlin and Ruth Zook, July 19, 1980.
[5] Ray F. Downs, "A Look at the Third Culture Child," *Japan Christian Quarterly*, Spring 1976, pp. 66-71. This article is chiefly a summary and evaluation of research done by Ruth A. Unseem of Michigan State University.

In a letter to the author, September 1980, Margaret Willms Evans wrote that she feels she has led "two separate lives." She indicated that she feels this especially since returning to the United States. Except for a few mementos, the first fourteen years of her life seem "hardly even there." She goes on, "In the United States my life goes back only eleven years. In Japan, it only goes up to fourteen. No wonder I feel as though there aren't twenty-five years to my life."

[6] For a discussion of the homogeneous unit concept and the "we-they" mentality, see C. Peter Wagner, *Our Kind of People* (Atlanta: John Knox Press, 1979).
[7] Willms interview.
[8] Zook interview.
[9] Thelma Book, "When Color Counts," *Visitor*, March 27, 1967, p. 7.
[10] Interview with J. Earl Musser, July 1, 1980; Mission Minutes, August 15, 1960.
[11] Mission Minutes, August 15, 1960.
[12] Mission Report, Willms Annual, 1960.
[13] Peter Willms in *Handbook of Missions* (Nappanee, Ind.: Evangel Press), 1961, p. 29. Edna later became Mrs. William Hart and presently resides with her husband in Upland, California.
[14] Mission Minutes, August 15, 1960.
[15] Mission Report, General, 4th Quarter, 1960; 1st Quarter, 1961; 1st and 2nd Quarters, 1962; and Pre-Conference, January 5, 1961.
[16] Mission Minutes, October 1961; Mission Report, General, 2nd Quarter, 1962.
[17] Willms interview.
[18] Thelma Book, "Battle for Absolutes," *Visitor*, February 11, 1966, p. 7.
[19] In the earlier years of the mission the personal allowance was $10.00 a month for an adult and $5.00 for a child.
[20] Interview with John and Lucille Graybill, June 28, 1980.
[21] Willms interview.
[22] For a general discussion of missionary children on furlough, see Beth L. Frey, "Children of Brethren in Christ Missionaries and their Adjustment to Life" (unpublished thesis), pp. 8-9.
[23] Willms interview.
[24] See *Visitor*, May 22, 1967, p. 6.
[25] Graybill interview with Barbara Graybill letter, 1980.
[26] Margaret Willms Evans wrote: "Because of the advanced educational system in Japan, any adjustment to the U.S. was made infinitely easier. At a time when I was so self-conscious about everything, at least I didn't have to worry about school work. Poor grades might have made me drift apart, ultimately to be a very unhappy person. But fortunately, thanks to excellent training in Japan, school was no problem, and good grades carried me right along to the point where, by the time I was beginning to adjust to the U.S., my grades were good enough to put me anywhere I wanted to be."

In a letter to the author, November 7, 1980, Edward Graybill wrote: "I believe the academic level of CAJ was quite superior to that of most high schools in America. As a result I feel it provided a solid foundation for future life and study."

[27] Eleven of the thirteen children from the four original mission families have returned to the United States.

Margaret Willms Evans works in personnel at the University of Massachusetts and takes in typing. Husband, John.

Bonnie Willms taught in Japan on a Fulbright grant and is a business analyst in the Foreign Affairs Division of General Motors.

Kenneth Willms is in home construction in Pennsylvania.

Charity Book is a performing musician and teaches piano and electric bass.

Stephanie Book is a piano performance major at the University of Redlands.

Michael Graybill is a Ph.D. candidate at Harvard University. Wife, Holly, two children.
Brenda Graybill Custer works as a technician for a chiropractor. Husband, Dale, two children.
Edward Graybill has an M.Div. from Westminster, an M.A. from Villanova, and is teaching in China.
Debra Graybill Valentin is a secretary with Four Seasons. Husband, Manuel, one child.
Barbara Graybill graduated with a major in art and will enter graduate school.
Brian Zook completed two years at Messiah College and is continuing studies at Goshen College.
Both Elaine Zook and Stephen Zook are enrolled at Christian Academy in Japan in Tokyo.

In an article in *The Japan Times*, February 21, 1985, entitled, "My Son, The Interpreter," Ruth Zook reports that Brian's fluency in Japanese made him in demand in the States in negotiations between an American and a Japanese company. She adds, however, that it is not easy to get similar jobs in Japan. It seems that most people feel uncomfortable with a "gaijin" of light skin and fair hair being so skillful in the language.

Bonnie Willms, as an employee of General Motors, has been an intepreter in business dealings with Japanese firms.

[28] *Handbook*, 1956, p. 98; Peter Willms to Doyle Book, December 30, 1981.
[29] John Z. Martin, "General Report to the Foreign Mission Board," August 1954, p. 10.
[30] Mission Report, Willms, October 1955.
[31] *Handbook*, 1956, p. 98; Mission Report, Willms, October 1955.
[32] Interview with Yasuo and Kikuyo Miyamoto, August 7, 1980.
[33] Mission Report, Willms, October 1955.
[34] Interview with Hiroko Kanakubo Hataya, July 26, 1980; Mission Report, Willms, October 1955.
[35] Mission Report, *ibid*.
[36] Thelma Book, personal journal, November 28, 1955, p. 28.
[37] *Ibid*., October 8, 1955, p. 21 and September 16, 1956, p. 59.
[38] *Handbook*, 1956, p. 100.
[39] Mission Report, Willms, October 1955.
[40] Seiichiro Aburatani, personal journal in 12 volumes (unnumbered) in English.
[41] Miyamoto interview.
[42] *General Conference Minutes* (Nappanee, Ind.: Evangel Press), 1957, p. 80.
[43] *Handbook*, 1958, p. 109.
[44] Peter Willms to Hiroko Kanakubo, November 14, 1957.
[45] Peter Willms, "The Japan Brethren in Christ Mission—Its First Seven Years," Spring 1961.
[46] For a calendar of the main activities of the mission families during the first ten years see page iii.
[47] *Handbook*, 1958, p. 109.
[48] *Visitor*, October 21, 1957, p. 7.
[49] Carl J. Ulery to Peter Willms, July 30, 1955.
[50] Mission Minutes, September 7, 1957.
[51] *Ibid*., November 7-9, 1957.
[52] Mission Report, Willms, October 1955.

Chapter 6

[1] Interview with Koichiro Sugiyama, July 20, 1980. The reference was to another individual.
[2] Interview with Henry N. Hostetter, June 30, 1980.
[3] *General Conference Minutes* (Nappanee, Ind.: Evangel Press) 1957, p. 73.
[4] Hostetter interview; Interview with Henry A. Ginder, July 2, 1980.

197

[5] John Z. Martin, "General Report to the Foreign Mission Board," August 1954, p. 8; Mission Minutes, February 13-16, 1960 and October 31-November 3, 1967.

[6] Board Minutes, December 28-29, 1965; Mission Minutes, October 31-November 3, 1967.

[7] Peter Willms, "The Japan Brethren in Christ Mission—Its First Seven Years," Spring 1961; *Handbook of Missions* (Nappanee, Ind.: Evangel Press), 1956, p. 98. See also Roland Allen, *The Spontaneous Expansion of the Church* (Grand Rapids: Eerdmans, 1962), pp. 143, 150.

[8] *Handbook*, 1958, p. 108; *Evangelical Visitor* ("Look") (Nappanee, Ind.: Evangel Press), June 16, 1958, p. 2; *Handbook*, 1959, pp. 44-45.

[9] Martin Report, p. 9; "Japan Brethren in Christ Mission Policies 1954," Sec. III, 3.

[10] Willms, "Seven Years."

[11] Peter Willms, "A Case for Lay Leadership," April 1961.

[12] *Ibid.*

[13] *Ibid.*

[14] Mission Minutes, September 7, 1957 and December 7-10, 1965; Board Minutes, December 25-29, 1965.

[15] Mission Minutes, December 4-8, 1963, p. 6 and December 7-10, 1965, p. 5. For the visits of board representatives, see minutes of the respective years.

[16] Hostetter interview.

[17] *Visitor*, September 9, 1957, p. 8.

[18] Board Minutes, June 8-15, 1953; Henry Hostetter to Peter Willms, July 15, 1968; Mission Minutes, November 27-December 1, 1966; Mission Minutes, February 17, 1975.

[19] See Mission Minutes, December 7-10, 1965, for a summary of mission and personal items and the actions taken regarding them over the years.

[20] Mission Policy for Japan, September 2, 1959.

[21] Mission Minutes, November 21-24, 1959.

[22] *Ibid.*, February 13-18, 1960.

[23] Peter Willms to Henry Hostetter, May 19, 1959.

[24] Interview with Peter and Mary Willms, June 24, 1980.

[25] Board Minutes, June 8-15, 1953.

[26] Henry Hostetter to Peter Willms, February 13, 1954. See also the report of the special committee "Appointed under the Board Minutes of December 28, 1953-January 1, 1954, regarding the work in Japan," January 19, 1954.

[27] Board Minutes, June 8-15, 1953.

[28] Carlton O. Wittlinger, *A Quest for Piety and Obedience* (Nappanee, Ind.: Evangel Press, 1978), p. 194.

[29] Board Minutes, December 28, 1953-January 1, 1954.

[30] Henry Hostetter to Peter Willms, January 13, 1954.

[31] Peter Willms to Carl J. Ulery, February 1, 1954.

[32] Hostetter interview.

[33] Martin Report, p. 3; Mission Report, Pre-Conference, June 5, 1961; Mission Minutes, October 1961 and December 4-8, 1963; Carlton Wittlinger to Peter Willms, 1961.

[34] Hostetter interview.

[35] Wittlinger, *Quest*, p. 195.

[36] Mission Report, Book, October 8, 1959.

[37] Mission Report, Willms, 1968.

[38] Willms, "Seven Years."

[39] *Handbook*, 1964, p. 79, 1962, p. 70, and 1963, p. 34.

[40] Mission Minutes, December 4-8, 1963.

[41] Mission Minutes, October 1961.

[42] Mission Reports, Book, First Quarter 1962 and Third and Fourth Quarters 1962; Mission Report, Willms Annual, March 2, 1962.

[43] Willms, "Seven Years"; Willms, "Lay Leadership"; Mission Report, Pre-Conference, June 5, 1961. See also *Visitor*, May 14, 1962, p. 11.

[44] Mission Report, Pre-Conference, June 5, 1961; Mission Report, Annual 1963, January 25, 1964; Willms' class records.

[45] Peter Willms, "From the Land of the Nipponese," *Visitor*, October 8, 1956, p. 7; Thelma Book, personal journal, August 14-22, 1955, pp. 58-59.

[46] Doyle Book, "Japan General Report," *Handbook*, 1960, p. 67; Peter Willms, "Summer Camp Pays Off Again," *Visitor*, April 15, 1963, p. 9; Thelma Book, "Many Believed," *Visitor*, December 12, 1960, p. 5.

[47] Peter Willms, "Radio Tapes Speak Good Japanese," *Visitor*, June 30, 1958, p. 7; *Handbook*, 1959, p. 44.

[48] Peter Willms, "Radio Responses Reach a New High," *Visitor*, April 1, 1963, p. 7.

[49] Mission Minutes, January 4-5, 1965, November 27-December 1, 1966, February 8, 1971, October 18-20, 1971, November 6-8, 1972, November 24-25, 1975 and November 25-26, 1977. In 1966, 80,000 yen equalled approximately $222.00. With the later decrease in the rate of exchange, the late 1980 level of 20,000 yen was about $93.00 The subsidy was finally terminated at the end of 1980.

[50] Seiichiro Aburatani, personal records.

[51] Mission Report, General, Fourth Quarter, 1960; Dorothy C. Haskin, "A Converted Liquor Store," *Visitor*, April 3, 1961, p. 9.

[52] *Handbook*, 1961, p. 30; Mission Minutes, February 13-16, 1960 and October 1961.

[53] Mission Minutes, February 13-16, 1960; Seiichiro Aburatani, personal records; Mission Report, Graybill, June 12, 1967.

[54] Mission Minutes, November 28-December 1, 1966, October 20-22, 1969, January 24-27, 1969, February 27-28, 1970, March 21, 1970 and April 20-21, 1970.

[55] See Chapter 5.

[56] See articles by Don McCammon, Norman Wingert and Peter Willms in *Mennonite Life*, October 1957.

[57] *Visitor*, January 20, 1964, p. 17.

[58] *Visitor*, August 25, 1978, p. 9.

[59] See Melvin Gingrich, "The Mennonite Peace Witness in Japan," *Mennonite Life*, October 1957, p. 185; *Visitor*, December 31, 1956, p. 13.

[60] Mission Report, Pre-Conference, 1960; Mission Minutes, February 13-18, 1960.

[61] Mission Report, Book, Third and Fourth Quarters 1962; Mission Minutes, November 12-13, 1963.

[62] *Handbook*, 1961, p. 29; John Graybill, "Brethren in Christ Host All-Mennonite Fellowship in Japan," *Visitor*, December 28, 1960, p. 8; Mission Report, General, Fourth Quarter 1960.

[63] See *Visitor*, March 11, 1957, p. 13, March 25, 1957, p. 6, and June 17, 1957, p. 3.

[64] John Graybill, "Voluntary Service Report—Japan," *Visitor*, October 20, 1969, p. 11.

[65] Mission Minutes, June 14-15, 1969.

[66] Mission Report, Andrew Stoner, 1969.

[67] Mission Minutes, October 20-22, 1969.

[68] Mission Report, Dwight Thomas, October 1971.

[69] Mission Report, Timothy Botts, January 1971.

[70] Mission Report, Thomas, October 1971; *Handbook*, 1972, pp. 46-49; Mission Minutes, November 10-12, 1970.

[71] Interview with Andrew Stoner, July 2, 1980; Timothy Botts to Doyle Book, May 25, 1980; Interview with Dwight and Carol Thomas, July 3, 1980; Miriam Bowers to Doyle Book, June 5, 1980. See also Timothy and Nancy Botts, "Japan Is . . . ," *Visitor*, February 10, 1970.

[72] John Graybill, "An Accurate Picture of the Tokyo, Koganei Church" (unpublished paper), June 12, 1980.

Chapter 7

[1] Mission Report, Willms to FMB, circa July 1954.
[2] Mission Report, Graybill, 1st quarter 1959.

[3] Mission Report June 5, 1961; *General Conference Minutes* (Nappanee, Ind.: Evangel Press), 1962, p. 93; "A Walk of 20 Years," October 10, 1973 (in Japanese); Mission Report, General, 2nd quarter 1961.
[4] Henry N. Hostetter diary, October 18, 1961, p. 8.
[5] Mission Report, Book, October 8, 1959 and January 20, 1960; "A Walk of 20 Years."
[6] *Handbook of Missions* (Nappanee, Ind.: Evangel Press) 1957, p. 43; 1958, p. 108; 1959, p. 45; 1960, p. 67; Mission Report, Annual 1960.
[7] Mission Report, General 1959; *Handbook* 1960, p. 67.
[8] Mission Report, Book, January 21, 1960; Interview with Yasuo and Kikuyo Miyamoto, August 7, 1980.
[9] Mission Report, June 5, 1961.
[10] Seiichiro Aburatani personal records.
[11] Thelma Book, personal journal, April 13, 1956, p. 45; Thelma Book, "Baptism at Hagi, Japan," *Evangelical Visitor* (Nappanee, Ind.: Evangel Press), October 21, 1957, p. 6; Interview with Hajime and Yaeko Kaneshige, August 9, 1980. See also *Visitor*, March 4, 1963, p. 7.
[12] Peter Willms, *Firewood Field of Japan* (Women's Missonary Prayer Circle), 1965.
[13] Interview with Masaharu Okano, August 7, 1980.
[14] See *Visitor*, December 11, 1961, p. 6. The Hagi church led an evangelistic campaign by itself and paid all the expenses.
[15] Peter Willms, "Divide and Multiply," *Visitor*, August 2, 1965, p. 11.
[16] "A Walk of 20 Years."
[17] Mission Report, Willms Annual, 1968. Among those who transferred to the other church were the Miyamoto family, Mr. and Mrs. Aburatani and Mrs. Tsuchiko Fujita.
[18] "A Walk of 20 Years."
[19] *Handbook* 1959, p. 45.
[20] Doyle Book, "Believers Added to the Hagi and Senzaki Churches," *Visitor*, December 28, 1959, p. 8.
[21] John Graybill to Doyle Book September 20, 1960.
[22] John Graybill, "Our First Christmas in Nagato," *Visitor*, April 3, 1961, p. 7.
[23] Mission Reports, General, 1st quarter 1961 and 1st quarter 1962; *Visitor*, May 13, 1963, p. 6.
[24] *Visitor*, September 14, 1964, p. 9.
[25] *Visitor*, November 22, 1965, p. 9; May 23, 1966, p. 6; May 8, 1967, p. 6 and May 5, 1968, p. 10.
[26] Mission Minutes, January 24-27, 1969.
[27] For other information and heartwarming stories about the early years in Nagato see the following *Visitor* issues: June 12, 1961, p. 11; May 27, 1963, p. 6; August 3, 1964, p. 7; October 26, 1964, p. 6; January 18, 1965, p. 17; April 12, 1965, p. 6; June 21, 1965, p. 6; December 20, 1965, p. 7; January 17, 1966, p. 6; March 28, 1966, p. 6; October 10, 1966, p. 10; December 9, 1966, p. 6; September 25, 1967, p. 7; and July 1, 1968, p. 15.
[28] John Graybill, "Outreach," *Visitor*, July 23, 1962, p. 9; Hiroto Okazaki, personal records.
[29] John Graybill, "Outreach," *Visitor*, July 23, 1962, p. 9.
[30] John Graybill, "Evangelistic Effort at Takibe (Japan)," *Visitor*, October 23, 1963, p. 7.
[31] Hiroto Okazaki, personal records.
[32] Thelma Book, "I Read the Book You Left," *Visitor*, October 7, 1968, p. 5.
[33] *Visitor*, August 10, 1970, p. 10.
[34] Other details concerning Agawa are given in *Visitor*, September 26, 1966, p. 10 and November 7, 1966, p. 6. See also Mission Records, Nagato Pre-Mission Meeting 1965 and Willms, November 21, 1966 and Seiichiro Aburatani personal records.
[35] Melvin Gingrich, "The Anabaptist Vision in Japan," *Mennonite Life*, October 1957, p. 192.
[36] *Handbook*, 1968, p. 37.
[37] Peter Willms, "They Must Increase but We Must Decrease," *Visitor*, February 26, 1968, p. 11; *Handbook*, 1969, p. 37.
[38] Mission Report, October 16, 1967; Peter Willms, "The Call of the Campus," *Visitor*, July 3, 1967, p. 16 and "Through an Economics Seminar," *Visitor*, July 17, 1967, p. 10.
[39] Mission Minutes, October 31-November 3, 1967, August 7, 1968, and November 27-December 1, 1966.
[40] Marlin Zook, to John Graybill, February 20, 1969.

[41] Mission Minutes, June 14-15, 1969.
[42] Interview with Marlin and Ruth Zook, July 19, 1980.
[43] Marlin Zook, "What is Your Thinking About God?" *Visitor*, May 10, 1976, p. 8.
[44] Interview with Goro Shibata and Masaharu Okano, August 7, 1980.
[45] The date of the original action is not clear. Marlin's appointment, however, was affirmed in various discussions and correspondence, including John Graybill to Marlin Zook, March 9, 1970; Mission Minutes, February 8, 1971 and Marlin Zook to church leaders, February 24, 1971.
[46] The testimony of Mrs. Yamamoto appears in Chapter 11.
[47] Mission Minutes, November 15-19, 1962; Mission Reports, Annual, March 2, 1963; Willms, November 25, 1963 and Book, Nagato, 1963.
[48] Mission Reports, Nagato, June 2, 1964; Nagato Station 1965 and Field, June 12, 1967.
[49] Thelma Book, "After Searching," *Visitor*, January 2, 1967, p. 6.
[50] The class was introduced in the Prologue. See also *Handbook*, 1972, pp. 8-11.
[51] Mission Report, Book, 1969.
[52] Mission Reports, Shimonoseki, November 1970 and October 1971; Doyle and Thelma Book, "Patterns in Shimonoseki," *Visitor*, February 25, 1971, p. 8.
[53] Mission Minutes, February 27-28, 1970 and April 26, 1974; Marlin Zook, "Dedication at Shimonoseki," *Visitor*, November 25, 1974, p. 8. See also Ruth Zook, "Our Cup Runneth Over," *Visitor*, April 25, 1975, p. 9.
[54] "A Walk of 20 Years."
[55] *Visitor*, August 20, 1962, p. 8 and April 27, 1964, p. 7.
[56] Mission Minutes, October 1961.
[57] Mission Minutes, May 21, 1964 and January 18, 1965; *Visitor*, April 27, 1964, p. 7; John Graybill, "Our Beginnings in Tokyo," *Visitor*, June 7, 1965, p. 17.
[58] Interviews with Koganei members. See Ito story in *Handbook*, 1973, p. 26.
[59] Mission Report, Tokyo, November 15, 1965; John Graybill, "Our Beginnings in Tokyo," *Visitor*, June 7, 1965, p. 17; "Outreach Into Homes," *Visitor*, July 4, 1966, p. 10 and "Prayer Cell Evangelism in Tokyo," *Visitor*, February 13, 1967, p. 6.
[60] Mission Report, Tokyo, November 3, 1970. See Matoba story in *Handbook*, 1973, p. 43 and *Japan Harvest*, Winter 1972, p. 26.
[61] Interview with Masanori Tange, July 17, 1980. See M. Tange, "How I Became a Christian," *Visitor*, April 7, 1969, p. 8, and *Handbook*, 1974, p. 20. See also Chiyoko Horiuchi, "Surprised by Joy," *Visitor*, October 25, 1970, p. 8 and David Nagashima, "What God is Doing," *Visitor*, May 10, 1978, p. 9.
[62] Mission Report, Tokyo, November 3, 1970; John Graybill, "The Koganei Church," *Visitor*, September 10, 1973, p. 9 and "A First for the Church in Tokyo," *Visitor*, June 25, 1977, p. 8; and interview with John Graybill, March 15, 1981.
[63] Mission Report, Tokyo, January 26, 1970; John Graybill, "An Accurate Picture of the Tokyo, Koganei Church," (unpublished paper), June 12, 1980.
[64] Marlin Zook to Doyle Book, October 20, 1980.
[65] Peter Willms to Henry Hostetter, May 21, 1954; Board Minutes, June 7-14, 1954.
[66] Samuel Wolgemuth to Peter Willms, March 18, 1966. A great deal of correspondence on the matter can be found throughout 1966. See Willms or Board files.
[67] Paul Peachey, "The Christian Church in Japan," (unpublished paper), July 4, 1959.
[68] *Handbook*, 1955, p. 69; *Conference Minutes*, 1955, p. 15; *Handbook*, 1964, p. 79; Mission Report, Annual, January 25, 1964; Mission Minutes, January 30-31, 1966.
[69] Peter Willms to Henry Hostetter, May 21, 1954.
[70] Peter Willms to Samuel Wolgemuth, June 7, 1966.
[71] Seiichiro Aburatani personal records; Shibata and Okano interview; Mission Minutes, October 31-November 3, 1967 and December 4-8, 1963.
[72] Mission Minutes, January 24-27, 1969, Appendix I.
[73] Shibata and Okano interview; Interview with Asao Nishimura, August 1, 1980.
[74] For a devastating criticism of Swedenborgianism see Enoch Pond, *Swedenborgianism Reviewed* (Portland, Me.: Hyde, Lord and Duren, 1846). For a brief treatment of the cult see Doyle Book, "The Atonement and Emanuel Swedenborg," (unpublished paper), May 1979.

[75] See Minutes of the Yamaguchi Brethren in Christ Conference for the respective dates, church or mission files, Nagato or Tokyo.
[76] Interviews with Nagato members. For additional information on Iwamoto or on the formation of the conference see Mission Minutes, May 21, 1971 and August 16, 1971; *Visitor*, August 10, 1971, p. 9, and *Handbook*, 1975, p. 13.
[77] Shibata and Okano interview.
[78] *Handbook*, 1976, p. 26 and Marlin Zook to Doyle Book, January 13, 1981.

Chapter 8

[1] *Handbook of Missions* (Nappanee, Ind.: Evangel Press) 1964, p. 78.
[2] John Graybill to Doyle Book, April 23, 1980.
[3] Information taken from John Graybill, "An Accurate Picture of the Tokyo, Koganei Church" (unpublished paper), June 12, 1980.
[4] *Ibid.*, p. 7.
[5] Interview with Masanori Tange, July 17, 1980.
[6] Graybill to Book, April 23, 1980.
[7] Marlin Zook, "Face-Lift in Yamaguchi," *Evangelical Visitor* (Nappanee, Ind.: Evangel Press), February 25, 1980, p. 8.
[8] Mission Report, Willms Annual, 1968.
[9] Interview with Asao Nishimura, August 1, 1980. Other stories will be recounted in Chapter 11.
[10] Graybill, "An Accurate . . . ," p. 2.
[11] Peter Willms, "Victorious Notes from Japan," *Visitor*, March 16, 1964, p. 7; *Visitor*, April 27, 1964, p. 7; Thelma Book, "God Working at Nagato—Japan," *Visitor*, April 12, 1965, p. 6.
[12] Graybill, "An Accurate . . . ," p. 11.
[13] LaVerne Snider, *It's Happening in Japan Today* (Osaka: Japan Free Methodist Mission, 1980).
[14] Peter Willms, "The Japan Brethren in Christ Mission—Its First Seven Years," Spring 1961. The uneasiness returned from time to time. Pete was aware of certain principles of strategy such as receptivity. He had felt originally that it would be wise to locate in an urban area, win and train converts there, and then send them into the country areas. But he deferred to the decision and "older and wiser brethren." Even after some years in the country, he wondered if he should press for a change of policy, but he was afraid this might suggest a lack of dedication to the needy in the "difficult" rural areas. (Peter Willms to Doyle Book, December 30, 1981)
[15] Interview with John Graybill, June 28, 1980; Interview with Peter Willms, June 24, 1980.
[16] It is recognized that by this time the mission's responsibility for the country could not be avoided. Churches had been formed and nurture must be provided. To provide this nurture was part of the call and qualifications of Marlin Zook. One feeling in the mission was that any new missionary residence needed to be established apart from existing churches which were now under the direction of national leaders. Thus Nagato, although strategic in location, was to be avoided. Since the Willmses were in Yamaguchi City, it was felt that there was no better new location than Nishiichi. In this choice, whether or not a new church might be established was considered a secondary matter. (Willms to Book, December 30, 1981)
[17] Interview with Tsutomu Kuboe, July 26, 1980; Interview with Goro Shibata and Masaharu Okano, August 7, 1980.
[18] Mission Minutes, October 18-20, 1971; Marlin Zook to Church Leaders, February 24, 1971.
[19] Interviews with Hajime Kaneshige, August 9, 1980, Shibata, Okano and others.
[20] Peter Willms, "A Case for Lay Leadership," 1961, p. 6.
[21] C. Peter Wagner, *Your Church Can Be Healthy* (Nashville: Abingdon, 1979), p. 90.
[22] Snider, p. 141.
[23] *Handbook*, 1968, p. 36.
[24] Interviews with Takanobu Tojo, July 28, 1980 and Hiroko Kanakubo Hataya, July 26, 1980.
[25] Nishimura interview.

²⁶Interview with J. Earl Musser, July 1, 1980.
²⁷Snider, pp. 8, 30, 36, 86, 132. See also Neil Braun, *Laity Mobilized* (Grand Rapids: Eerdmans, 1971).
²⁸Graybill, "An Accurate . . . ," pp. 3, 9.
²⁹Snider, pp. 35, 121, 140, 141.
³⁰Musser interview.
³¹Tojo, Shibata and Nishimura interviews.
³²Program of the twentieth anniversary of the Yamaguchi Brethren in Christ Churches, October 10, 1973 (in Japanese).
³³Marlin and Ruth Zook, "Japan Camping Weekend," *Visitor*, November 10, 1975, p. 10; Yukiko Yamamoto, "I Found the Holy Spirit Ruled the Service," *Visitor*, August 25, 1978, p. 10.
³⁴Asao Nishimura, "What Is on My Mind at the 20th Anniversary," *Visitor*, October 10, 1973, p. 8.

Chapter 9

¹Adapted from John Graybill, "Prayer Cell Evangelism in Tokyo," *Evangelical Visitor* (Nappanee, Ind.: Evangel Press) February, 1967, p. 6.
²Neil Braun, *Laity Mobilized* (Grand Rapids: Eerdmans, 1971), p. 160.
³LaVerne Snider, *It's Happening in Japan Today* (Osaka: Japan Free Methodist Mission, 1980), pp. 15, 25, 27, 39, 60.
⁴Braun, pp. 160-161.
⁵Thelma Book to Mrs. C. R. Heisey, November 16, 1956.
⁶Braun, pp. 49, 29.
⁷Peter Willms, "The Japan Brethren in Christ Mission—Its First Seven Years," Spring 1961.
⁸*Visitor*, May 14, 1962, p. 11.
⁹Snider, p. 81. For further discussion on the principle of "training during and through ministry," see pp. 84-88. See also Fred Holland, *Teaching Through TEE* (Kisumu, Kenya: Evangel Press, 1975).
¹⁰Interview with Tsutomu Kuboe, July 26, 1980.
¹¹Interviews with Hajime and Yaeko Kaneshige, August 9, 1980, Masaharu Okano, August 7, 1980 and Kimiko Nishimura, August 1, 1980.
¹²Snider, p. 15. Takanobu Tojo said of the Shimonoseki church: "The mission of this church is young men." Many young men have been baptized in the Shimonoseki group and two of them have gone to seminary.
¹³Interview with Marlin and Ruth Zook, July 19, 1980. They referred to Buddy Stott of the Cumberland Presbyterian Mission.
¹⁴Kimiko Nishimura interview.
¹⁵Shibata and Okano interview.
¹⁶Interviews with Masanori Tange, July 17, 1980, and Takanobu Tojo, July 28, 1980.
¹⁷Tojo interview.
¹⁸Robert Hempy, "A Cure for Conflict" (sermon at Upland, Calif.), October 26, 1980.
¹⁹Interview with Henry N. Hostetter, June 30, 1980.

Chapter 10

¹Marlin Zook, "Friendship Evangelism in Tokyo," *Evangelical Visitor*, (Nappanee, Ind.: Evangel Press) July 10, 1981, pp. 8-9.
²John Graybill, "Church Planting, Partnership Style," *Therefore*, (Mount Joy, Pa.: Brethren in Christ Missions), March/April 1982, p. 6.

[3] *Ibid.*
[4] Interview with John Graybill, March 9, 1985.
[5] *Ibid.*
[6] Karen Dehyle, "The Struggle of Learning Japanese," *Therefore*, March/April 1982, p. 9.
[7] Dan Dehyle, "Deciding What's Best," *Visitor*, February 25, 1982, p. 1.
[8] Paul Hostetler, "Impressions of Japan," *Visitor*, January 1984, p. 15.
[9] Marlin Zook to Donald Zook, November 11, 1985.
[10] Connie Lofthouse, "The Joys of Tokyo Travel," *Visitor*, April 25, 1981, p. 8.
[11] Mary Brubaker, "Teaching and Learning," *Visitor*, April 25, 1981, p. 8.
[12] Dora Myers, "Spreading the LIght," *Visitor*, April 25, 1981, p. 9.
[13] Dora Myers Kawata, "Living as a Family at Miyoshi-cho," *Visitor*, April 1984, p. 16. Because of personal reasons, Mr. Kawate quit his company job and on July 24, 1985, the Kawates left Japan with ten-month-old Mark for a new life in the United States.
[14] Jean Maedke, "Teachers in English—Ambassadors for Christ," *Visitor*, December 1984, p. 18.
[15] Marlin Zook to Donald Zook, November 11, 1985.
[16] Peter and Laura Shaida, "Japan Meets Lancaster," *Visitor*, January 1985, p. 16.
[17] Minutes of the Board for Missions, December 2-4, 1982, pp. 213, 215.
[18] Arlene Miller, "Looking Onward: Brethren in Christ Missions," *Visitor*, February 10, 1980, p. 4.
[19] Board Minutes, p. 215.
[20] Report of the Pioneer Evangelism Committee, February 26, 1985, Article 3.1.
[21] Report of Takanobu Tojo to Doyle Book, February 1985.
[22] Confession of Faith, Japan Brethren in Christ Church, November 1984.
[23] Tojo Report, February 1985.
[24] *Ibid.*
[25] Pioneer Evangelism Committee Report, February 26, 1985.
[26] Hirokawa, Hock, Okano and Tojo, "Sow in Tears, Reap in Joy," *Visitor*, October 1984, p. 12.
[27] *Ibid.*, p. 14.
[28] Marlin Zook, "Who Are You?", *Vsitor*, June 1983, p. 17.
[29] Marlin Zook to Donald Zook, November 11, 1985.
[30] Dora Myers Kawate, "Living as a Family at Miyoshi-cho," *Visitor*, April 1984, p. 16.
[31] Hirokawa, Hock, Okano and Tojo, "Sow in Tears, Reap in Joy," *Visitor*, October 1984, pp. 13-14.
[32] *Handbook for World Christian Intercessors*, (Missions Prayer Fellowship: Mt. Joy, PA), August 1985.
[33] Dan Dejyle to Doyle Book, July 10, 1985.
[34] *Ibid.*
[35] Interview with John Graybill, March 9, 1985.
[36] Marlin Zook, "Mrs. Matsuura's Testimony," *Visitor*, August 25, 1980, p. 6.
[37] Marlin Zook, "Face Lift in Yamaguchi," *Visitor*, February 25, 1980, p. 8.
[38] Sachie Hashimoto, "Meeting the Brethren in Christ in Yamaguchi," *Visitor*, August 25, 1981, p. 11.
[39] Takanobu Tojo to Doyle Book, February 1985.
[40] John Graybill to Doyle Book, September 2, 1985.
[41] Eiji Suzuki, "A Report and Testimony," *Visitor*, August 1984, p. 18.
[42] John Graybill to the Members of the General Conference Preparation Committee and the Pioneer Evangelism Committee, June 20, 1983. 1984 statistics for Japan are given in *1984 Annual Reports*, Brethren in Christ Missions, page 6, as follows:

Home Meeting Attendance	17.6
Cooking Class Attendance	18
Ladies Meeting Attendance	26.7
Church Leaders	18
Seekers	57
Baptized in 1984	5

203

Church Members	156
English Class Attendance	197
Bible Study Attendance	69.3
Prayer Meeting Attendance	38.2
Sunday School Attendnace	75.2
Worship Attendance	143.7
Offerings	$73,467.

[43] Board Minutes, p. 215.
[44] *Ibid.*, p. 216.

Chapter 11

[1] Interview with Yukiko Yamagata Yamamoto, July 27, 1980.

[2] Interviews with Izumi Hasegawa Awaya and Kimiko Ueda Nishimura, August 3, 1980. Written by Thelma Book, adapted by the author. Kiyoko experienced yet another crucial operation in the spring of 1984. She has recovered and is in better condition than before. Although she must still be careful, she is attending school regularly. Her father received the Lord and was baptized. He gave his personal testimony at the annual retreat for the Yamaguchi churches in November 1984. He is a member of the Yamanota Church where he serves as Prayer Leader.

[3] Inteviews with Asao and Kimiko Nishimura, August 1, 1980.

[4] Interview with Toshiki Funaki Takahashi, August 10, 1980. Written by Thelma Book, adapted by the author.

Epilogue

[1] The three vignettes which appear here were adapted from the following sources: Thelma Book, "Can God . . . ?" *Evangelical Visitor* (Nappanee, Ind.: Evangel Press), September 25, 1967, p. 7; Interview with Peter and Mary Willms, June 24, 1980; Miriam Bowers, "I Hear the Soft Voices of the Women as They Pray," *Handbook of Missions* (Nappanee, Ind.: Evangel Press), 1972, pp. 36-37.

Index

Abe, Setsuko, 112
Abe, Yoshito or Reiko, 113, 119
Aburatani, Seiichiro, 33, 35, 60-61, 75, 77, 93, 102, 104, 109, 119
Agawa Church, 109, 110, 119
Akidomi, Makiko, 108
Akidomi, Taro, 107, 108, 119
Akimoto, Masako, 112
Arita, Chisako, 104
Arita, Toshiaki or Emiko, 108, 119
Awaya, Kiyoko, 173-176
Awaya (Hasegawa), Izumi, 172-176, 178

Bearss, Beth, 98, 186
Bert, Eldon and Harriet, 85
Book, Charity (Chari), 69-70, 72, 73, 74, 98, 186, 195
Book, Doyle, 40-41, 55, 57, 58-59, 61, 63-64, 65, 66-67, 68, 70, 71, 73, 75, 76, 77-78, 79-81, 85, 91, 92, 95-97, 101-102, 105-109, 110, 111-113, 119, 120-121, 171-172, 178, 179-180, 181-182, 186
Book, Stephanie, 70, 72, 186, 195
Book, Thelma, 40-41, 55, 56-57, 58-59, 61, 63-64, 65, 66-67, 68-69, 70, 71, 73, 75, 76, 78, 79-81, 85, 91, 95, 96-98, 101, 105-107, 108, 110, 111, 112-113, 119, 121, 171-172, 178, 179-180, 181-182, 186
Botts, Tim or Nancy, 97, 98, 116, 186
Bowers, Miriam, 98, 116, 186
Brubaker, Mary, 98, 157-159, 187
Buddhism, 56, 77, 110, 150, 163, 165
Burkholder, Alvin C., 3

Canadian Church, 18, 25
cell groups (house churches), 82, 90, 112, 114-115, 144-145
children's education, 70-73, 91, 113
Christian home, 149, 151, 172, 177
church buildings, 87, 101, 107, 113, 114-116, 146
communism, 15

denominations, 83, 117-122, 135-137, 144
Deyhle, Cameron, 186
Deyhle, Daniel and Karen, 156, 158, 164-165, 186

Deyhle, Douglas, 186
Dehyle, Vaughn, 186
Dohner, Elam, 88
Dourte, Alice, 159, 166, 187
Dourte, Eber, 22

Ehara, Akira, 107-108
Engle, Charles or Kathryn, 22, 29, 31
English teaching, 9, 31-32, 39, 71, 77-78, 87, 95-99, 112-113, 114, 116, 151-152, 156, 157, 158-160, 161, 164
evangelism—country vs. city, 19-20, 100, 126-131
Ezaki, 104, 109

family loyalty, 56, 148-149
felt needs, 150-151
Fuchu, 98, 111, 114, 116, 133, 156, 157, 159-160, 161, 164
Fujita, Kiyoshi, 103, 104, 165
Funaki (Takahashi), Toshiko, 106, 114, 179-182
Furuta, Masashi, 136, 160, 161-163, 164, 166
Furuya, Michiko, 92

General Conference (Japan), 161-163, 167
gift giving, 55
Ginder, Henry A., 8, 9, 11, 22, 24-26, 28-30, 35, 82
Gingrich, Melvin, 94-95
Goto, Susumu, 105
Graybill, Barbara, 66, 69, 72, 74, 186, 196
Graybill, Brenda, 71, 74, 186, 196
Graybill, Debra, 58, 74, 186, 196
Graybill, Edward, 71, 186, 196
Graybill, Holly, 98, 186
Graybill, John, 41-43, 58-59, 61, 62, 64-66, 68, 71, 73, 79, 80, 85, 89, 91, 96-97, 99, 101, 102, 105-106, 107, 113-116, 124, 134, 136, 156-158, 160, 162, 164-165, 167, 169, 178, 186
Graybill, Lucille, 41-42, 43, 58-59, 63, 64-66, 71, 73, 79, 80, 86, 91, 96, 101, 105-106, 107, 113-114, 116, 124, 156-158, 178, 186
Graybill, Michael, 71, 98, 186, 196

Hada, Takaichi, 75, 90

Hagi, 6, 8, 9-10, 19-20, 28-33, 71, 75, 79-80, 82-83, 93, 98, 101-104, 108, 109-111, 119-120, 123, 126, 127, 130, 161, 165, 166, 178
Haldeman, Anna, 62
Haruyama, 110
Hasegawa, Izumi (see Awaya)
Hashimoto, Hirotoshi, 116, 135-136, 162, 166
Hashimoto, Sachie, 116
Hashimoto, Tatsumi, 92, 105
Hatano, Yoshiko, 108
Hataya, Hiroko (Kay) (see Kanakubo)
head covering, 22-23, 88-90
Hepzibah Mission, 17
Herr, Pauline, 3, 25
Hirokawa, Kazuyuki, 136, 158, 161, 163, 164, 166
Hock, Amy, 156, 186
Hock, Jason, 156, 186
Hock, Ray, 156, 158, 186
Hock, Winnie, 156, 158, 186
Holland, Steve, 159
Hoover, Kenneth, 116
Hori, Tomie, 113
Horiuchi, Chiyoko, 115
house churches (see cell groups)
Hostetter, C. N., Jr., 95
Hostetter, John N. or Nellie, 21, 22, 29
Hostetter, Henry N., 7, 22-23, 39, 44, 67, 82, 85-86, 89, 101, 117, 154, 178
Howard, Stanley, 6
Huggins, Farris, 162

Ichikawa, Uno, 32, 36, 38, 75, 101
Igeta, Toshiharu, 104, 165
indigeneity, 36, 82-85, 107, 144, 146
Ishii, Masako, 106
Ishii, Yoko, 105
Ito, Teriko, 114, 182
Iwakura, Ritsu, 32, 35, 38, 75
Iwamoto, Takeko, 106-107, 120-122

Johnson, Gordon, 4, 18, 22
Joseph, Kenny, 6

Kanakubo (Hataya), Hiroko, 76-77, 78-79, 103
Kaneda, Mitsuko, 114
Kaneko, Michiko, 111, 113, 175
Kaneshige, Hajime, 92, 102-104, 110, 119, 136
Kaneshige, Yaeko, 77, 94, 103-104, 110
Kansas, 16-17
Kato, Mitsuko, 111, 113
Katsura, Emine, 32, 34-35, 37, 76, 92, 94
Kawakami, 90
Kawakami, Tomiyo, 38
Kawate, Toru, 159, 164

Kennedy, Kathy, 159-160, 187
Kilbourne, Edwin, 6
Kodaira (Yayoidai), 116, 122, 124, 156, 158, 159, 166
Koganei, 97, 114-116, 122, 123, 124-125, 127, 133, 134, 156, 158, 161, 166, 179, 182
Kogo (evangelist), 106
Komiyama, Rinya, 162
Kuboe, Tsutomu or Setsuko, 108
Kuodera, Toshiyuki, 162
Kuroda, Mamoki, 162, 166
Kyodan, 14, 15

Lady, Jesse F., 4-5, 18, 25
language study, 55, 61, 70, 91
lay ministry/leadership, 16, 83-85, 106, 112-113, 115-116, 120, 128, 131-133, 144, 145, 146-148, 165-166
leadership training, 91-92, 106, 128, 131-133, 147-148, 178
literature evangelism, 93-94, 102
Lofthouse, Connie, 98, 116, 157, 158-159, 187
Long, Jeremiah L., 17
Long, Mary E., 17

MacArthur, Douglas, 3, 14, 15
Maedke, Jean, 159, 160, 164, 187
Mandai, Tsuneo, 107
Martin, John Z., 35-37, 41, 75-76, 82, 83, 85, 88
Masaoka, Yoshiko, 108
Matoba, Chie, 114, 115
Matoba, Setsuko (see Kuboe)
Matsuo (Kimoto), Yoshiko, 111
Matsuya, Ryuzo, 166
Matsuura, Noriko, 92, 105, 106, 114, 166
Matsuyama (evangelist), 108
Mennonite Central Committee, 41, 77, 94, 95, 102-103
Mennonite Missions, 36, 37, 70, 91, 94-95, 103, 115
Messiah College, 4, 43, 98, 110, 136, 156
Midori Ward (see Nagoya)
missionary qualities, 152-154
Miwa, Yasuko, 77
Miyamoto, Kikuyo, 38, 75, 76
Miyamoto, Yasuo, 35, 38, 39, 76, 77, 171
Miyoshi Cho (see Fuchu)
Moody, John, 159, 160, 187
Morioka, Toshio, 112
Morken, Dave, 4
Musser, Earl or Sue, 158
Musser, J. Earl, 85, 116
Myers, Dora, 98, 116, 157, 158, 159, 187

Nagai, Moriya, 119
Nagashima, David, 115

Nagata, Kazuyo, 105
Nagata, Sachiyo, 105
Nagato, 71, 82, 83, 90, 93, 98, 104-107, 108, 110-112, 119-122, 126-128, 130, 161, 165, 178-181
Nago, 37, 76, 90
Nagoya, 157-158, 160, 163, 164-165
networks, 149-150
Niagara Christian College (see Ontario Bible School)
Nishihara (see Fuchu)
Nishiichi, 97-98, 107, 108, 110-111, 130
Nishimura, Asao, 106-107, 119-121, 126, 135-136, 161-162, 165, 176-179, 180
Nishimura, Kimiko (see Ueda)
Nukui (see Koganei)

Oba, Jihichi, 38, 77, 94, 101-102
Odani, Noriaki, 112-113
Oe, Suteichi, 101, 106, 107
Ogori, 10, 20-21, 41
Oka, Keijun, 105
Okano, Kikumi, 92, 103-104, 180
Okano, Masaharu, 92, 103-104, 126, 135-136, 161-162, 165, 180
Okazaki, Hideko, 107-108
Okazaki, Hiroto, 107-108, 119, 165-166
Okuaki, Kenji and Kazuko, 106
Onaka, Miyako, 105-106
Onimura, Hajime (see Kaneshige)
Onimura, Kikumi (see Okano)
Ontario Bible School, 3-4, 14, 23, 25

Pacific Broadcasting Association, 93
partnership, 157, 161, 163, 164, 167-169
Peachey, Paul, 94-95, 118
Pioneer Evangelism Committee, 162, 163, 167-168
Pye, Phyllis, 4, 25

radio evangelism, 93, 111
Reid, Augusta, 159
Royer, Richard, 85

Saito, Masae, 65
Sakamoto, Tomoichi, 32, 35, 36-37, 38, 62
Saltzman, Royce, 4, 18, 22
Sato, Masako, 165
self-support, 16, 115, 120, 132-133, 144, 147
Seno, Morio, 114
Senzaki (see also Nagato)
Shafer, R. Donald, 133-134
Shaida, Peter or Laura, 158-159, 160, 187
Shibata, Goro, 103-104, 119, 126
Shibata, Yaeko, 103

Shimonoseki (see also Yamanota), 97-98, 107, 108, 111-113, 119, 123, 126, 136, 147, 158, 160, 163, 165, 176
Shin-Shimonoseki, 158, 161, 163, 164
Shintoism, shrine, etc., 14-15, 56, 102, 150-151, 163, 164
Sherk, Dorothy, 3, 25
Sider, Roy V., 161, 168
Smelser, F. L., 17
Smith, Jay, 98, 187
Stoner, J. Andrew, 96-97, 98, 110, 116, 186
Sugata, Hidetsugu and Makiko, 157-158, 164, 166
Sugiyama, Koichiro, 32, 35, 75, 102
Sugiyama, Seiko, 92, 105-106
Sugiyama, Shizuko, 105
Susa, 90, 109
Suzuki, Eiji and Hiromi, 116, 162, 166
Suzuki, Hiroyuki and Yasue, 113, 162

Tachikawa, 116, 122, 158, 166
Takahashi (interpreter), 29
Takahashi, Toshiko (see Funaki)
Takamura, Shizue, 105
Takamura, Takashi, 71, 105-107, 119
Takeshita (lawyer), 9, 30, 33
Takibe, 90, 98, 107-108, 110, 112, 119, 165-166
Tamachi Church, 38
Tange, Masanori, 115
Tange, Yachiyo, 115
Tarnowsky, Rosalind, 97, 186
TESL (Teaching English as a Second Language), 159
tensions, missionary, 54-55, 57-58, 63-64
Thomas, Dwight and Carol, 97-98, 113, 186
Thomas, Erwin, 22
"Three Sisters," 157, 158
Tojo, Takanobu, 112-113, 120, 135-136, 161-162, 166, 172
Tokaichi (see also Hagi), 34, 41
Tokyo, 91, 113-116, 122, 123-125, 161-162, 164
Tomoe Inn, 8, 10, 25, 31, 44

Uchida, Eiji or Eiko, 113, 120
Ueda (Nishimura), Kimiko, 92, 106, 107, 121, 126, 173-175, 178-179, 180
Ulery, Carl J., 5-6, 19-21, 35, 85, 90, 101
United Christian Church, 41
Upland Church, 4, 18, 25, 40
Upland College, 3, 4, 40

voluntary service, 70-71, 95-99, 116, 158-159

Wakabacho (see Tachikawa)
Welch, Alice, 159, 187
Willms, Bonnie, 69, 71-72, 186, 195, 196

Willms, Kenneth, 69, 71, 186, 195
Willms, Margaret, 69, 71, 186, 195
Willms, Mary G., 3-5, 7-8, 9-11, 22, 24, 25-27, 28-35, 39, 41, 57, 58, 59, 60-64, 66-67, 68-69, 70-71, 74-77, 79-80, 83, 88-89, 92, 101, 103-105, 109-111, 117, 119-120, 171, 177, 186
Willms, Peter, 3-5, 7-11, 14-15, 18-19, 22-24, 25-27, 28-40, 41, 54, 57, 59, 60-65, 66-67, 68, 70, 74-77, 79-81, 83-85, 88-90, 91-92, 93, 95-96, 100, 101, 103-105, 109-111, 117-120, 129, 131, 132, 171, 177-178, 186
Winger, Marshall, 4, 18, 25
Wingerd, Edna, 70-71, 96
Wingert, Norman or Eunice, 22, 41, 67, 76, 94
Wittlinger, Carlton O., 16, 90
Wolgemuth, Grace, 21
Wolgemuth, Mark, 22, 29
Wolgemuth, Samuel F., 4-8, 15, 18-19, 20-21, 28, 90, 117
Worcester, L. B., 17
World Congress on Evangelism, 7, 9, 21-22, 28, 31, 34

Xavier, Frances, 13

Yadomi, 76, 90
Yamada, Keiko, 112
Yamada, Takashi, 103
Yamagata, Yukiko (see Yamamoto)
Yamaguchi, 104, 109-110, 119
Yamamoto, Akiko, 103
Yamamoto (Yamagata), Yukiko, 111, 113, 171-172, 174
Yamane, Hosaku, 92, 119
Yamanota (see also Shimonoseki), 97, 112-113, 158, 161, 164, 165-166, 175
Yamazaki, Hisako, 77, 94, 119
Yasumura, Teruyo, 108
Yayoidai (see Kodaira)
Yoshinaka, Tasuko, 92
Yoshioka, Kyosuke, 112
Yoshizu, Kiyo, 105, 114
youth camps, 92-93, 95, 103
Youth for Christ, 4, 12, 18, 22

Zook, Brian, 69, 186, 196
Zook, David W., 17-18
Zook, Elaine, 70, 108, 186, 196
Zook, Marlin, 43-44, 63, 64, 68, 71, 97-98, 103, 104, 106-107, 108-111, 113, 116, 130, 156, 157, 158, 160, 162, 164, 172, 174-175, 186, 201
Zook, Ruth, 43-44, 63, 64, 68, 71, 97-98, 103, 106, 108, 110-111, 113, 116, 130, 156, 157, 164, 172, 186, 196
Zook, Stephen, 186, 196

Doyle Curtis Book was born in Kansas in 1929 and moved to Upland, Calif., in 1936. He graduated from Upland College and married Thelma Heisey of Union, Ohio, in June 1951. In 1955 they went to Japan as missionaries, where they served until 1972. Their two daughters, Charity and Stephanie, were born in Japan.

He entered the School of World Mission of Fuller Theological Seminary in 1975, receiving a M.A. degree in 1977 and the Doctor of Missiology degree in 1981. From 1973 to 1982, he served as Assistant Professor in Missions and Church Growth and as Spiritual Life Coordinator at Melodyland School of Theology in Anaheim, Calif.

He is presently Director of the English Language Institute at Azusa Pacific University, Azusa, Calif., where he also teaches occasional courses in missions and New Testament. In addition, he is an instructor in "Problems in Cross-Cultural Communication" with Operation Impact of Azusa Pacific University, serving in Kenya in 1984 and in Ecuador, Bolivia, Peru, and Guatemala in 1986.

He is currently a member of the Board for World Missions of the Brethren in Christ Church, and chairs the Board of Directors of Dialogue Ministries and The People Place, Claremont, Calif. An ordained minister in the Brethren in Christ Church, he serves as deacon in the Chino Hills Community Church in Chino, Calif.